THE WORLD'S GREAT
RIFLES

THE WORLD'S GREAT
RIFLES

ROGER FORD

BROWN
BOOKS

Published by Brown Books
an imprint of Brown Packaging Books Ltd
Bradley's Close
74–77 White Lion Street
London N1 9PF

ISBN: 1-897884-33-8

Editor: Chris Westhorp
Design: Colin Hawes
Picture Research: Chris Westhorp

Printed in Hong Kong

Picture Credits
Ian Hogg: 153 (both), 159, 168, 172-173 (bottom), 173, 174
Military Archive and Research Services: 20-21, 36, 48-49
Peter Newark Military Pictures: 6-7, 8-9, 13, 17, 18, 19, 28-29, 44-45, 61
Small-Arms Research & Publicity Service: 154, 155, 156, 157, 158 (both), 158-159,
   160-161 (top), 163, 164, 166-167 (both), 169, 170-171 (both), 172-173 (top)
Salamander Picture Library: 10, 11, 21 (middle), 25 (both), 26-27, 31 (both), 33,
   34 (both), 37, 38-39, 40, 40-41, 42, 46, 47, 50-51, 54-55, 56-57, 64, 66, 67, 71, 73,
   77 (top), 78, 100 (top), 104-105, 105 (bottom left) 109 (bottom), 110 (top), 112, 139
TRH Pictures: 21 (top & bottom), 58-59, 63, 75, 76, 77 (bottom), 80, 82-83, 83, 87, 89,
   94-95, 95, 96, 97, 98-99, 100 (bottom), 102, 103, 105 (right), 106 (bottom), 107,
   109 (top), 110 (bottom), 114, 115, 117, 118, 119, 121, 123, 125, 127, 128, 130, 132,
   133, 135 (both), 137, 138, 140, 141, 142, 144, 145, 148, 149, 150-151, 152,
   160-161 (bottom), 162-163 (both)
TRH Pictures via Espadon: 106 (top)

Artwork Credits
Aerospace Publishing: 110-111
John Batchelor: 8-9, 10-11, 16-17, 22-23, 62-63, 64-65, 68-69, 70-71, 72-73,
   74-75 (both), 78, 78-79, 80-81, 86-87, 88-89, 90-91 (top), 100-101, 102-103,
   108-109, 128-129, 130-131 (top)
De Agostini: 112-113, 114-115, 116-117, 120-121, 122-123, 124-125, 126-127,
   130-131 (bottom), 134-135, 146, 154-155, 166-167, 168-169
Roger Ford: 146-147
Bob Garwood: 14-15, 42-43, 84-85, 90-91 (bottom), 92-93
Salamander Picture Library: 12-13, 32-33, 46-47, 52-53, 164-165

CONTENTS

LEFT: Infantry formed squares – this is the 28th Foot at Waterloo – primarily in order to bring concentrated all-round firepower to bear. Each face consisted of up to 150 men in three ranks.

CHAPTER 1

FROM MUZZLE-LOADERS TO THE BRASS CARTRIDGE

A gun which doesn't shoot straight is next to useless except at close quarters; and during the years of development nothing occupied gunmakers like the quest for accuracy. The first and most important step was to impart spin to the projectile to stabilise it in flight.

Four major forces act on a bullet fired from a gun. The most dramatic is the force created by the rapid translation of the propellant charge into gas, driving the projectile on a vector based on the axis of the gun's barrel. But even as the projectile leaves the protection of the barrel, the other forces come into play, and these are negative influences which tend to send it off its line.

The most important of the misguiding influences is gravity, which exerts its pull towards the centre of the planet on the projectile just as surely as it does on all other things – the projectile drops vertically at a rate which increases by just over 9.75 metres (32ft) per second, every second, until it is brought up short or falls to earth. This factor is at least constant in both force and direction, and that means that we can compensate for it simply by aiming high. We can minimise it, too, by increasing the velocity of the projectile so that its vulnerable period is reduced. The resistance of the air, which slows the projectile and gives the force of gravity more time to work, is a factor too. We can take it as a constant, since it varies only by very little, and we can

effectively ignore it as a separate influence – though those who are concerned with the performance of very big guns with maximum ranges measured in many tens of kilometres, and flight times measured in tens of seconds, have to consider it.

Secondly, if there is a wind exerting a side pressure it will tend to blow it off course. There is no satisfactory way of compensating for windage other than by aiming off to a degree dictated by experience, for the degree of force exerted changes second by second (if not much faster) and mechanical devices are of little use. High-velocity rounds are less affected once again, of course.

NATURAL LAWS

Thirdly – and this is the most significant factor – the projectile has a tendency to try to rotate its heaviest and densest 'side' to the fore. This presents a different sort of problem, for each projectile certainly has a different combination of impurities and dimensional inaccuracies, ensuring that the geometrical centre and the centre of gravity are not just in different places, but that they are in different places every time, and that the deviation in the flight path caused as the two circle each other (which sets the projectile wobbling as it turns) will be random. Happily, there is a simple but effective solution: set the projectile

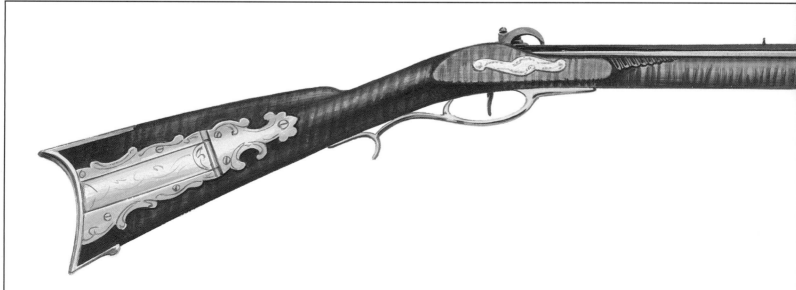

■LEFT: The death of American General Warren at Bunker Hill in June 1775. The American War of Independence was one of the first in which organised bodies of riflemen took part.

spinning around the axis of its path and you create an artificial equilibrium just like that found in a gyroscope, and you stabilise it.

SPIN THE BULLET

Archers solved the problem of the directional instability of their arrows and bolts by setting their flights at an angle, causing the shaft to rotate around its axis, long before firearms were invented, and we can assume that it was not long before a curious gunsmith decided to try the same trick by imparting spin to the projectile before it had left the barrel of the gun.

The gunsmith achieved this by cutting a succession of parallel spiral grooves down the length of the barrel, and casting slightly over-sized projectiles, which had to be rammed and hammered home so that they were gripped tightly by the raised ribs, or lands, between the grooves. The results of the experiment must have exceeded his most optimistic expectations, for not only was the new rifled gun very much more accurate than the 'old' smooth-bore, but it also carried much further thanks to the projectile being a better fit and more of the propellent gases being employed effectively (the tight fit also meant that the ball didn't skip and bounce around in its passage down the barrel, of course, and that factor contributed significantly to the improvement in accuracy, too).

It is estimated that just one-fifth of one per cent of the energy produced when a cartridge is fired goes to rotating the bullet, while friction in the barrel accounts for another three per cent (20 to 30 per cent goes to propelling the bullet, 30 per cent goes in heat to the barrel and 40 per cent goes in muzzle blast).

We have to guess at the history, because there are no clear contemporary accounts that put names, dates, and places to the innovation. We can be sure that it happened around the end of the fifteenth century, for a rifled firearm from that period, once owned by the Holy Roman Emperor Maximillian, exists to this day; we can guess that it took place in Central Europe, probably in Germany or Bohemia (Nürnburg, Vienna, and Leipzig all have their claims), and some believe either August Kotter or Gaspard Koller to have been responsible, but that can only be speculation, for this was a time when few men left written records.

The internal grooving of their barrels aside, the early rifles were no different in basic character from the smooth-bore guns of the time. They used the same variety of actions – Maximillian's rifle was a snapping matchlock; later guns were wheel-locks, snaphaunces, miqueletes, and flintlocks – and were of a similar calibre, often as large as 19mm (.75in), and overall length – and naturally had the same sort of wooden furniture; though not surprisingly, given the fact that they cost so much more, many were finished to a higher standard, and were often intricately decorated, a feature which began to disappear from everyday weapons as rifles became more commonplace.

Pill-Lock Kentucky Rifle

Calibre: .40in, .55in (10mm, 14mm)
Weight: Circa 6kg (13lb 4oz)
Length: Circa 1500mm (59in)
Barrel length: Circa 1100mm (43in)
Effective range: Circa 120m (390ft)
Configuration: Single-shot, muzzle-loading
Muzzle velocity: Circa 180mps (585fps)
Country of origin: United States

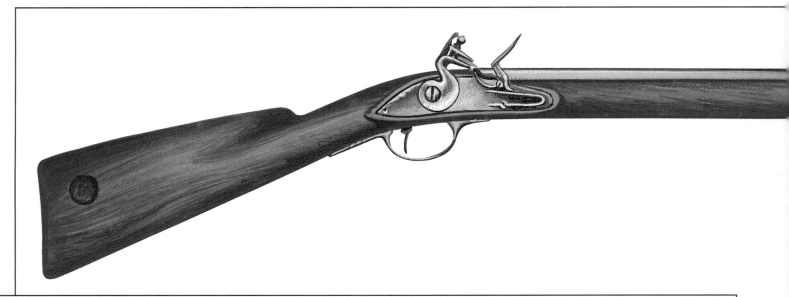

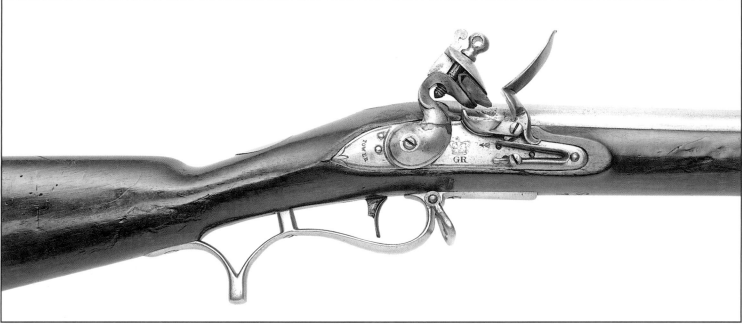

■ **ABOVE: The rifle produced by Ezekiel Baker was adopted by the British Army and used (in limited numbers) from 1808. It was designed to be loaded with either a patched or a naked ball.**

The rifling itself was shallow at first (often so shallow as to be barely discernible now, after prolonged use and the passage of centuries) but became more deeply incised as the technology to produce it developed; it had a multiplicity of grooves, rarely fewer than six and often 12 or more (four is normal today, but so-called 'micro-groove' systems, which use 16 and more, are also in production). Some would-be innovators tried other arrangements – barrels bored oval or polygonal, the whole bore of which twisted – but the most important (and most successful) of those fall into a later period, by which time much more

sophisticated machine tools had been developed.

FANCIFUL NOTIONS

As with so many other phenomena known during the period in question, there was no contemporary understanding at all of the real reasons why rifling actually worked and made for a more accurate, further-reaching weapon.

One of the earlier theories was theological and concerned devils; it was known that devils, which of course had a propensity for evil and would make mischief wherever possible, could not perch on a spinning object and could thus not use their malign influence to throw it off its line (after all, were the celestial bodies, which span, not free of them? And was the Earth, which of course did not, not infested with them?).

The two other widely held, rather more down-to-earth theories – while perhaps less colourful – were still really no nearer the truth. One had it that the spinning bullet actually drilled its way through the air, while the other held that the rifling exercised a resisting and retarding effect on the projectile while it was still in the barrel, allowing the propellant charge to develop its full potential. The latter notion does actually contain a germ of truth, if only thanks to the by-product improvement in obturation (as 'gas–tightness' is properly known) but in practice trying to exploit it as a virtue just made the rifle even harder to load and that actually delayed its acceptance as a battlefield weapon. There's no disproving a theological precept, of course, no matter how ludicrous it may be, but at least both the latter theories were shown to be false

Pennsylvania Mountain Rifle

Calibre: .69in (17.5mm)
Weight: Circa 6kg (13lb 4oz)
Length: Circa 1500mm (59in)
Barrel length: Circa 1100mm (43in)
Effective range: 120m (390ft)
Configuration: Single-shot, muzzle-loading
Muzzle velocity: Circa 150mps (485fps)
Country of origin: United States

when the Newtonian theory of gravitation, first presented in 1684, was better understood.

TO THE NEW WORLD

The eighteenth century was a turbulent period in much of Europe, and that, along with the much readier availability of shipping and a huge upswing in intercontinental trade, meant that migration overseas began to look attractive to many people.

British North America, as we may call the Thirteen Colonies which stretched down the Atlantic seaboard from New England to Georgia, was the chosen destination of the vast majority of the emigrants from Europe, no matter what their origins, despite the fact that the colonies in question were in their infancy still, their very existence threatened by the peoples they were trying to displace. At a stroke, men who went to live there, who had perhaps never used a gun for other than the essentially peaceful purpose of keeping meat on the table, began to find themselves in furious

fighting where the quality of their marksmanship and their skill at arms, and ultimately the quality of the weapons they used, meant the difference between life and violent death for themselves and their families.

THE AMERICAN RIFLE

The American rifle – the Kentucky rifle as we generally know it today, without any good reason at all – was developed relatively rapidly, during a period when conservatism was the norm, in towns like Lancaster and Reading in Pennsylvania – where the majority of German immigrants had congregated – a colony which had been established only in 1681 and which was still very much frontier territory 40 years on. The German rifles from which it evolved were definitely very superior to anything else available, but they had considerable practical drawbacks. They weighed anything up to nine kilograms (20lb), a burden which was further increased by the sheer weight of accoutrements, shot, and powder – probably another seven

kilograms (15lb), all told, for a reasonable reserve – and were thus unsuitable for anything other than static defence. Many were wheel-locks, with 20 or more moving parts, which were impossible to repair or even maintain satisfactorily in the backwoods, and this action very soon gave way to the much simpler and straightforward flintlock, which was to become characteristic of the new gun. The set trigger/hair trigger combination – which had been developed as early as the mid-sixteenth century and which allowed the weapon to be discharged with only the smallest degree of movement – was relatively simple to manufacture and was retained (and showed up both in many Kentucky rifles and in successors), while the same simple fixed vee-and-bead sights were also carried through, at least for everyday use (though aperture sights

■BELOW: The Baker Rifle was short by contemporary standards and was thus not as accurate over longer ranges. It fired a .61in (15.4mm) calibre ball and was issued with a sword bayonet.

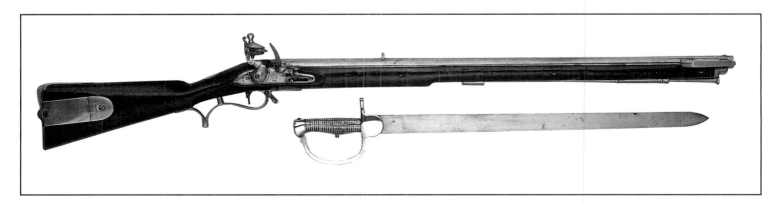

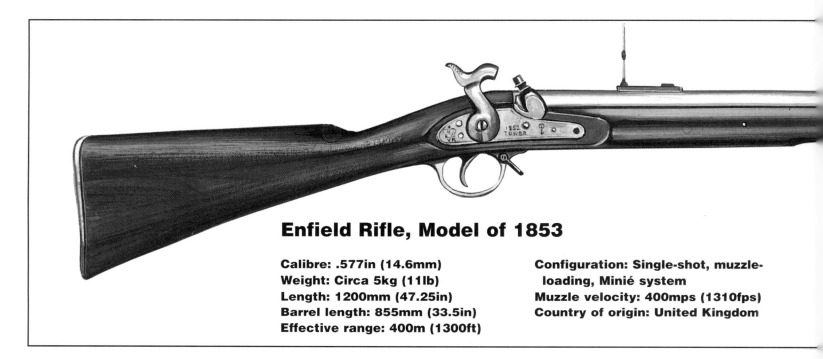

Enfield Rifle, Model of 1853

Calibre: .577in (14.6mm)
Weight: Circa 5kg (11lb)
Length: 1200mm (47.25in)
Barrel length: 855mm (33.5in)
Effective range: 400m (1300ft)

Configuration: Single-shot, muzzle-
loading, Minié system
Muzzle velocity: 400mps (1310fps)
Country of origin: United Kingdom

were not uncommon in German rifles, and telescopes, too, were seen occasionally, they were rarely found on American rifles).

LIGHTER AND SMALLER

The trend towards simplification and weight reduction went further. The calibre of the new rifle was reduced to between 10mm (.40in) and 14mm (.55in), which dramatically increased the number of rounds of ammunition one could carry, and the barrel – still octagonal in external cross-section, as that of its predecessor had been – was lengthened, typically by more than 15 per cent, to somewhere between 1070 and 1220mm (42 and 48in), both to improve accuracy at longer ranges and so that the powder charge had a better chance to burn cleanly and completely and maximise the propellant force. The stock was slimmed down to the bare minimum, and most decoration removed from it (instead, decorative woods such as curly maple, with its characteristic intricate grain pattern, were used in place of the more mundane walnut). More widely-applied decoration began to creep in again as the eighteenth century drew on, but most connoisseurs rate the early rifles more highly for their clean lines and simple elegance. The angle the butt-stock made with the axis of the barrel was altered too, becoming considerably steeper, on the principle that the recoil would tend to try to align the barrel with the butt and cause it to rise before driving the gun back into the shooter's shoulder, thus reducing the blow he had to absorb; sling

swivels disappeared because these men soon learned that the place for one's gun was in the hand (or in the crook of an arm), not slung over the back. By contemporary European standards, the American rifles were workmanlike but little more. Their locks, for example, were crude in comparison to those being manufactured in London and the German gunmaking centres, but they had the advantage of simplicity, which made them easy to repair with only the crudest tools and workshop facilities.

The slimming-down process which produced the American rifle was necessary for reasons other than just a reduction in the weight a hunter or soldier had to carry – both the lead which went into the bullets and the saltpetre (potassium nitrate, KNO_3) for the powder were difficult to obtain and thus very expensive. Saltpetre, the active constituent of gunpowder, along with carbon and sulphur (and forming no less than 75 per cent of its mass by the late eighteenth century), is a ready source of oxygen, which combines with carbon to form carbon dioxide, the gas produced so readily and in such copious quantities when gunpowder burns that it provides the motive force to push the projectile out of the barrel at a speed of many hundreds of feet per second.

OF POWDER AND BALL

Saltpetre occurs in nature as a by-product of the decay of vegetable matter – but not in any large quantities. As demand for it increased, an intensive process of nitre farming, as it was known,

■ RIGHT: Coldstream Guardsmen armed with 1853 Pattern Enfield rifles storm the Heights of Alma on 20 September, 1854. The new rifle proved deadly and much easier to load.

came into being: farmyard manure was laid in shallow trenches, kept warm, covered with light soil, and raked and stirred regularly to ensure that the bacteria which released the nitrates had a sufficient supply of air; then wood ash was added so that the potassium it contained could replace the hydrogen in the weak nitric acid the bacteria produced, forming potassium nitrate. The admixture of soil, manure, and ashes was then washed and allowed to soak, which dissolved the saltpetre, and the resulting solution was evaporated to leave crystalline potassium nitrate. It was the scarcity of potassium nitrate which had prompted Napoleon Bonaparte to set the eminent chemist Claude Louis Berthollet searching for an alternative; Berthollet discovered the alternative oxygen source, potassium chlorate, in 1786, and also produced fulminate of silver. Gunpowder only became easier to produce after the middle of the nineteenth century when vast deposits of nitrates were discovered in Chile (albeit in the form of less-reactive sodium nitrate, which still had to be treated with potassium chloride to produce saltpetre), and later still with the invention of a process to fix nitrogen directly from the air, though ironically, those discoveries almost coincided with the invention of new explosives such as nitro-glycerine and nitro-cellulose which

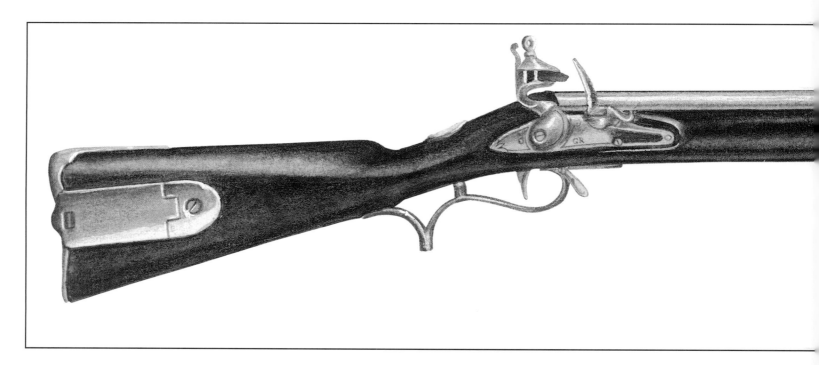

soon took over from gunpowder and killed the demand for potassium nitrate anyway.

MAKING GUNPOWDER

Gunpowder is a perfectly adequate explosive, but it has two distinct drawbacks: because it is a simple mixture made up of three rather disparate substances, it tends to unmix itself in bulk and is difficult to handle, and when burned it produces copious quantities of smoke together with a considerable solid residue which settles in the barrel and renders any gun employing it unuseable until it is cleaned. The second problem is inherent in the nature of the material and there is nothing to be done about it, but the first could be alleviated by 'mealing' or 'corning' it – mixing it into a paste with water, drying it, and then grinding it into tiny, evenly-sized fragments, each of which has the same homogenous composition as the overall admixture – an approach which was adopted as early as the sixteenth century.

BREECH-LOADERS

Far more important than finding a new propellant was the search for a way to get around the slow business of loading a rifle with a tight-fitting projectile via the length of its barrel. There were two main avenues to be explored: loading it through an opening breech, and using a loose-fitting bullet which could simply be dropped into place and then expanded to fit once it was there.

The most successful breech-loaders of the period were Ferguson's screw-breech

(a development of a method devised by a Frenchman named Chaumette) and Hall's tipping-breech (also a development of an earlier, unsuccessful invention, this time from an Italian named Crespi). Ferguson's rifle had a large-diameter vertical plug through the breech, with a screw thread cut into it; it could be lowered, ball and charge inserted and then screwed back into position. It was used with some success during the Revolutionary War in America. Hall's method used a short breech chamber which tipped up for loading and was then locked back into the barrel's axis. A rifle and carbine he designed were adopted by the US Government in 1819, and saw action in the Mexican War.

EXPANDING BULLETS

The alternative – a loose-fitting bullet which was somehow expanded to take the rifling before it came back up the barrel – took a surprisingly long time to perfect after an English army officer named John Norton suggested in the 1820s that a suitably shaped under-size ball – one with a marked recess cut in the surface it presented to the charge – would be expanded by its detonation and would thus take the rifling. After a succession of false starts, success finally came when Greener in England and Delvigne in France improved on the original idea by proposing elongated cylindro-conoidal bullets with indentations in their bases, solving the problem of getting the cut-out in the right place, and finally Claude Minié, yet another French army officer, popularised the system and gave it his

name (while at the same time introducing other features which were less than successful and soon abandoned). Rifles using the Minié system began to reach front-line troops in the early 1850s, and at their best were quite excellent – the Swiss Federal Carbine, Model 1851, in 10.5mm (.41in) calibre and charged with 4g (62 grain) of black powder, produced a muzzle velocity of around 400 metres (1310ft) per second (enough to pierce three one–inch thick wooden boards at a thousand paces) and were accurate enough to hit a one and a half metres square target 50 times out of 50 at one-third of that distance. Rifled muzzle-loaders on the Minié system were the most common longarms of the American Civil War.

FORWARD IN MANY DIRECTIONS

By the start of the nineteenth century, the flintlock was almost universal (though in some parts of the world, particularly Japan and Central Asia, matchlocks remained more common; and there were many wheel-locks still in service, too, especially in Africa). Simpler and more reliable than the other methods of igniting gunpowder at the breech by means of a spark struck by flint on steel, they were still prone to misfiring, even in good weather and when maintained in perfect order, and were next to useless when dirty or in the wet.

The sequence of operations leading to the projectile leaving the muzzle was complex. The trigger released the sear, which in turn released the cock, either directly or via a tumbler; propelled by a

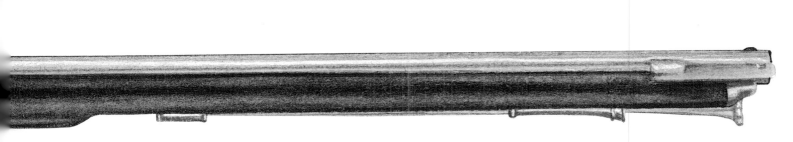

Baker Rifle

Calibre: .625in (15.9mm)
Weight: 4.5kg (10lb)
Length: 1100mm (43.25in)
Barrel length: 750mm (29.5in)
Effective range: Circa 150m (500ft)
Configuration: Single shot, muzzle loading
Muzzle velocity: Circa 150mps (500fps)
Country of origin: United Kingdom

spring, the cock travelled forwards through about one-eighth of a turn before the flint clamped in its jaws struck the steel, pushing it, and the priming pan cover connected to it, forwards out of the way, overcoming the pressure of another spring and opening the pan itself to expose the priming charge; sparks from the action of flint against steel (which have a measurable, though short, life) fell upon this charge, igniting it (if it were perfectly dry) and causing the propellant charge proper, exposed to the flash via the touchhole, to ignite in turn (pre-supposing that it, too, was perfectly dry). Contained as it was by the chamber and the projectile, this ignition resulted in an explosion and a sudden (though not quite instantaneous) release of copious quantities of gas which propelled the projectile down the barrel. Needless to say, all this happened in the blinking of an eye – but even the blinking of an eye takes an appreciable time.

FOIBLES OF THE FLINTLOCK

Modern experience with flintlock weapons – and they have an enthusiastic following, particularly in the United States – shows that in a good-quality gun in pristine condition, the action of pulling the trigger and the gun discharging will seem as one, but that assumes that every one of the set of conditions described above is met absolutely. Naturally enough, that was very often not the case at all. In the field, improperly maintained and in less than expert hands (just the sort of conditions under which a weapon of war, in particular, was most likely to

be used), the eighteenth century gun was a fallible piece, and even if it did fire successfully (as it did just seven times out of 10, on average, in a soldier's hands), there was often a noticeable delay between the cock falling and the discharge taking place; during that delay the gunman often faltered and allowed his weapon to drift away from the point of aim or, worse still, an animate target, seeing the spark, could actually get out of the line of fire.

FULMINATE PRIMING

Tradition has it that it was frustration at being thus eluded – by wildfowl – which led Alexander John Forsyth, Rector of Belhelvie, some miles north of Aberdeen in Scotland, to reflect upon the nature of this aspect of the gun's operation. Forsyth knew of the existence of a set of unstable explosive salts known as fulminates, obtained by dissolving metals in acids. (Fulminate of gold, for example, is mentioned in Samuel Pepys' diary of 11 November 1663; fulminate of silver, so volatile that 'when it has been once obtained it can no longer be touched' was produced by Berthollet in 1788, two years after he had synthesised potassium chlorate and shown how it could be used as a substitute for saltpetre in gunpowder.)

Following Edward Howard's fabrication of the rather more docile fulminate of mercury in 1800, Forsyth began to experiment with it and with potassium chlorate, hoping, it seems, to produce a new faster-acting and self-detonating propellant to supplant

gunpowder. This soon proved impractical (though that didn't stop others from later going down the same road) and Forsyth instead turned his thoughts to using the tiny explosive force of the fulminate to set off the gunpowder.

FORSYTH'S LOCK

After experimenting with a simple iron tube, he produced a gun action with a hammer in place of the flintlock's cock and replaced the priming pan with a small dispenser, in shape and operation much like a perfume flask, which, when tipped up, fed a measured quantity of powdered fulminate directly into the touchhole and onto an adjacent enclosed 'anvil'. At last, and still in very imperfect form, there was an alternative to the glowing match or fallible flint and steel.

PERCUSSION CAPS

Many gunmakers purchased fulminate locks from Forsyth (and his licensees in London and Edinburgh) and used them to convert otherwise sound flintlock weapons to the new system, but curiously enough the Scot made no attempt to improve on the means of delivering the detonating powder to the breech (particularly in that the fulminate was very corrosive; the use of it in powder form necessitated very regular cleaning of the lock and some means of enclosing it was clearly needed). That was left to others, and soon fulminate primers were on offer in a variety of forms. The best of all of them was the percussion 'cap', so-called because it was shaped to fit over a nipple fixed in what had been the touchhole, and it was that system which prevailed, though tape primers – pockets of fulminate sandwiched between two strips of paper, fed to the breech by a simple escapement, as devised by an American dentist named Maynard – were also briefly popular.

The best claim to have invented the percussion cap is that of an English emigrant to the USA, the artist Joshua Shaw. He obtained a patent in the USA in 1822, but always maintained that he had actually perfected the invention some five years earlier. This was the first time an important step forward in the state of the gunmaker's art was made outside Europe, the first of many to be made in the United States. Shaw's original caps were made of steel but he soon switched, first to pewter and then to copper. It was soon clear that the percussion cap was a notable improvement over other percussion systems and few examples of the others have survived.

THE BRASS CARTRIDGE

The Minié system was current for just two decades before the rifled muzzle-loader was overtaken by the breech-loader (though an effective breech-loader, the work of von Dreyse, had actually been adopted in Prussia some 10 years before the expanding bullet was widely accepted; see below), and the changeover came not as a result of some innovation in engineering, which suddenly permitted gunsmiths to manufacture a gas-tight breech, but with the realisation that a working seal could be obtained by another means: by containing the propellant in a soft-metal cartridge, which would itself prevent the leakage of gas to the rear by expanding to seal the gap between the moving and standing parts of the breech.

Of course, there was nothing new about the idea of cartridges, but previously they had been paper tubes; only a means of containing a pre-measured weight of powder, which were opened and the charge poured into the muzzle of the gun. The projectile was then tamped in afterwards, usually on top of the paper wrapping, which served a useful second purpose as a containing wad. Additionally, the paper could be impregnated with grease, usually tallow or animal fat, which served as a lubricant.

UNITARY CARTRIDGES

These first cartridges were something of an improvement over loose powder

Plains Rifle, Circa 1800

Calibre: Circa .45in (11.4mm)
Weight: Circa 6kg (13lb 4oz)
Length: 1500mm (59in)
Barrel length: 1100mm (43in)
Effective range: Circa 120m (390ft)
Configuration: Single-shot, muzzle-loading
Muzzle velocity: Circa 150mps (485fps)
Country of origin: United States

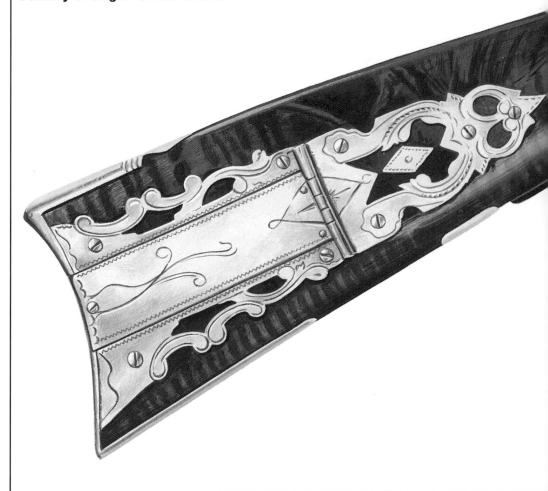

carried in a horn or flask, but not much; it was not until they began to appear with the wrapping rendered highly inflammable, it having been soaked in a saltpetre solution in exactly the same way as the slowmatches of a bygone day, that they really started to make the shooter's life easier, because now they could be inserted whole. Cartridges of this sort became popular with pistol shooters (who had previously tended to stick to the use of powder flasks and loose balls) after about 1850. As an alternative to being wrapped in nitrated paper, the charge was sometimes formed entirely of gunpowder which had been made into a thick paste with collodion (a syrupy solution of a nitro-cellulose named

■RIGHT: Black powder produced smoke in copious quantities. After several volleys, neither side's infantrymen could have seen the other, leading to costly blind attacks on fixed positions.

pyroxylin in ether or alcohol), moulded and then allowed to dry, the bullet – by now usually cylindro-conoidal or cylindro-ogival (that is, either a short cylinder with a straight-walled, cone-shaped point or a short cylinder with a rounded head) rather than spherical – attached to it by means of either collodion or regular glue. This latter approach produced a cartridge which was waterproof enough – an important consideration – but which was brittle and fragile.

demand – the American Civil War alone saw to that. One of the most impressive statistics to come out of that conflict concerns the number of pistol cartridges it consumed: for the 19 types of handgun it issued to its troops, the Union Army alone bought no less than 68,385,400.

INCORPORATING A DETONATOR

None of these cartridges contained a primer/detonator, of course, though that idea too had been around for almost half a century, thanks to the pioneering work of Samuel Johannes Pauly (or Pauli), a Swiss based in Paris, towards the end of the Napoleonic War. In fact, Pauly's chief interest was in improving the breech-loader, but in order to do that he believed he first had to devise a means of containing projectile, charge, and detonator in one cartridge. In 1810 or 1811 he produced a cartridge with a rimmed base of soft metal and a body of paper, like shotgun shells were until the 1960s, or of brass, in which case they could be reloaded. Priming was more primitive for, the percussion cap having not yet been invented, the only method available was to place a small amount of fulminate in an open pan in the head of the cartridge. In order to make sure the priming stayed in place, Pauly was forced to utilise a flush standing-breech, pierced to take a spring-loaded firing pin, and the hammer-like extensions seen on his guns are in fact just cocks for concealed strikers. Pauly employed a young Prussian gun-lock maker, Johann Nikolaus von Dreyse, to make the guns he designed; the employee was to go on to become rather better known than his master. Curiously, the fact that his brass cartridge bases expanded to form a gas-tight seal at the breech – far and away the most important aspect of his work – seems to have gone unremarked for years.

RIM-FIRE CARTRIDGES

Some 30 years after Pauly had left Paris, Louis Flobert produced there the prototype of the less important of the two types of metallic cartridge still in everyday use today: the rim-fire cartridge. It started out as a drawn copper case little bigger than a percussion cap, in which the priming

Pistolmaker Robert Adams in London experimented with thin-walled metal tubes, a projectile loosely crimped into one end and the open base sealed with nitrated paper; and William Eley and Samuel Colt improved on that (independently of each other) in the mid-1850s by wrapping the charge in thin tinfoil, sealing the joint with waterproof cement, and attaching the projectile by means of a spot of glue – but both approaches left metal residue in the chambers which had to be removed before they could be reloaded. The following

year a British naval captain, John Hayes, filed a patent application for what became known as the skin cartridge (though that was something of a misnomer, as the material involved was actually gut). William Storm improved on Hayes' patent in 1861 when he treated the dried-gut cartridges with gutta-percha varnish, which rendered it both completely waterproof and brittle when it dried, so that it fragmented when being forced into the chamber by the rammer.

Imperfect though cartridges like these were, they were nonetheless in huge

■RIGHT: These two Union soldiers were photographed in Virginia in 1864, supposedly on picket duty, but note that neither's Model 1855 rifle-musket is cocked.

fulminate acted as propellant, shooting low-mass, small-calibre projectiles which were used for indoor target practice and disposing of garden pests. Flobert showed his invention at the Great Exhibition in London in 1851, and though his cartridges aroused considerable interest they never established themselves in Britain as they did in France and Belgium (nor, until much later, at the time of the Boer War, did indoor target shooting as a sport attain any popularity there).

An American gunsmith, Daniel Wesson, thought enough of Flobert's work to turn his own hand to rim-fire cartridges, concentrating on .22in calibre and increasing the case length somewhat to accommodate a small (three or four grain) additional charge of black powder. Wesson had better tooling available to him than Flobert had had, and succeeded in forming a true rim to the cartridge where the Frenchman had only managed a slight swelling, placing the fulminate priming there instead of simply depositing a blob of it somewhere in the head of the cartridge. The rim served not only to aid ejection, but also to regulate the headspace – the distance between the breech block and the struck face of the cartridge. Pauly's cartridge had achieved that, but succeeding designs had not; misfires were common as a result.

The basic defect of the rim-fire cartridge was one of material strength. In order for the blow from the hammer to be able to detonate the primer, the case of the cartridge had to be both thin and soft, but in larger calibres the charge necessary to propel the projectile often then proved sufficient to split the case. In addition, it was difficult to ensure the even distribution of primer around the cartridge's rim, and this often resulted in misfires, while the relatively high proportion of primer to propellant necessary frequently caused the rim to split and even to separate from the case proper, which normally rendered the weapon useable without the attention of an armourer.

These problems were to cause the demise of the rim-fire cartridge in all but .22in calibre, but initially, at least, the genre took over; rim-fire rifles and pistols

chambered for calibres as large as .50in were produced, though the most popular were .32in – and pistols chambered for this round were produced until 1963 – and .41in, the latter being used in the famous Remington Double Derringer, the preferred hide-away gun of gamblers, whores, outlaws, and lawmen alike throughout the 'Wild West' of the United States. One of the most famous rifles of that same era, the Winchester Model 1866, the Henry rifle from which it was developed, and the Spencer, the outstanding repeating rifle of the

American Civil War, were also chambered for rim-fire cartridges.

CENTRE-FIRE CARTRIDGES

In the end, there were to be many false starts made and not a few false paths followed before the reloadable cartridge with a replaceable primer became a practical reality, even though all the components of a successful design, and all the workshop techniques to realise it, were available as early as 1840, or even before. Noting the contributions made by George Morse, who constructed tubular

■ABOVE: Heavy Union casualties at the Battle of Fredericksburg in December 1862 showed the military effectiveness – and human cost – of accurate rifle fire from entrenched defensive positions.

brass cartridges with wire 'anvils', against which percussion caps could be detonated (the annular gap left when the cap was fitted being filled with a rubber retaining ring), we can pass on to the work of two men, both military officers, one British and the other American: Colonel Edward Mounier Boxer, of the Royal Laboratory at Woolwich, and

Colonel Hiram Berdan, late of the elite Sharpshooters Regiment of the Union Army. It was these two – with considerable help from assistant technicians, who no doubt contributed much to the development process while actually doing the work involved in manufacturing prototypes; neither Boxer nor Berdan was an engineer or gunsmith – who designed and produced the first truly effective reloadable centre-fire cartridges with set-in primers: Boxer in 1866, Berdan two years later.

In practice, Boxer's cartridges (which were made up of coiled brass walls, a

drawn brass head cup drilled to take the primer and a separate anvil to strike it on, and a perforated iron disk which served as the extraction and seating rim) proved to be less than perfect under the rigours of active service. On firing, the cases often swelled and jammed in the chamber, and the iron rim was all too easily torn off by the extractor claw.

■RIGHT: Along with the rifle-musket, 1855 saw the introduction of a standard rifled pistol in the same .58in calibre, issued with a detachable stock for use primarily by cavalrymen.

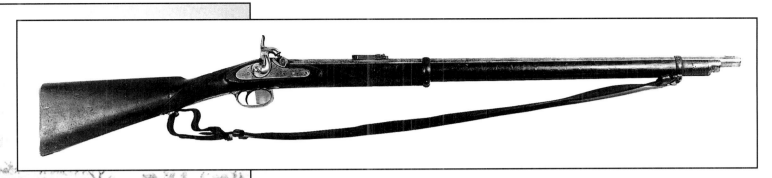

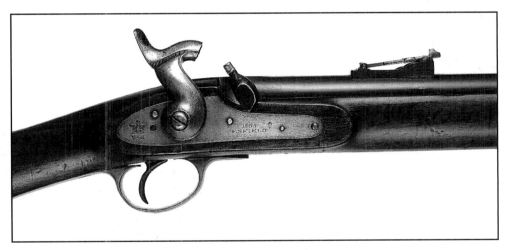

ABOVE: This fine example of a Whitworth rifle, with its very expensive spiralling hexagonal bore, was probably intended as an officer's personal weapon – note the chequering decor.

They were also assembled by hand, and inevitable faults meant misfires; annoying on the firing range, life-threatening in battle, as the British found out to their cost all too often.

Berdan's major contribution was to see that the anvil for the primer could be formed as part of the case itself, but he also used solid drawn cases right from the start, thus avoiding the major problems which beset Boxer's early ammunition. Surprisingly, Berdan didn't take the obvious next step and patent the design for a primer to fit his cartridge cases; that was left to A.C. Hobbs of the Union Metallic Cartridge Co. in 1869. In Europe, Werder in Bavaria (and somewhat later the Mauser brothers in Germany) also began to devise unitary cartridges on the Boxer/Berdan model, and within just a few years it became clear that a de facto standard had evolved. At this stage, all cartridges were rimmed or flanged, the rim rather than

BELOW: This view of an Enfield 1853 Pattern rifle-musket shows very clearly how much simpler was the percussion cap than the flintlock system, with its cock, flint, frizzen, pan and touchhole.

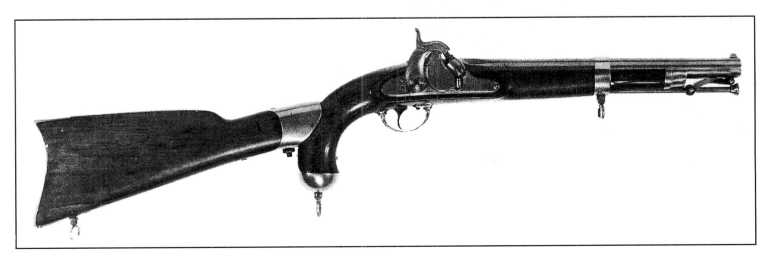

the form of the cartridge and projectile locating the round in the breech. This continued to be convenient until the advent of guns with box magazines, when it became somewhat of a liability: if rimmed rounds are wrongly packed into a box magazine, they simply won't feed. The answer to both these problems was the rimless round, the neck of the cartridge case (which of course is of slightly greater diameter than the projectile it contains) and its overall length determining its accurate seating within the chamber, with all that entails for headspacing and extraction, but it was some years before this was suggested by the Swiss, Rubin.

The shape and make-up of the projectile itself began to change from around this time, too. The first improvement was the move away from the round ball of the early muzzle-loader to the cylindrical bullets with a more or less rounded nose used in the non-unitary cartridges, a form which carried over into the unitary cartridge, and later to what was to become the standard form, the sharply-pointed so-called 'spitzer' rifle bullet (the name is derived from the German word '*spitz*', which simply means pointed), introduced for the Model 1898 Mauser, of which much more later. There was also a move towards projectiles with greater stopping power for a given velocity – softnose, hollow-point and partially-deformable rounds in particular, as well as fragmenting and exploding bullets. The use of these latter was universally condemned – but only against white men, not against the coloured races, a widespread racist sentiment which harks back to Pope Innocent II's banning the use of the crossbow against Christians but permitting its employment against infidels.

Later the composition of projectiles also began to change, particularly with the introduction of repeater arms which fed rounds into the chamber mechanically from a magazine. Pure lead gave way to an alloy of lead with a hardening agent – usually tin or antimony – in an attempt to cut down distortion and resultant misfeeds, and the ultimate solution to that problem was the introduction of bullets fully or partially 'jacketed' with steel or cupro-nickel, another of Rubin's innovations. In modern times, only .22in rim-fire rounds are generally to be found with pure lead projectiles.

NEEDLE-GUNS
The first 'modern' breech-loading rifle actually pre-dated Boxer's metallic cartridge by three decades, and we can trace its ancestry back to Pauly's work in France via the small town of Sömmerda,

Ferguson Breech-loading Rifle

Calibre: .75in (19mm)
Weight: Circa 5kg (11lb)
Length: Circa 1200mm (47.25in)
Barrel length: Circa 800mm (31.5in)
Effective range: 150m (485ft)
Configuration: Single-shot, screw-plug breech-loading
Muzzle velocity: 200mps (650fps)
Country of origin: United Kingdom

a little way north of Erfurt in Prussia, Nikolaus von Dreyse's home town. He returned from Paris and presumably worked as a journeyman gunsmith for the next decade before setting up in partnership with one Collenbusch to begin the manufacture of percussion caps, just two years after Shaw's US patent for them was granted. We may suppose that this was simply a way of feeding his family, for within three or four years (the actual date remains unclear) he had devised and produced a new type of rifle and put it into limited production.

VON DREYSE AND PAULY

Von Dreyse's work in Pauly's shop had centred around producing rifles to his master's design, utilising a standing breech and a spring-loaded firing pin, and the first innovation he produced of his own was to elongate that pin and

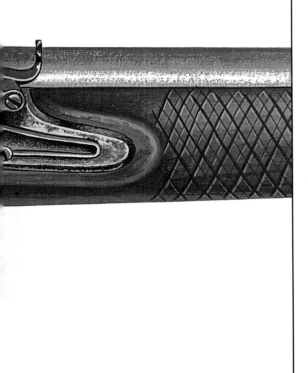

sharpen it, so that under pressure from the spring which drove it forward it would pierce the charge in the chamber through its entire length, and strike a percussion cap embedded in the rear cavity of the projectile, a Minié-type cylindro-ogival bullet. Von Dreyse's first needle-guns were muzzle-loaders employing a separate charge and projectile, but very soon he adopted a fabric-wrapped cartridge which contained both bullet and charge.

The next step was to devise a form of opening breech, to simplify and speed up the loading process. He discarded Pauly's tipping block mechanism, and instead introduced a cylindrical iron rod travelling horizontally in a bored-through receiver, with a small lever set at right angles to its axis to permit it to be moved backwards, to expose the chamber and allow the cartridge to be loaded, and then forwards to close it. The unlocking and locking was performed (though, it must be said, imperfectly) by a simple partial rotation through a quarter turn which freed or located the root of the lever/handle in the rear of the loading recess in the side of the receiver, against the forward edge of what can, if one stretches a point, be considered as a locking cam. It was no more sophisticated in design than the bolt holding closed a door or garden gate – though, of course, it was machined to the closest tolerances then obtainable – and that was how it became known.

THE FIRST BOLT-ACTION RIFLES

Von Dreyse patented his development in 1836, and five years later the Prussian Army adopted his breech-loading rifle in 13.6mm (.53in) calibre, despite the fact that with a muzzle velocity of just 300 metres (985ft) per second it was only really effective to 200m, and that its firing pin – which was, of course, embedded in the propellant charge when it exploded – was prone to rapid deterioration thanks to the effects of heat and corrosion, and frequently broke or bent. Its shortcomings notwithstanding, the Prussians used the needle-gun to good effect, defeating Denmark in the war to decide the fate of Schleswig-Holstein in 1864, and routing Austria two years later in a lightning campaign which lasted just seven weeks. Most of the other German states followed Prussia's lead after 1866 and adopted the needle-gun themselves, and when Prussia and its allies went to war against France four

years later it was still the regulation infantry arm.

PRUSSIAN CHASSEPOTS

The forces the Prussians faced when they chased a wildly over-optimistic invading French army out of the Rhineland and back into France in August 1870 were armed with a basically similar but far better (though still imperfect) bolt-action breech-loading rifle in 11mm (.43in) calibre, the brainchild of Antoine-Alphonse Chassepot, an engineer at the Chatellerault Arsenal. Chassepot moved the percussion cap to the head of the cartridge, thus both shortening the firing pin/needle and allowing it to be more robust, and removing it from the hostile environment of the charge itself. He also added a rubber sealing ring, known as the de Bange gas stopper, on the bolt face, which although it hardened rapidly and became progressively less effective with every round fired, prevented gas leakage surprisingly well initially. His method of locking the bolt in position was no more sophisticated than von Dreyse's, though in fairness to both of them, there seem to have been few enough instances of failure, thanks to the relatively light propellant charge both guns employed.

The Chassepot, which achieved a muzzle velocity of 410 metres (1345ft) per second, was effective at twice the range of the Dreyse needle-gun, and was also somewhat quicker in operation (though the French High Command's assumption that its infantrymen could maintain a rate of aimed fire of 10 rounds per minute proved to be woefully optimistic), but in the hands of what was certainly the illest-led army of the time, the advantages it conferred were simply not sufficient. The Prussians captured perhaps as many as 600,000, along with many of the men who had carried them, and after the unification of Germany the following year, they were allocated to sections of the enlarged army. As early as 1868, the Mauser brothers had successfully reworked Chassepot rifles to accept brass cartridges (and also improved the operation of the bolt mechanism), and their work was to form the basis for a modification programme resulting in the captured weapons being transformed into the Adapted Chassepot Carbine Model 1871 (*Aptierter Chassepot-Karabiner* M/71), chambered for the Werder unitary cartridge and – considerably more importantly – for the Mausers' own Model 1871, the first bolt-action rifle from the Oberndorf firm with which the genre was to be inextricably linked ever afterwards. State arsenals in Bavaria and Saxony also produced modified Chassepot rifles cut down to the dimensions of carbines, and so, belatedly, did the Prussian state itself. In some parts of Germany, modified Chassepot carbines were in use until late in the century with 'home guard' units.

SHARPS' OLD RELIABLE

Even while the innovative Dreyse needle-gun and Chassepot rifle were making their mark on the continent of Europe, across the Atlantic a rather more conventional breech-loader which used paper cartridges with separate percussion primers and projectiles, but which didn't suffer too badly from gas leakage, was going from strength to strength. And since we began this chapter by tracing the genesis of what was to be the first in a long line of great American rifles, it is perhaps fitting that we close it by looking at what most would consider the second: the guns Christian Sharps made from 1848 until his retirement (to devote himself to breeding trout in captivity) in the 1870s.

Sharps learned his trade under the tutelage of John Hall at Harper's Ferry, and it was his master's breech-loader which inspired him to build a more effective version himself in the workshop he set up in Cincinnati, Ohio. When it came, it was somewhat simpler than Hall's design: a breech block slid vertically (perpendicularly in some models, at an angle in others) in a mortice cut in the receiver, the (extended) trigger guard acting as a lever to lower it and raise it again. With the block lowered, the chamber was exposed; after a projectile and cartridge were inserted, the block was raised again, its sharp upper front edge acting as a guillotine to cut off the back end of the cartridge and expose the powder within to the flash from the primer, which was in the form of a disc which was fed to the nipple automatically as the hammer fell. Many Sharps rifles intended for precision shooting were equipped with a set trigger, but most were not.

Sharps' design was still subject to some leakage of propellant gases, but was basically so strong that it would withstand the effect of a heavy charge of powder, thus making good the deficiency. His first rifle, in .52in (13.2mm) calibre, soon became known as 'Sharps' Old

Reliable', and was purchased in considerable numbers, not least by anti-slavery campaigners in the northeastern states, who were even then financing and equipping a guerrilla war, between those who held slaves and those who would free them, which was being fought out largely in Kansas and the state of Missouri. One such Kansas free-stater, John Brown of Osawatomie, was equipped with slant-breech, brass-bound Sharps carbines of 1852 and 1853 vintage when he raided Harper's Ferry so famously in 1859 'with his eighteen men so true', and that type of gun has been known to collectors – of which there are many – as the John Brown Sharps ever since.

CIVIL WAR FAVOURITE

In the civil war which was soon to follow, Sharps' rifles and carbines were perhaps the most popular, if not the most widely used, longarm on the Union side (it has been suggested that upwards of 200 different small arms of all sorts were officially procured by one side or the other during the war, and that number doesn't sound unreasonable). The most widely-issued rifles among northern forces were the .58in calibre muzzle-loading Model 1860 and Model 1863 rifle-muskets, which had started life with the Maynard tape priming system as the Model 1855, and which were set to continue in service for some time to come, many of them being converted to accept rim-fire metallic cartridges according to the Allin system, of which more later. (Not a few British Enfield 1853 Pattern rifle-muskets in .577in calibre were also procured for Union troops.) In all, the government in Washington purchased 9141 rifles and 80,512 carbines from Sharps, the latter for use by cavalrymen, the former by hand-picked, first-class shots who went to make up such units as Colonel Hiram Berdan's famous Sharpshooters. This particular unit's prowess was so linked with the rifles it used that its name was frequently corrupted to 'Sharps' Shooters' in contemporary newspaper reports. Some of those carbines were equipped for a bizarre dual purpose: in their butt-stocks was located a small mill, turned by a cranked handle which emerged from the right hand side; this was intended to serve as a grinder for issue coffee. In any event, 'coffee grinder' Sharps carbines are very rare, and much sought-after by collectors as a result. Copies of Sharps rifles and carbines were manufactured in

■ **RIGHT: A fine Ferguson rifle, made by Durs Egg in London around 1780. Using the extension to the trigger guard as a handle, the screw-plug was wound down to give access to the breech.**

the Confederacy, too, more or less successfully.

WORLD-BEATER

With the war between the states over, attention turned to the largely unexploited land west of the Mississippi. Here, the only animals which had cropped the pasture for many thousands of years were the North American bison – the so-called buffalo – and these ponderous beasts soon became targets for professional hunters who had designs both on their hides, for the production of carriage robes, and on their meat, to feed the armies of construction workers flooding into the area to build the railways which were to become the arteries of colonisation. Once again it was the Sharps rifles, accurate in the right hands out to the best part of a thousand yards (900m), which were the tools of choice for those hunters, since they allowed them to pick off individual animals from far enough away that the sound of the shot hardly carried as far as the herd, and thus did not alarm the rest of its members. There are not a few recorded instances of well over 100 buffalo being dispatched at a single stand, and in many cases, the 'bag' was limited only by the number of cartridges at the hunter's disposal.

Even though the Sharps falling-block coped adequately with the leakage of propellant gases, paper- or fabric-wrapped cartridges had other drawbacks too, notably their fragility. During the 1860s, as brass cartridges become more easily available, many local gunsmiths transformed Sharps rifles to accept them – it was no difficult matter for a skilled craftsman. After the end of the American Civil War, the self-same conversion was undertaken in the factory. Then in 1877, the German gun designer Hugo Borchardt, who had emigrated (originally to Canada) in 1860, was lured away from Winchester to oversee the development of an entirely new Sharps rifle, a task which he carried out very efficiently indeed, producing a hammerless rifle with an enclosed firing pin and a heavy elongated octagonal barrel which was phenomenally accurate. (At Winchester Borchardt had designed a swing-out

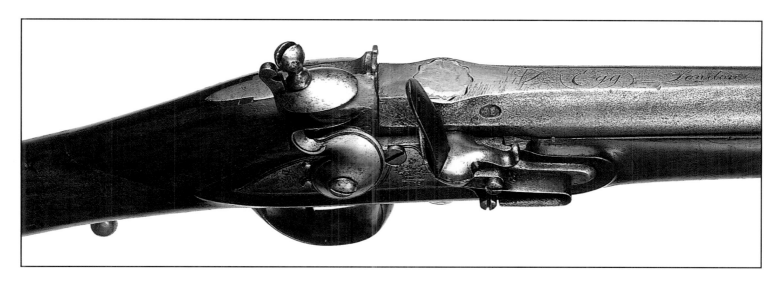

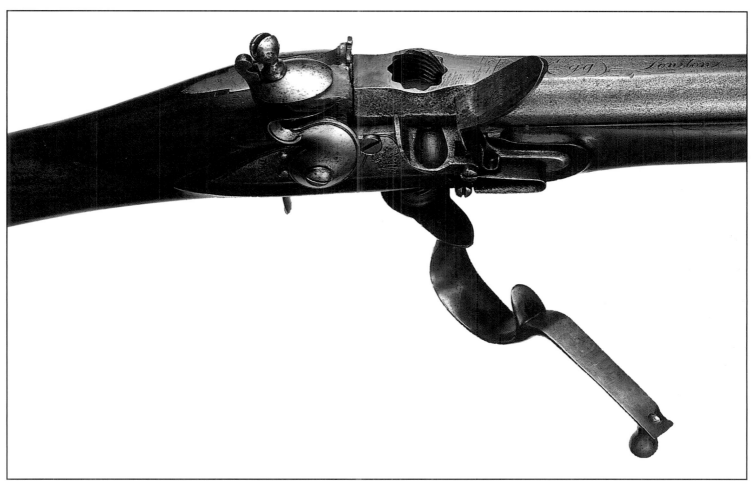

cylinder revolver to rival Colt's Single Action Army Model of 1873; it is perhaps coincidental – and perhaps not – that Colt had had an under-lever repeater rifle very similar in character to Winchester's own Model 73 in development at the time, and that neither the Colt rifle nor the Winchester pistol ever reached the market. . .) On 13 and 14 September that year, the six-man United States team won the World Championship Rifle Match at Creedmoor, Long Island; three of the team used the new guns (the other three used

Remington Rolling Block rifles, of which more below, while their closest opponents, the Irish, who held the title, used muzzle-loaders), and the *London Sporting Gazette* commented that 'in the Sharps rifle the Americans seem to have secured at last a match rifle which, for accuracy at long ranges, is unsurpassed, perhaps unequalled'. Despite such success, two years later the Sharps Rifle Company shut up shop, its new (and very expensive) product having been unable to compete with the excellent low-cost repeaters flooding the market.

■OVER: **For 30 years from the late 1840s until they went out of business, Christian Sharps' rifles were much sought-after weapons. Initially chambered for paper or linen cartridges with separate percussion caps, the later models were adapted to take unitary brass cartridges. All the rifles and carbines shown here are pre-Borchardt models, with exposed hammers. Some have the longer, heavier barrel, and these would have been accurate out to 913m (1000yds) and more in expert hands.**

SHARPS RIFLES

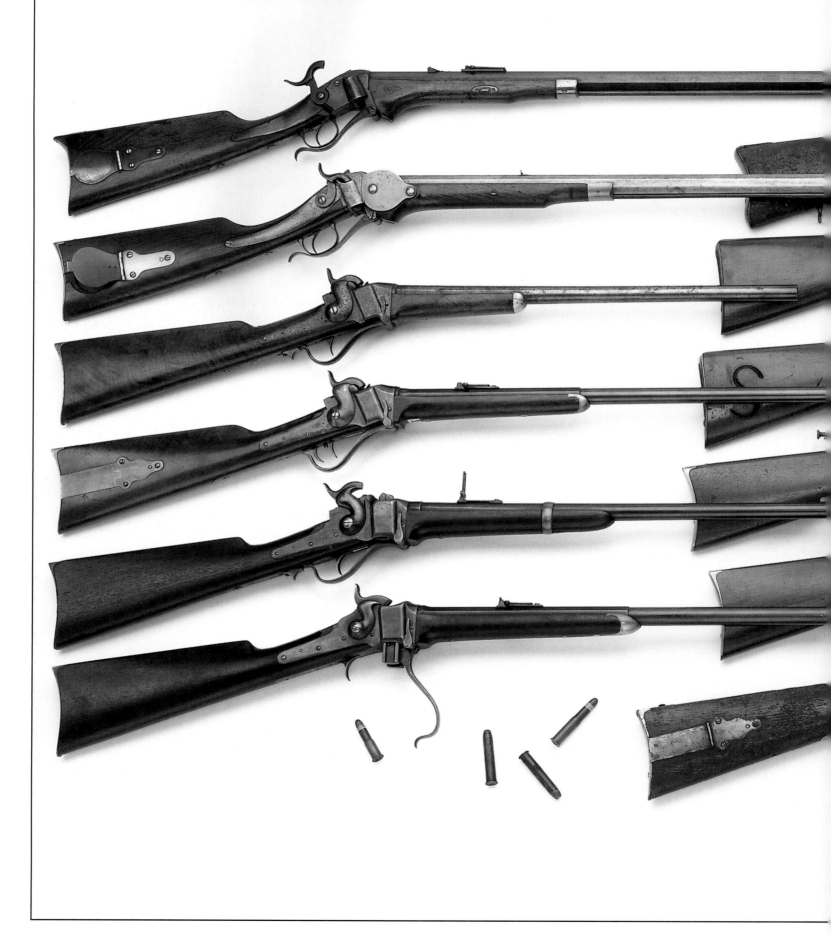

CHAPTER 2
THE RIFLE IN TRANSITION

Until two-thirds of the way through the nineteenth century, the gun was still a very imperfect device, slow to load and prone to malfunction; hardly suited at all, then, to the rigours of the battlefield – but the invention of the unitary cartridge changed all that.

The perfection of the metallic cartridge eliminated the last reason for championing the muzzle-loader. It also meant – though this was very much a secondary effect – that repeating rifles, which stored unused rounds in a magazine of some sort and fed them into the breech as required, were now a feasible possibility (multi-shot cap-and-ball revolver rifles such as those produced by Samuel Colt had been around for some time, but were never either truly effective or widely popular). It was to be some years before repeating arms would be generally adopted by the world's armies, but private individuals were to take to them readily, particularly in the United States where the move to open up the country west of the Mississippi was in full swing. To start with then, state arsenals and would-be government contractors concentrated on producing single-shot breech-loading weapons utilising a wide variety of different actions, many of them extremely simple modifications designed to bring up to date some of the millions of muzzle-loading rifles already in existence, others modifications to actions devised for earlier, less-than-perfect breech-loaders, which could now be dramatically improved.

In that first category, the two most important modifications – and they were very similar in character, and took place

LEFT: The Battle of Reynau. Having intemperately declared war on Prussia in 1870, the French soon found themselves totally outfought, despite being for the most part better armed.

at very nearly the same point in time – were those devised to update the service rifles of the British and United States armies. Up to 1865, the British Army was equipped with muzzle-loading rifle-muskets in .577in (14.6mm) calibre, the Enfield 1853 Pattern. Somewhat surprisingly, given the high standard of gunmaking in the United Kingdom, the degree of innovation and the very extent of the industry there, it was a modification suggested by an American, Jacob Snider of New York, which was chosen to transform it into a breech-loader. Snider's modification was simple in the extreme; it called for a section of the breech something over seven centimetres (three inches) long to be milled out, and a breech block, hinged along its right hand edge, set in its place. This was retained in the closed position by a simple latch, and contained an inclined firing pin onto which the original hammer fell.

SNIDER'S MODIFICATION

The modification was simple and straightforward, both to carry out and when in use, and its only serious drawback was the poor design of the extractor contained within the breech block, which, because of the angle at which it had to work, only drew the spent case part-way out of the breech (the accepted procedure thereafter was to turn the rifle upside down and shake it). All too often, especially after a spell of rapid firing, when heat-induced expansion would cause the spent case to jam, the extractor claw would rip off its iron rim – the cartridge in question was the composite Boxer, of course – and the rifleman could only try to dig the remains out with a knife; if that expedient failed, it was a matter for the armourer. (Not surprisingly, this didn't inspire confidence on the battlefield, but the situation was improved when much more robust solid-drawn cartridges became the standard issue in 1885.) Despite this shortcoming the Enfield-Snider, as the rifle became known, was to remain in front-line service for six very turbulent years, having made its combat debut in 1868 during Sir Robert Napier's punitive Ethiopian campaign, before a satisfactory replacement was identified; it was still to be found in second-line units well into the 1880s.

ALLIN'S TRAPDOOR

The approach the US Army chose for the modification of its Springfield Model 1860 and Model 1863 rifle-muskets was basically similar to that adopted at Enfield. Erskine S. Allin, the Master Armourer at Springfield, milled the breech of the muzzle-loader open in just the same way, and also installed a breech block, but this time it was hinged at the front, secured to the barrel by two screws, and opened upwards and forwards. Its similarity to a trapdoor gave the rifle its sobriquet (in Europe, such conversions were known as *tabatière* rifles, a tabatière – a snuffbox – opening in just that same way).

Like that of the Snider conversion, the Allin breech block housed an inclined, spring-loaded firing pin which transferred the impact of the hammer to the percussion cap. A simple extractor operated manually by a lever set on the right hand side of the breech proved somewhat more reliable than that devised for the Enfield-Snider, but was subsequently replaced anyway by a U-shaped spring which operated automatically when the breech was opened. Initially, the modified trapdoor Springfield rifle was chambered for rim-fire cartridges, but within a year of it being issued the switch to more reliable (but still less-than-perfect) Boxer-type centre-fire cartridges was made, and at the same time the calibre was reduced to .50in (12.7mm) by the simple expedient of boring out the rifle's barrel and brazing in a reduction tube.

In 1873 the calibre was reduced still further, to .45in (11.4mm), and a propellant charge of 4.54g (70 grain) of black powder was standardised. In that

form, and now known as the Springfield .45in-70 (this combination of calibre, in decimal parts of an inch, and propellant load, in grain, was the standard method of describing a type of cartridge in the United States at the time) the rifle was to stay in service almost until the end of the century (and some state militia units still had it at the outbreak of World War I), though it was functionally obsolete long before then, due as much to its reliance on black powder as its propellant as to the nature of its action.

REMINGTON'S ROLLING BLOCK

During the long currency of the trapdoor Springfield, a succession of attempts was made to identify and introduce a replacement for it. The first centred on another single-shot rifle, the Remington Rolling Block, which had a somewhat simpler and very much stronger action. The brainchild of Leonard Geiger and Joseph Rider at Remington's factory in Ilion, New York, the new rifle was developed in the closing months of the American Civil War and perfected by early 1866 – just too late to secure a share of the most lucrative market for firearms the world had ever known, much to Remington's frustration (though the company need not have feared a dearth of orders; the rifle – and, somewhat surprisingly, at a time when the revolver pistol was just coming into its own, the single-shot pistol it produced with the same action – was to go on to become very popular indeed, and to be selected, at the Imperial Exposition held in Paris in 1868, as the best rifle in the world. In all, Remington was to sell well over one million rolling block rifles over the coming years, and keep the action in limited production until 1933; later, replicas became very popular, as indeed did copies of the trapdoor Springfield (both for display and to shoot).

The action was simple and strong, designed so that pressure in the chamber forced the standing breech and the rolling block together more tightly. To open the action, one merely thumbed back the hammer to full cock, which in turn permitted the breech to be rolled back, extracting a spent case in the process if there were one in the chamber. A fresh round was then inserted, and the breech was rolled up to the closed position, which aligned the firing pin with the hammer and the primer in the centre of the head of the cartridge case. A practised rifleman could keep up a very rapid rate

of fire indeed – 15 rounds a minute was certainly attainable under the right conditions. As for its strength, a trial which took place in the Belgian city of Liège, one of the gunmaking centres of the world, showed that the rifle was effectively unbreakable with the sort of propellant charges then available. A test piece was loaded with a charge of 48.6g (750 grain) of black powder – 10 times the normal load – and 40 over-size balls, so that the barrel was completely filled; when it was fired, 'nothing out of the ordinary happened', according to the director of the proof house.

In all, the armies of over a dozen different countries were to be equipped with the Remington rifle, but that of its homeland was not to be one of them. The US Navy came closest, when, in 1870, the Naval Ordnance Board placed an order for 10,000, but due to a manufacturing error the rear sight on these pieces was mis-aligned, and it was then discovered that the fault could not be rectified without weakening the barrels. All was not lost for, it is said, the 10,000 rifles were sold to France just prior to the outbreak of the war with Prussia (though French sources suggest that only around 1000 rifles were actually supplied, and that they arrived at the port of Le Havre on 4 September, by which time the French emperor had already surrendered to Bismarck). The US Army did order a small number of Remingtons for trials purposes, but declined to swap its trapdoor Springfields for a rifle which was only marginally superior.

THE FALLING BLOCK

The British Army, on the other hand, had always considered the Snider conversion of the Enfield rifle-musket to be nothing more than a stop-gap measure, and even while the conversion programme was under way it had begun looking for a replacement, testing, according to some accounts, around 120 different submissions with no less than 49 different cartridge configurations before settling in 1871 on a rifle with a falling block action, the Martini-Henry.

The falling block action (which was only superficially similar to that employed to such good effect by Christian Sharps, but nonetheless hardly inferior to it) was the brainchild of a Bostonian named Henry O. Peabody, who obtained a patent for it in 1862. Actuated by the forward motion of a lever which formed a rearwards extension of the trigger guard,

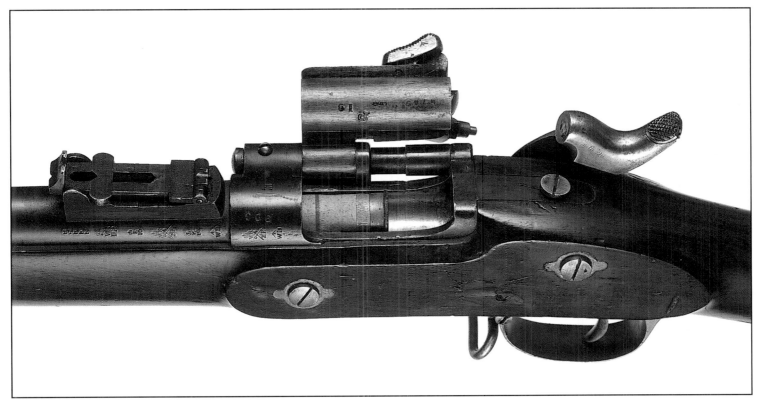

and which was shaped to allow the easy insertion of a thumb, the breech block, which was hinged at its lower rear edge, tipped down to expose the chamber while its smooth concave upper surface – by now inclined at an appropriate angle – acted as a guideway for the introduction of a fresh round. Peabody found a ready market in Canada and in a number of European countries, but the US Army rejected the new rifle (along with many others) in 1865 in favour of modifying its Springfield rifle-muskets. That same year the Swiss Army commenced a

competition to choose a breech-loading rifle, and it, too, rejected the Peabody, but during the course of the exercise the arm attracted the attention of a Swiss (or perhaps Austrian), Frederich von Martini, of the firm of Martini, de Frauenfeld, which was occupied in a very non-martial trade: it made lace.

THE MARTINI-HENRY

Martini recognised that there were flaws in Peabody's design and set about rectifying them, removing the exposed hammer (which the shooter was forced to

■ **ABOVE: Jacob Snider's simple conversion of the Enfield 1853 Pattern rifle-musket was cheap and effective, though it was never seen as anything but a stop-gap measure.**

thumb back manually), and the set-through firing pin upon which it acted, in favour of a concealed striker actuated directly by the trigger mechanism which was brought to the cocked position by the single act of lowering the block and then returning it to battery. Martini submitted his modified rifle to the commission of

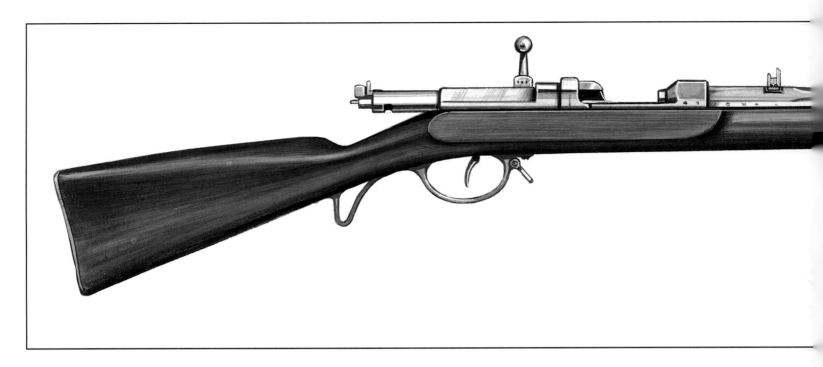

officers set up to select a new service rifle for the British Army in 1867, and was successful in part – the British liked the falling block action, but not the rifling method Peabody had adopted, which Martini had left unchanged. Instead, they chose the rifling devised by Benjamin Tyler Henry for the under-lever rim-fire repeating rifle he had produced for Oliver Winchester some seven years previously. In mid-1868, the Superintendent of the Royal Arsenal at Woolwich, Colonel Dixon, was instructed to construct a specimen rifle combining the two elements in .45in (11.4mm) calibre, chambered for a rimmed centre-fire cartridge.

The test piece was delivered on 21 October. During the rapid-firing trials which followed, a sergeant-instructor of musketry named Bott got off 20 rounds in 53 seconds; then there was the exposure trial, in which the test piece was immersed in dirty water and mud for seven days and nights, being periodically retrieved and cursorily cleaned so that a total of 400 rounds could be fired. Lastly, a second musketry instructor, this time a captain named Mackinnon, was called upon to replicate Bott's earlier feat as closely as possible, and got off his 20 rounds in 63 seconds. The new rifle was approved and put into production at Enfield; deliveries to infantry regiments began in 1871. It was to continue in front-line service until the introduction of the first model Lee-Metford bolt-action magazine repeating rifle (the Rifle, Magazine, Mark 1) in 1888, and formed the basis for a series of unsuccessful

attempts to convert the falling block action from single-shot to magazine-fed repetition. The Martini action was subsequently adopted for many custom-made target rifles in .22in calibre, and the Birmingham Small Arms Co. (BSA) in the United Kingdom (and others) kept such rifles in production until well into the 1960s.

THE BAVARIAN WERDER

The British were not alone in choosing the falling block action for their new service rifle. The Bavarian Army also selected the system, this time in the guise of a rifle designed by Johann-Ludwig Werder, director of the Cramer-Klett Machine Factory in Nürnberg. The Werder rifle in 11mm (.43in) calibre, known as the M/69 but not actually issued to most of the troops of Germany's second-largest state until they returned from the war with France in 1871, differed from the Martini chiefly in that its inventor did away with the rear-mounted manual actuating lever and substituted a spring-loaded device operated by a short lever resembling the trigger, set just ahead of it within the trigger guard and with its curvature reversed, to be actuated by the back of the trigger finger to open the breech. Ejection and extraction were automatic, as they were with the original Peabody and Martini falling block actions. The breech was subsequently closed and the action set up for firing (and the leaf spring which served to open the breech block was also set) by manually thumbing back the exposed offset

hammer tail (the hammer itself was concealed in a rear extension to the breech block housing) to the full-cock position; bringing it to half-cock rendered the rifle safe.

FEWER COMPONENTS

One of the most important features of Werder's rifle was its small number of components – its lock or action had just 13 parts, including side panels; Martini's action as used by the British had 27 parts, and the repeating Henry had no fewer than 49. This was an important factor, for not only did it make maintenance and the armourer's job considerably easier, but it also kept down the cost of manufacture. As originally issued, they enjoyed wide popularity with the troops who used them. This was due to their being able to get off up to 20 rounds per minute from a rifle which was accurate out to 600m (1970ft) and effective to twice that distance, thanks to the 385 metres (1265ft) per second muzzle velocity (almost exactly the same as that of the Martini-Henry) produced by the M/69 Long cartridge, with its 4.5g (70 grain) black powder charge and 22g (340 grain) round-headed lead bullet (there was a less-powerful M/69 Short cartridge too, developed for the M/69 carbine and a single-shot pistol using the same falling block action).

THE M/71 CARTRIDGE

That all changed later, when it was decided, in an attempt to introduce an element of unification throughout the Reich, to re-chamber the existing M/69

Dreyse Needle-Gun

Calibre: 13.6mm (.53in)
Weight: 4.6kg (10lbs)
Length: 1100mm (43.25in)
Barrel length: 700mm (27.5in)

Effective range: 200m (975ft)
Configuration: Single-shot,
  bolt-action, breech-loading
Muzzle velocity: 295mps (960fps)
Country of origin: Prussia

rifles then in Bavarian service – 127,000 of them – to take the more powerful M/71 cartridge (see below), developed at Spandau for the Mauser-designed M/71 bolt-action rifle then coming into use in Prussia; the modification (which consisted primarily of lengthening the cartridge bed in the chamber, and then fitting re-calibrated sights) was all too often carried out very badly, leading to frequent jamming and incomplete extraction. This was a bad enough fault in a bolt-action rifle, or even in one with a vertical breech block like the Sharps, but was a very serious problem indeed in one with a hinged falling block; it could not be rectified in the field, but required that the jammed piece be returned to the armoury for repair.

Proof that it was not a basic trait of the M/69 rifle was soon forthcoming when new guns manufactured to the new specification – 25,000 of them were supplied – proved as good with the new cartridge as the originals had been before modification (or more accurately, rather better, since the new round was an improvement on the original and gave a

muzzle velocity of 430 metres/1410ft per second), but by that time, the damage had been done. There was a very real concern that should Bavaria have to go to war to defend herself (a possibility which could never be dismissed during that period), the result would quite literally be a walkover, since the modified M/69 rifle could not be considered, in the words of the enquiring commission set up under HRH Prince Luitpold, Master of the Bavarian Ordnance, 'as a weapon fully usable for war'.

The outcome of this fiasco was Bavaria adopting the bolt-action Prussian M/71 service rifle in place of its Werder rifles. Luitpold, conscious of the strategic implications, originally demanded that the Bavarian state arms factory at Amberg immediately increase production of the M/69nM (*neuer Modell*) rifles chambered for the M/71 cartridge to re-equip the Army, but was told that that would be impossible since its entire production was now taken up with supplying M/71s to Prussia under what had looked at the time like a very advantageous contract, and that the few

M/69nM rifles available were in fact being manufactured by Josef Werndl at Steyr, in Austria, who had no more capacity either (this despite the fact that it was the biggest arms factory in the world). Luitpold had no option but to accept the Mauser rifle, a decision which was the first step along a road which led to de facto dominance for the Oberndorf-developed bolt action – though in truth, like many another of the time, it was a rutted road strewn with rocks and pitted with holes.

THE MAUSER BROTHERS

The Mauser brothers were born four years apart, Wilhelm in 1834 and Paul (who is sometimes known as Peter-Paul) in 1838, the 11th and 13th children of Andreas Mauser, a semi-skilled parts filer at the Royal Württemburg Rifle Factory in Oberndorf am Neckar. By the

■ BELOW: Like the Enfield-Snider, the Allin-modified 'trapdoor' Springfield was a way of updating a muzzle-loading weapon (the Model 1863 rifle-musket) to permit it to use unitary cartridges.

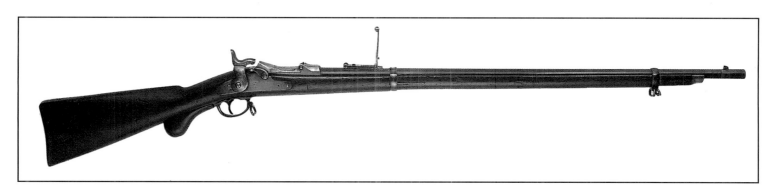

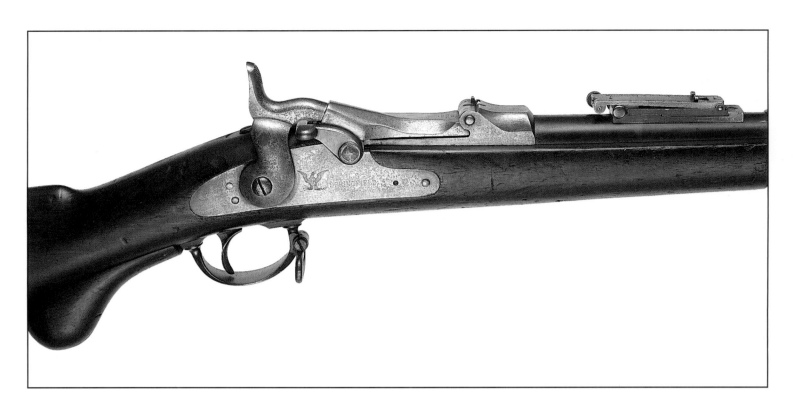

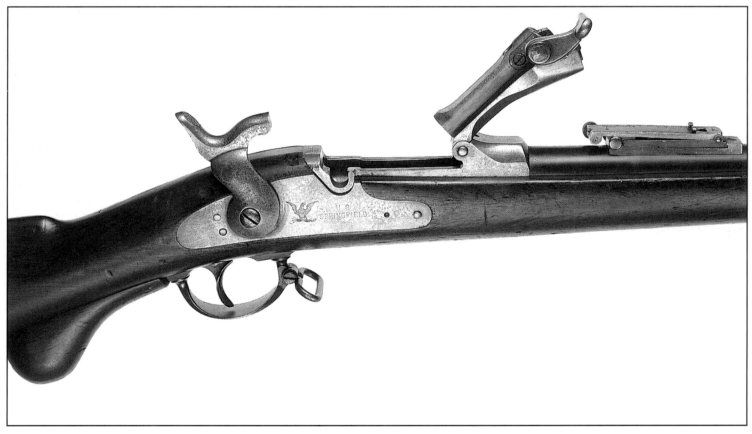

■ABOVE: A beautifully preserved Allin-modified 'trapdoor' Springfield. These rifles were issued from the late 1860s and were not entirely superseded until well into the twentieth century.

time each was 12 years old, he was at work in the factory himself. Clearly, the Mauser brothers had ambition beyond that normally found in factory workers,

for no sooner had they attained the necessary sort of skill levels than they were at work on designs of their own, apparently using the factory's facilities but in their own time. From the start, they were to concern themselves with producing a bolt-action, presumably as a result of having worked on countless Dreyse needle-guns, and by the mid-1860s had come up with a design of their

own, which they showed not just to the superintendent at Oberndorf, but to representatives of foreign governments at the various embassies located in Stuttgart, the state capital.

THE FIRST MAUSER DESIGN
The novelty of the first Mauser design lay in its bolt handle – fabricated in two pieces and split along its length, the two

portions were held together by a countersunk set-screw through the head of the handle. The rear portion, which was fabricated from spring steel, was held back by the cocking cam on the trigger sear as the bolt was pushed home and acted as the mainspring, being released by the trigger to impact with the firing pin, which in turn acted on the primer of the centre-fire cartridge for which the rifle was chambered. Both Prussia and Bavaria rejected the rifle, the former in the person of the ambassador, who it is safe to say knew absolutely nothing about the subtleties of firearms design, who advised the Mausers that his government was not then looking for a replacement for its Dreyse needle-guns (a statement which was, equally certainly, blatantly untrue), the latter after rather greater consideration from the Hand Firearms Commission in Munich which cited design deficiencies that could not be rectified. Only in Austria was the new gun received at all favourably (though it was still rejected, the Imperial Government having decided only the year before to commit itself to a programme to convert its vast stock of existing Lorenz muzzle-loaders, very similar in character to that which was even then under way in Britain and the United States), and the war minister also took it upon himself to show the sample to Samuel Norris, the European agent for Remington and Sons.

THE MAUSERS MOVE TO LIÈGE
The Mauser design's real attraction lay in the fact that it was applicable to the conversion of muzzle-loaders and it is clear that Samuel Norris was acting on his own behalf and hoping to gain entry to a very lucrative, if short-lived, market, rather than for Eliphalet Remington and his son Philo, his employers.

He travelled to Oberndorf in September 1867 and started negotiations with the elder Mauser (from the start, Wilhelm was the better businessman of the two, Paul the more talented designer, though their partnership was clearly synergetic), convincing the brothers to move to Liège to work for him. In the sort of deal not uncommon at the time, the Mauser brothers signed over the rights to their inventions (though since they had not succeeded in obtaining patents, exactly what rights they had is unclear) in return for the sum of 60,000 Francs, payable in instalments over 10 years.

In the end, Norris failed to sell the Mauser conversion and reneged on his promise as a result, but by that time the Mausers had reaped a much more lucrative benefit, for, in what was certainly one of the most important gunmaking centres in the world at the time, they had become intimately acquainted with machine tools and production methods quite unknown to the factory in Oberndorf. And they also – and this was to be just as significant – became acquainted with important men at the Prussian Military Gunnery School at Spandau, Berlin, where many of the significant opinions regarding small arms manufacture and procurement in the state originated, and which was to go on to occupy the same position in the entire Reich after unification in 1871

THE MAUSER-NORRIS RIFLE
Much of the Mausers' early work at Liège centred on developing a conversion for Chassepot rifles to enable them to accept brass unitary cartridges; within a year of their arrival they had perfected a design, and were able to obtain a patent for it in 1868. This was to have considerably greater significance than they probably imagined when, two years on, the German states found themselves in possession of vast numbers of these same guns and began converting them along the lines that the Mausers had devised, though just how much Wilhelm and Paul gained financially is rather moot – European governments of that period still had absolute power, and a tendency to ignore patent protection in a fairly arbitrary way when it suited them.

The brothers broke with Norris in 1869, but not before they had produced a revised rifle with a more conventional bolt-action which owed a considerable debt to the Chassepot, which their American partner managed to have selected for trials the Prussian Rifle Testing Commission was holding to find a replacement for the by-then fairly venerable (and certainly obsolete) Dreyse needle-gun. The Mauser-Norris, as the rifle was briefly known, thus took its place alongside the new falling block Werder M/69 and Martini, and the Chassepot, the Swiss Vetterli and long-forgotten designs from Holland and Belgium, as well as one from Hiram Berdan, who had by now left the US Army and set himself up as a designer of firearms, all the latter being cylindrical-breech bolt-action arms.

Having had some 35 years' experience of a rifle with a cylindrical breech by then, the Prussians were somewhat prejudiced against the Martini and the Werder from the start. It was the bolt-action designs which attracted them the most, and the favourite among those, there was good reason to believe, was the Mauser-Norris.

MAUSER *MODELL* 1871
In May 1870 Wilhelm Mauser went to Spandau to gauge the situation for himself, and wrote to his brother Paul: 'That a new rifle is sought in Prussia is definite, and ours is surely at the head of the list. In terms of simplicity it stands alone. . .' but it was not exactly what the commission wanted.

As spring turned to summer, Paul Mauser made many small modifications to the design, in line with constructive criticism relayed from Spandau by Wilhelm, working in the small shop he had set up behind his father-in-law's house in Oberndorf, and over the weeks and months a better and better rifle emerged. But the trials proceeded very slowly, and, long before any substantive decision even looked likely, the war with France intervened.

It was late summer of the following year before any further progress was made. During the war the Werder rifle had shown up very well in the hands of the four Bavarian Jäger battalions which had been armed with it, and, despite the prejudice against, it was still in contention as a result, but by the end of September it had been eliminated, along with the American, Belgian, British, and Dutch contenders (and also the Vetterli, an 11-shot repeater with a tubular magazine which was a few years ahead of its time), and the revised bolt-action Mauser emerged as a clear winner, with the proviso that Paul Mauser re-design the safety mechanism within no more than two months.

Mauser beat the time limit handsomely, and on 2 December 1871 the Prussian Royal Arsenal at Spandau was instructed to produce 2500 Mauser *Infanteriegewehr Modell* 1871 rifles in 11mm (.43in) calibre for extended testing. On 22 March 1872 a note from the War Ministry to the Mausers informed them that 'His Majesty the Kaiser and King. . . has condescended to approve the test of the Infantry Rifle M/71 and to command most graciously that rifles of this type be produced for the re-armament of the infantry.' The Mausers had found success

■ABOVE: A French infantryman of the Second Empire period with his Chassepot needle-gun. The Chassepot was introduced in 1866 in reply to the Dreyse needle-gun.

at last, but all too soon discovered that it was little more than an illusion.

POOR EJECTION MECHANISM

The basic action of the M/71 rifle was very similar to that developed by von Dreyse and Chassepot, and the all-important locking system was hardly more sophisticated, even though the M/71 cartridge developed for it was very much more powerful than anything seen a generation earlier. The bolt had a straight handle which was attached to a raised rib; when the action was closed, it stuck out at right-angles. Bringing it up to stand vertically turned the body of the bolt through 90 degrees and allowed it to be withdrawn to the rear, the guide rib passing through a slot machined in the upper surface of the receiver, its rearwards motion being arrested when a stop (which was really nothing more than a set-screw with an over-thick washer) in the rib was obstructed by the rounded shoulders of the receiver bridge. The cocking process commenced towards the end of the rearward stroke, when the cocking piece at the rear of the bolt – an external extension to the spring-loaded firing pin, though not connected to it – engaged the cocking cam on the trigger sear; it was completed on the forward stroke, when the cam restrained it and held it off against the pressure of a secondary spring. The safety catch, which Paul Mauser had had belatedly to modify, was no more than a stop which was interspersed between the cocking piece and the bolt body, retained by a pin which was located in the rear of the bolt guide, engaged and disengaged by the simple act of turning it through 90 degrees. In the process of pulling the bolt back, the spent case, the rim of which was gripped firmly by the extractor claw

spring-mounted on the bolt head, was extracted from the chamber, but, inexplicably, the ejection mechanism – a spring-loaded lever in the receiver bed – present in earlier generations of the design was absent from that which was to become the M/71 and the rifleman was forced to turn the weapon over and tip out the spent case before he could manually load a fresh round, pushing the bolt back home to seat it in the chamber and completing that process by turning the bolt handle back down so that the rear of the guide rib (essentially, the root of the bolt handle) engaged the camming surface on the front of the receiver bridge, seating the cartridge, completing the seal (by means of a ring-shaped flange on the bolt head) and locking the action. As we have seen, the Dreyse and Chassepot needle-guns used this same, rather perfunctory, one-sided locking method; but what had been acceptable with the relatively low-power charges they employed was to be less reliable in the future. In the case of the M/71 rifle employing the M/71 round, the result was to be a tendency for the rifle to pull to the right, rendering it less accurate than it might have been, and it was a fault which was to be perpetuated and accentuated in the first Mauser repeater rifle.

AN UNHAPPY OUTCOME
Despite the fact that they actually had no production facilities of their own, the Mauser brothers were surprised to discover that they would not receive a contract to produce the M/71 rifle. They had fondly imagined that a substantial order would allow them to set up a factory of their own, but instead the Royal Rifle Factories at Spandau, Erfurt, and Danzig got the work – and to make matters worse, when they could not keep up with demand, additional orders were still not placed with Mauser, but with the Bavarian Royal Rifle Factory at Amberg, with Spangenberg & Sauer, Schilling, Haenel in Suhl, Josef Werndl's Osterreichische Waffenfabrik Gesellschaft (Austrian Weapons Manufacturing Company) in Steyr, and the National Arms & Ammunition Co in Birmingham, England. All the Mausers themselves actually produced in the end were a few thousand rear sights.

In keeping with the practices of the day in Germany, the Mausers had not even agreed a development fee with the Prussian Government in advance (though 60,000 Talers – equal to 180,000 Marks, £9000 Sterling, US$45,000 – had been suggested and apparently approved by the Prussian Rifle Testing Commission's president, Colonel Kalinowski), and were eventually forced to settle for 8000 Talers (24,000 Marks). Worse still, the Prussian Government immediately declared the design of the new weapon a state secret, so they could not even try to obtain export orders for 'their' rifle, and to add insult to injury they were denied a patent, so there could be no question of them demanding a licence fee. As compensation for this, Kaiser Wilhelm granted the brothers an 'unconditional authorised cash gift' amounting to a further 12,000 Marks.

MAUSER BROTHERS & CO.
The story eventually had a slightly less unhappy outcome, however, for at the end of 1873 the Württemberg State Government gave the Mausers an order for 100,000 M/71s to be produced over the next five years at a rate of 22 Taler (66 Marks) for the first 11,000 and 18 Taler, 55 Groschen (about 55 Marks) for the rest; this latter price was almost identical to the one the non-Prussian producers charged the Berlin government. More importantly, the Württemberg

government also agreed to sell the Royal Rifle Factory at Oberndorf to the brothers; the needed capital came from the Württemberg Union Bank, and on 5 February 1874, Gebrüder Mauser & Cie was established.

CARBINE M/71
The self-same thing was to happen to the Mausers again in 1875, when the shorter carbine version of the M/71 was produced for issue to the cavalry (apart from shortening the barrel from 860mm to 485mm – 34in to 19in – and deleting the cleaning rod, the only real modification to the design saw the bolt handle bent through 90 degrees, so that when the action was closed it lay down the side of the woodwork): Prussia ordered 60,000, from Werndl at Steyr, and Saxony acquired 10,000 from the same source, while Spangenberg & Sauer, Schilling, Haenel supplied 14,000 to Bavaria (taking a similar number of Chassepot rifles in part-exchange). Mauser Brothers & Co. were able to supply only 3000, for the Royal Württemberg Cavalry.

The year Mauser Brothers & Co. came into existence matters started to improve, however, for the 'state secret' status of the M/71 was lifted, giving them the chance to sell the rifle into other markets overseas.

The first export order came from China, for 26,000 M/71s, and a few years later, in 1878, came a much larger order from the newly-independent (from Turkey) Serbian Government for 100,000 of a slightly modified version, known as the Mauser-Koka Model 78/80, in 10.15mm x 63 calibre (the second figure

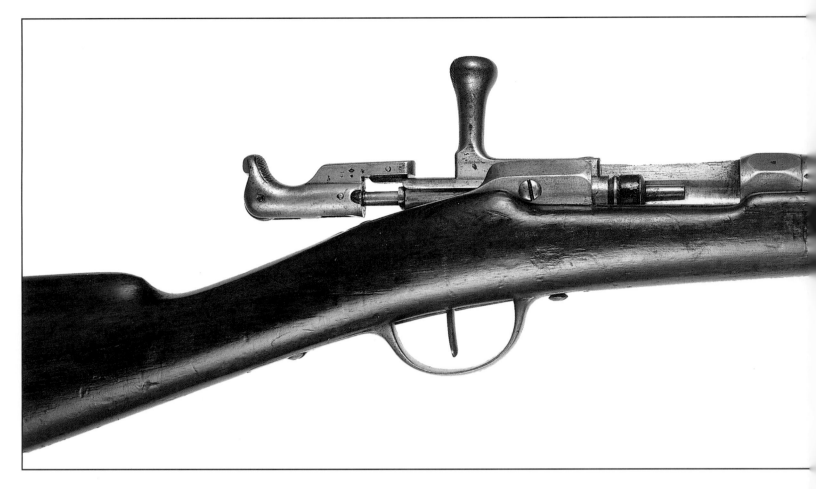

■ABOVE: This photograph of an early model Chassepot (note the 1867 date of manufacture stamped into the barrel) shows clearly the shroud protecting the needle-like firing pin.

is the length of the case, also in millimetres; it was – and still is – used as a subsidiary designator, there being many types of ammunition in similar calibres which are not interchangeable by virtue of the fact that they differ in length), with wedge rifling, the four lands of which decreased in width from 4.7mm (three-sixteenths of an inch) at the breech to 3.9mm (two and a half-sixteenths of an inch) at the muzzle, and the spring-loaded ejector the *Infanteriegewehr Modell* M/71 lacked.

WIND'S MODIFICATIONS

These were not the only modifications which had been applied to the basic design in the intervening period, but oddly, the inspiration for the most significant of them came not from Paul Mauser, but from a young Prussian infantry lieutenant named Wind. Early on, a niggling weakness had been detected in the Mauser M/71's 'igniting ability' – the force with which its firing pin struck the primer, in other words –

which caused infrequent misfires. Three solutions were put forward: strengthening the coil spring which propelled the firing pin forwards, which would have the slightly detrimental side-effect of increasing the effort needed to close the bolt; lightening the cocking piece, so that the firing pin had less weight to carry forward; and lastly – and this was Wind's suggestion – uniting the cocking piece and the firing pin into a single component. The problem was not serious, and the deliberations over which solution to adopt were rendered futile in 1876 anyway, when the convex primer caps in the original cartridge design were swapped for caps with a flat surface which required less energy to activate, but, nonetheless, Mauser Brothers adopted the modification for the rifles they produced for Serbia and for the M/71-84 repeater.

There were, however, further fundamental weaknesses to the design which could not be rectified. Firstly, the band which attached the fore-grip to the barrel near the muzzle, which was located and fixed by a set-screw passing through a lug below the barrel (this method had been adopted in order to provide a firm anchorage for the bayonet) prevented the barrel from vibrating freely

and caused the bullet's point of impact to deviate unpredictably from the point of aim. Secondly – and less crucially, or so it appeared – the one-sided locking of the bolt (by means of the bolt handle root being brought up against the locking surface on the front of the right hand side of the receiver bridge) also caused a degree of deviation, this time rather more predictably, for it caused the recoil to slew the rifle to the right, pulling it away from the point of aim. Neither of the two problems was anything like a disabling weakness, but they were present, and doubtless their very existence bothered Paul Mauser, who was nothing if not a perfectionist. The supposedly lesser fault of the two was to return to plague him later on.

THE FIRST REPEATING RIFLES

By the early 1870s all the world's major armies were equipped with breech-loading rifles effective out to a range of 500m (1640ft) and more, and as a result the nature of warfare was much changed from the way it had been even just one generation before. Already riflemen had begun to confront each other from cover, instead of standing-to in the open, in battles where like-levels of technology met; the contrast between the Crimean

War of 1853-56 and the American Civil War, less than a decade later, is both stark and compelling. ('Colonial' troops of the newly-important imperial powers – as well as the men of the US Army – continued to fight it out in the open with the indigenous peoples they set out to conquer, but that was largely because they usually managed to prevent the natives from getting their hands on modern firearms.)

But range is only one element of firepower; the rapidity with which an armed body can get off its effective fire is also vitally important, particularly in the last stages of an assault when the attacker must close with the defender and physically deprive him of his ground, either by killing him, disabling him, or by driving him away. We have already seen that in the hands of a skilled practitioner, the new breed of single-shot breech-loading rifle was able to produce a rate of fire approaching 20 rounds a minute, and this was already giving many strategists pause for thought, for it meant that an undisciplined private soldier could expend his entire ammunition supply in a matter of a very short period, and leave himself defenceless in the process. It was as a direct result of this fear that repeating rifles were not introduced

earlier to the European armies, even though their effectiveness was brought home with a very loud bang indeed during the second half of 1877 at a remote enough location in what is now Bulgaria, when 30,000 Turks besieged in Plevna held off 100,000 Russians for some months, thanks largely to the superior rate of fire of the Winchester repeaters with which they were armed over that of the single-shot bolt-action Berdan rifles in the hands of the Tsarist troops.

The Turks had no friends left in Europe, particularly after the massacres they had perpetrated in the Balkans as their grip there began to weaken, but their temporary and limited success at Plevna (Osman Pasha was driven out before the year's end, and by the spring the Russians were at the gates of Istanbul, then known as Constantinople) shook the world and sent gunmakers scurrying to refine designs for repeating rifles and governments flocking to buy them. To chart the progress of the type from the beginning, however, we have to retrace our steps, and return across the Atlantic to examine the almost-forgotten pioneering work of an almost-forgotten man, Walter Hunt, the rather better-known contributions made by Christopher M. Spencer and Benjamin Tyler Henry, and the decisive step forward taken by a man who is said never to have fired a gun in the entire course of his life. Oliver Fisher Winchester.

THE UNDER-LEVER RIFLES
In 1847 Walter Hunt of Brooklyn, New York, a professional inventor of some genius with literally hundreds of inventions of one sort and another to his credit – from sewing machines to safety pins – and hardly a dollar to his name, took out a patent for a self-contained cartridge which used a small charge of powder – some 0.42g (6.5 grain) – housed inside the hollow base of a .38in- (9.6mm) calibre cylindro-conoidal lead bullet which itself weighed 6.5g (100 grain), detonating it by means of a percussion cap acting through a hole in the cork plug which closed off the base aperture; by way of contrast, a relatively low-powered .41in- (10.5mm) calibre rim-fire round of the period used a 0.8g (13 grain) charge to propel a 8.4g (130 grain) bullet. Two years later, Hunt took out a US patent for what he called a 'Volitional Repeater', a gun with a tubular under-barrel

magazine using this ammunition (and a striker/firing pin energised by a helical coiled spring, in place of the then-standard leaf spring-actuated hammer, which was some years ahead of its time); lacking capital, he assigned the patent almost immediately, for an unknown sum, to a machinist named George Arrowsmith. An employee of Arrowsmith's, Lewis Jennings, worked on the gun design, simplified and strengthened it, and himself obtained an additional patent which he, too, assigned to Arrowsmith. Arrowsmith in turn sold both the Hunt and Jennings patents to Courtland Palmer, and Palmer contracted with the firm of Robbins and Lawrence, of Windsor, Vermont, to produce 5000 rifles to this design.

Over the next two years, two young journeymen-gunsmiths, Horace Smith and Daniel Baird Wesson, who had met while turning out gun barrels for Allen, Brown, and Luther in Connecticut, refined the design still further in their spare time and in 1854 they joined forces, together with Palmer, to manufacture it as both a rifle and a pistol.

THE VOLCANIC COMPANY
The following year, Smith, Wesson, and Palmer sold out to the Volcanic Repeating Arms Company, a consortium of some 40 investors from New Haven and New York, including clockmakers, carriage builders, shopkeepers, and a shirt manufacturer named Oliver F. Winchester. Volcanic continued to manufacture the rifles and pistols, the only major change being to the round they fired; instead of black powder, the base of the bullet was now charged with a fulminate-based percussion powder, which acted as a self-priming propellant, and did away with the need for a separate percussion cap. It was Daniel Wesson who had devised this charge, after Flobert (qv); still dissatisfied with its performance, he went on to develop a true centre-fire cartridge in 1854. The Volcanic Company acquired the rights to this cartridge along with the other assets of Smith, Wesson, and Palmer, but never put it into production – a serious oversight on its part.

That oversight was all the more lamentable since it was the original round's poor performance which eventually spelled disaster for the Volcanic rifle and pistol, and the company went into bankruptcy early in 1857 – though there may have been other forces

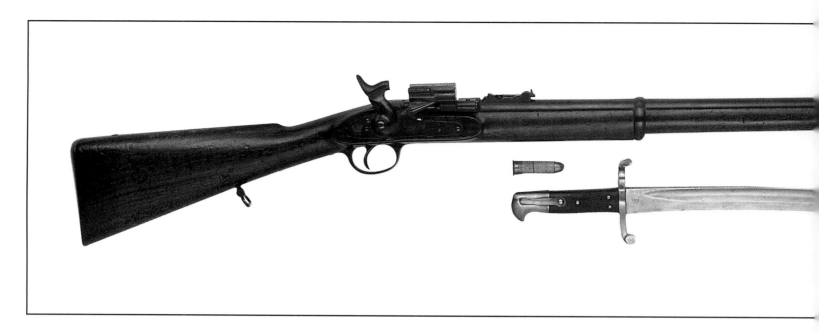

■ABOVE: The Enfield-Snider, while it was effective, had a distinctly anachronistic appearance – the bayonet, in particular, harks back to an earlier period.

at work, since on 19 March that year, Winchester, with the participation of just a few of the original investors, purchased its assets and assigned them to a new company, the New Haven Arms Co., with himself as president.

Knowing nothing whatsoever about firearms, Winchester brought in Benjamin Tyler Henry to run the manufacturing side of the business, and it was Henry who decided to abandon the pistol and concentrate instead on making essential improvements to the rifle, as well as devising the .44in- (11.2mm) calibre rim-fire unitary cartridge it was to fire, preventing the company from going the same way as Volcanic had and

■BELOW: While the Hunt/Jennings rifles were only marginally effective, they were the direct forerunners of the enormously successful and popular Winchester lever-action rifles.

producing one of the most famous lines of rifles ever seen in the process.

Essentially, the Volcanic was a bolt-action rifle, though in its case, and in those of the other under-lever rifles which followed it, the bolt was actuated, backwards and forwards, by the operation of a lever similar to that used by Peabody and Martini to open the falling block breech of their rifles. Purists argue that the method of locking the straight-pull bolt employed by the early under-lever rifles is less secure than the positive action of turning the bolt in its bed so that its handle is blocked by a locking cam, as employed by von Dreyse, Chassepot, and Mauser, and there might have been some grounds for concern if the original Hunt and Jennings rifles and the Volcanic had been chambered for a more powerful round. In any event, it was one of the first things Benjamin Tyler Henry addressed when he came to modify the rifle's design, introducing a pair of short horizontally-mounted rods, joined with a pivot to form a toggle which acted on the bolt to hold it closed by being forced over-centre by the cocking/loading lever.

There is an interesting testament to the ultimate strength of this innovation of Henry's, and a greater significance to it, which seems previously to have gone unremarked: it was a Winchester repeater which Hiram Maxim chose to modify when he wanted to prove that a rifle's recoil was enough to cycle the gun's action, to produce an automatic weapon which, once cocked, would continue firing as long as the trigger remained pressed and there was ammunition available (Browning chose a Winchester, too, when he wanted to demonstrate that a similar weapon could be made to work by tapping propellant gas off from the barrel and using it to actuate a piston, which in turn cycled the action). Maxim later adopted the over-centre toggle locking bar, suitably re-engineered and re-configured, to be the effective heart of his machine gun, the act of overcoming the mechanical disadvantage and breaking the toggle serving to delay the cycling of the action until the round just fired was clear of the muzzle, and the pressure in the chamber and barrel had dropped to a point where it was safe to open the breech. There must be a certain suspicion

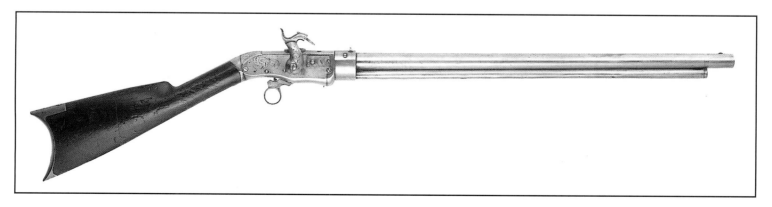

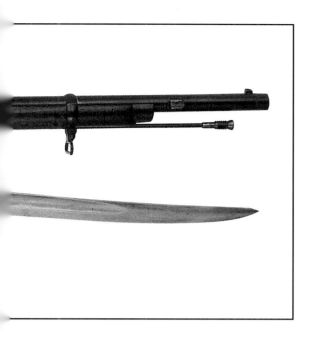

that it was Benjamin Tyler Henry's simple bolt locking device which gave him the idea in the first place.

THE HENRY RIFLE

As well as producing an effective cartridge, Henry also introduced a bifurcated firing pin which struck its rim in two places simultaneously, thus lessening the ever-present (in a rim-fire cartridge) risk of a misfire. He was able to obtain a patent on both this and his improved locking system, and the resulting rifle was originally marketed, from 1860, under his name.

Early models of the rifle were iron-framed, but from 1861 on he switched to brass (siver-plated frames, intricately engraved, featured on presentation models such as the ones Winchester gave, very publicly, to Secretary of War Simon Cameron and Secretary of the Navy Gideon Welles; Winchester was well aware of the power of publicity from the very start). Most of the production was dedicated to rifles, with a capacity of 15 rounds in the magazine under their barrels (and another in the breech; the original Henry's were advertised – widely – as 'sixteen-shooters'), but he also produced shorter, handier carbines with a 12-round capacity.

If the Henry guns had a major weakness, it lay in the way in which their magazines were charged – it was necessary to compress the spring in the magazine by way of a slot in the under-surface near the muzzle, whereupon the front section could be swung open and the magazine recharged from there. It was both rather slow and awkward, and all too often let mud and dirt in, but in

the view of too many senior US Army officers, the main drawback to the new weapon was its efficiency, for trials had shown that a practised rifleman could get off 120 rounds with it in five minutes and 40 seconds – and that included the time spent reloading. The spectre of the inexperienced young soldier firing off all his ammunition in a few minutes and then finding himself defenceless reared up, and killed the Henry dead as a military arm in the United States of the day, largely thanks to the prejudice of Brigadier General James Wolfe Ripley.

Brigadier General Ripley was director of the Board of Ordnance by the outbreak of the American Civil War, having previously been head of the Springfield Armory and having overseen the development and production of the Model 1855 rifle-musket and its transition from tape to percussion cap priming in 1860. As far as Ripley was concerned, there was not a rifle in the world to beat 'his', and he did everything in his considerable power to prevent the adoption of the Henry, ostensibly due to fears that ammunition would be consumed too quickly in battle (which was always a problem of discipline, and never one of technology). He succeeded in large measure, too, for only 1731 Henry rifles were procured by the Union Army during the entire civil war, and they were issued chiefly to units which saw little action until its very end. We shall encounter Ripley's wrong-headed obstructionism again, before long.

KING'S MAGAZINE

The residual problem with the magazine was cured by Nelson King, Henry's successor as superintendent of the New Haven Arms Co., in 1866 (by which time Henry had set up in business for himself, producing barrels with his own design of rifling), when he introduced a loading port on the right hand side of the receiver, fitted with a spring-loaded cover, which was both considerably more secure and easier to use and which allowed a partially-depleted magazine to be reloaded before it was fully discharged – something which was not possible with Henry's original design. The modification permitted a 50 per cent increase in the sustained rate of fire to be achieved – an average of 30 rounds a minute, including time for reloading. The modified rifle was offered for sale as the Model 1866, still under Henry's name, but on 30 March 1867, after just a few thousand had been

produced, Oliver Winchester re-incorporated the company as the Winchester Repeating Arms Co., and from that point Henry's name disappeared.

WINCHESTER REPEATERS

Sound – and hugely popular – as the Winchester '66 was, it had a flaw, and, ironically, it was to be found in the cartridge Henry had developed for the earlier model and which was still in use in the improved gun. As we have seen, rim-fire cartridges are constructed of much lighter material than the centre-fire rounds which succeeded them, since the material of the case itself has to be deformed by the striker or hammer so that it can set off the primer by its impact; as a result, Henry used copper for his cases. The effect of this was to limit the ultimate load of propellant they could use, which in turn limited the hitting power (and adversely affected the trajectory) of the projectile, for heavier loads led to split cases and, inevitably, to jams, which thanks to the closed-in design of the action were rather difficult to clear through the ejection slot on the top of the receiver (which provided the only access to the action short of stripping the gun right down).

There was a secondary drawback to the rim-fire cartridge, too: it could not be reloaded, but a centre-fire cartridge with a separate primer could; this was of little moment to a man who lived in reach of his gunsmith or general store, but more significant for anyone who set out to face the wilderness, who would probably have carried primers, black powder, a bar of lead, and a bullet mould and other simple tools, and reloaded his own cartridges.

THE GUN THAT WON THE WEST

It was Nelson King, again, who solved this problem, modifying the action of the '66 so that it would accept the soon to be almost ubiquitous centre-fire cartridge and producing ammunition to suit (Winchester was to be almost as famous for its ammunition as for its guns, later). The result was the Winchester Model 1873, the most famous of them all, which was to share with the Colt Single-Action Army (SAA) revolver of the same year the title of 'The Gun That Won The West'. The pairing of Colt pistol and Winchester carbine was made all the easier five years later when Colt started producing the SAA chambered for the .44in-40 Winchester Centre Fire (WCF) cartridge

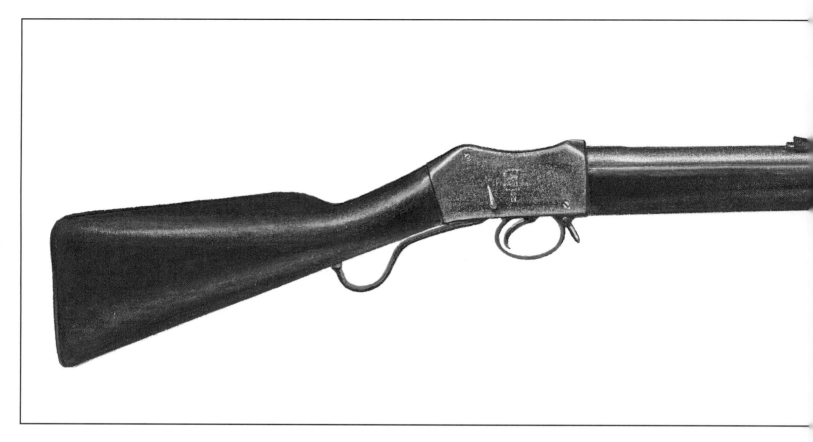

as the Frontier Model, allowing the same ammunition to be used in both (other revolver makers, notably Remington and Smith & Wesson, followed suit). Winchester was later to produce the '73 in a variety of other calibres including .32in WCF and .38in WCF; the

■BELOW: The Remington Rolling Block's action was popular even after effective repeaters made it obsolete. Its simplicity meant that a surprisingly high rate of fire could be maintained.

Winchester cartridges were easily distinguished by their slight 'neck', while most others of the period were straight. The Winchester '73 stayed in production until 1919, by which time almost three-quarters of a million had been produced. Curiously, the rim-fire Model '66 stayed in production alongside its more powerful successor until 1898, by which time 170,000 had been sold, many of them in Europe.

One of the real advantages Winchester had over his competitors was a finely

developed business sense. He was the first gunmaker to advertise widely, and it was the undoubted quality of his rifles which he stressed – selected guns with especially accurate barrels were fitted with set triggers (and often, aperture sights were added by discerning owners, mounted on the small of the butt). Carefully finished, the rifles sold at a premium price of US$100 (very expensive indeed at a time when European gunmakers were producing bolt-action tubular-magazine rifles at well under

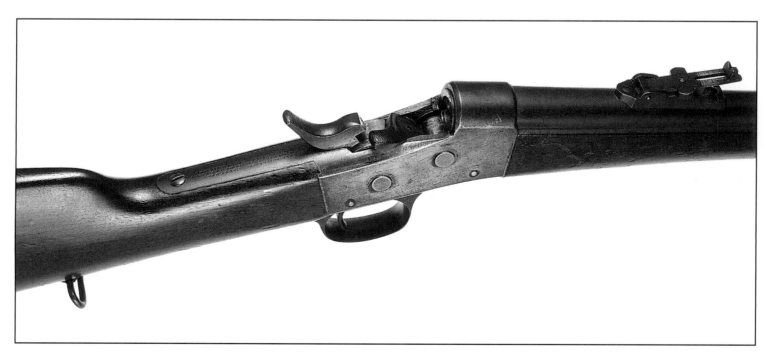

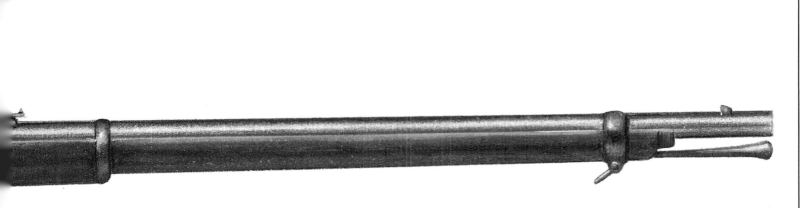

The Martini-Henry Rifle

Calibre: .45in (11.4mm)
Weight: 4.7kg (10lb 6oz)
Length: 1310mm (51.5in)
Barrel length: 850mm (33.25in)
Effective range: Over 400m (1310ft)
Configuration: Single-shot, falling block action
Muzzle velocity: 400mps (1310fps)
Country of origin: United Kingdom

one-fifth of that, admittedly for customers who only ever paid bottom dollar) as being 'One of One Thousand', with an engraved plate in the lower fore-stock to say so. The guns were very much sought-after then, and are probably even more so today.

Three years later, Winchester introduced a heavier, though basically similar, rifle and carbine (the only real difference between the two was usually the length of the barrel, though in the case of the Model 1876 the carbine had an extended fore-stock which reached almost to the muzzle and also an above-barrel handguard, both features normally found only on military rifles by this time. A true military version known somewhat confusingly as the Model 1876 Musket was of similar appearance; it was this latter which Turkish forces used to mete out such punishment to the Russians at Plevna).

WINCHESTER MODEL 1876
The Model 1876 was chambered originally for a .45in-75 round not dissimilar in its characteristics to that employed for the trapdoor Springfields, utilising a 22.7g (350 grain) bullet propelled by 4.86g (75 grain) of black powder, which produced more than twice the energy of the '73. The Model 1876 proved popular with those who wanted more stopping power than was provided

by the smaller rifle, and was eventually produced in .50in-95 Express, .45in-60 WCF and .40in-60 WCF calibres too. It was discontinued in 1897, by which time the market for black powder guns had all but disappeared. Theodore Roosevelt, perhaps the most flamboyant of American presidents, and an avid hunter of big game, favoured the '76, and many other hunters followed his lead; and the Royal Canadian Mounted Police adopted it as their official rifle to replace the Model '66. By the end of the 1870s, after less than a quarter of a century of operation, the Winchester Repeating Arms Co. was firmly established and a force to be reckoned with, having three excellent rifles in production.

THE SPENCER CARBINE
The other great innovator in the field of rifle design in the United States at that period could not have been more different in his background to Oliver Winchester, who was purely a businessman (though he had political ambitions, too, and served one term as lieutenant-governor of Connecticut in 1866 and 1867). Christopher Spencer left school at the age of 14 and went to work in the silk mills of his native Manchester, in that same state, and later in machine toolmaking and locomotive construction before going to work briefly for Colt in New Haven. Back in Manchester once more, he

obtained his first important patent (for a machine to wind silk thread) while still in his early 20s. Then, on 6 March 1860, six months before Henry, Spencer (who, curiously enough, was a Quaker, and could have been expected to have been a pacifist) obtained a patent for a repeating rifle. Like the other, it was a cylindrical breech action with a bolt connected to an under-mounted lever, but this time the rounds to be loaded – seven of them – were housed in a tube in the butt-stock.

SPENCERS FOR THE UNION
Spencer's design was marginally less efficient than the Henry, since the action was not cocked by the fore-and-aft movement of the under-lever which ejected a spent case and loaded a new round into the chamber, but had to be thumbed back by hand; but in its favour was its greater simplicity (we may remember that the Henry had no less than 46 moving parts), which made it both sturdier and cheaper to produce. It satisfied one body of criticism of the under-barrel tubular magazines – that the centre of balance of the rifle so equipped was changed with every round which was fired – and went some way towards making up for having only half the magazine capacity of the Henry by the speed with which it could be reloaded, particularly after the introduction of the Blakeslee Quickloader

– a pre-charged tube with the seven rounds already in it, 10 or more of which were carried in a modified cartouche the rifleman had on a cross-belt – which allowed the rifle to be fully recharged in one movement by literally pouring the cartridges into the magazine.

At the outbreak of the American Civil War in 1861, Spencer offered his carbine to the Union Army – and ran straight into Brigadier General James Wolfe Ripley who would have nothing to do with it. Spencer was luckier – or perhaps cannier – than Winchester, though, and secured the personal support of President Abraham Lincoln himself, who instructed

Ripley to place an order for the gun. Production delays held up delivery, and Ripley used this – and every other excuse he could think of – to limit the size of the contract. It was therefore 1863 before the Spencer carbine began to make a name for itself in the field, though soon both individual soldiers and even whole regiments were spending their own money to equip themselves with it, and still Ripley prevaricated.

It took a second intervention by President Lincoln to break the log-jam, but this time it was more effective; Spencer met Lincoln again on 18 August and both men shot the rifle, the gunsmith

having a slight edge over the statesman. Two weeks later, Ripley was out of a job and his replacement, George D. Ramsay, proved to be as supportive as his predecessor had been obstructive.

By the end of the American Civil War, 77,181 Spencer carbines and 12,471 rifles in .52in (13.2mm) calibre had been supplied to the Union Army, and perhaps as many again purchased privately.

THE END FOR SPENCER

With the end of the war, however, demand for the Spencer simply dried up, much as that for the rather simpler but harder-hitting Sharps rifle was to a

decade later. The last nail in the Spencer's coffin was the introduction of the improved Winchester '66 – with its smaller calibre, higher velocity, and greater capacity – which had considerably greater appeal to the new breed of 'cowboys' and frontiersmen. In 1869 the Spencer Repeating Rifle Co. was closed down, and its machinery and stock auctioned off (much of it to Oliver Winchester, who promptly sold it on to customers abroad).

Christopher Spencer died in 1922, having introduced many important innovations to machine tools – notably a screw-cutting attachment for a turret

lathe – in the later years of his life. Just as Winchester was essentially a man of commerce, the man who had once been his chief rival was an engineer from first to last.

BOLT-ACTION REPEATERS

While the United States was commencing a long-term love affair with the lever-action repeater rifle (and Winchester's rifles were only the beginning; as we shall see, three other gunmakers of genius, John Moses Browning, John Marlin, and Arthur Savage, were also to produce hugely popular lever-action rifles, and they were not alone), Europe displayed a predictable degree of conservatism. The turn-down bolt-action had proved itself to the satisfaction of many and there were still residual doubts as to the security of the lever action; on top of that there was the matter of the advantage the bolt had over the under-lever when firing from the prone position. In any event, when the Europeans began to turn their attention to repeaters, it was exclusively towards bolt-action rifles they looked, initially employing tubular magazines, like those found in the Winchesters, derived from the mechanism Hunt had used to store the ammunition in his Volitional Repeater.

THE VETTERLI REPEATER

We have noted that as early on as 1870, when the Prussians were still deliberating over the choice of a successor to the Dreyse needle-gun, the Vetterli tubular-magazine repeater was one of the weapons offered to them. Frederick Vetterli actually perfected it in 1866, using many of the components of the Henry and King Winchesters (notably the magazine arrangement, Henry's cartridge carrier, and King's loading gate); it won the competition which rejected the Peabody falling block action, single-shot rifle which Martini later modified, as we may recall, and the Swiss Federal Government adopted it, in 10.4mm (.41in) calibre, as its official rifle in 1868, becoming the first to approve a bolt-action repeater rifle for general service in the process. Firing a Boxer-type cartridge charged with 3.75g (57.9 grain) of black powder and a 20.4g (315 grain) bullet,

the muzzle velocity attained was around 410 metres (1335ft) per second, slightly superior to that of the Bavarian M/69 Long cartridge but inferior to that of the soon-to-be-introduced M/71. It stayed in service until it was replaced by the M1889 Schmidt-Rubin rifle which followed the trend started by the French in switching to a much smaller calibre, a development made possible by the introduction of much more powerful propellants, the last step in the evolution of 'modern' ammunition (actually, Rubini – he was a Swiss-Italian and it is unclear why his name is universally corrupted, but we will adhere to the accepted practice here – had nothing to do with the development of the rifle. He was a major in the Federal Army and director of its technical laboratory at Thun, and was the inventor of the rimless cartridge and the jacketed bullet, which he first produced in 1887 and for which the rifle was chambered).

THE KROPATSCHEK SYSTEM

The Henry/King method of presenting a fresh round to the chamber from a tubular magazine wasn't the only such. An Austrian, Kropatschek, produced one which appeared in a number of early European repeaters, most notably in the (rather later) French M1886, usually known as the Lebel, after the lieutenant-colonel of that name who chaired the committee which selected it (that was the accepted procedure in France at that time), in which it was combined with the bolt-action of the M1874 (which was essentially that of the Chassepot as extensively modified by another French Army colonel, Gras), while another Austrian, Ferdinand Früwirth, adopted a similar method for the rifle he produced for his country's gendarmerie as early as 1869. The most important of the genre, however, was the Mauser M71/84, not because it was particularly good of itself – it wasn't – but because of the numbers in which it was produced and the influence it had thanks to the power of the country for which it was developed.

Josef Werndl in Steyr offered the Prussian Rifle Testing Commission a repeating version of the Mauser M/71, fitted with a Kropatschek tubular magazine, as early as 1875, but it was rejected, as much as anything because of the fears of certain high-ranking officers that ill-disciplined troops would shoot themselves out of ammunition in minutes. (Werndl clearly didn't think

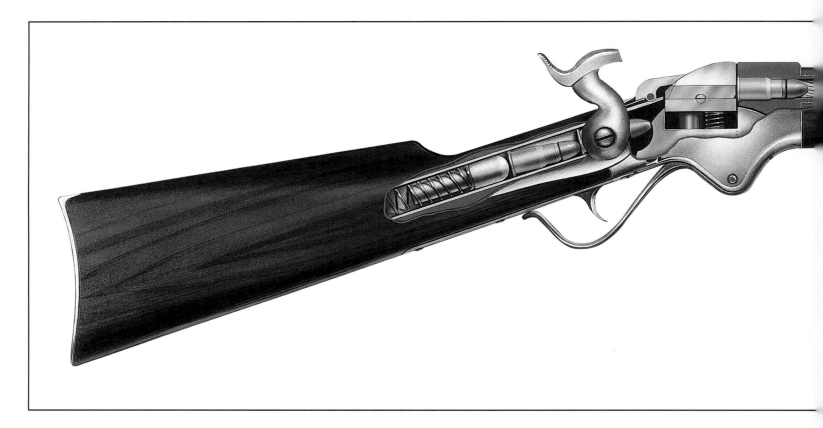

much of the Früwirth system. He bought Früwirth's company in 1869, transferred much of its machinery to Steyr and then closed it down; he put the Kropatschek magazine system into production in

■BELOW: The Spencer rifle was simple and straightforward, and well suited to employment as a weapon of war, but it was overshadowed in peacetime by the more advanced Winchester.

preference to the one to which he owned the rights himself.) Then came the Battle of Plevna. Actually there were four engagements fought during the Russian siege of Turkish-held Plevna between July and December 1877. Three were attacks on the defences, while the fourth was Osman Pasha's attempt to cut his way through the besiegers' lines. The Russians mustered 100,000 men, while the Turks could field 30,000. On 20 July

1877, the Russians attacked the defences north and east of Plevna, capturing some of the advanced trenches and driving the defenders back to the outskirts of the town. However, the Russians sustained heavy losses, losing two-thirds of their officers and nearly 2000 men. In the second battle, on 30 July, 30,000 Russians in two divisions attacked the Turkish redoubts. Though the Russians took two redoubts, by nighfall the Tutks

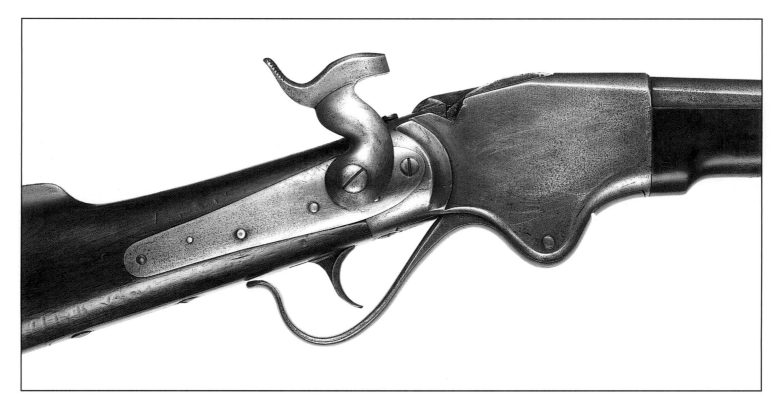

Spencer Model 1865 Carbine

Calibre: .56in (rim-fire) (14.2mm)
Weight: 4.2kg (9lb 4oz)
Length: 1025mm (40.25in)
Barrel length: 550mm (21.65in)
Effective range: 400m (1320ft)
Configuration: Seven-round tubular magazine, under-lever action
Muzzle velocity: 400mps (1320fps)
Country of origin: United States

had counterattacked and retook them, the Russians losing a further 169 officers and 7136 men. On 11-12 September, the Russians assaulted Plevna on three sides, but still their efforts were not enough. An attack on the Omar Tabrija redoubt cost them 6000 men, while in the southwest they fared no better. After two days of bitter fighting the Russians had lost 20,600 men, while the Turks had suffered losses of 5000.

On 10 December, Osman Pasha at the head of 25,000 Turks and a further 9000 wounded in carts, tried to cut his way through the Russian lines. He broke through the first line of enemy trenches, but Russian reinforcements drove the Turks back. The latter made a stand but were driven back into Plevna. In this final battle the Turks lost 5000 men and the Russians 2000. There was no escape for the defenders now, so they

capitulated. Total Russian casualties were 38,000 men.

Suddenly it became clear to even the most conservative that single-shot rifles were hopelessly obsolete. After all, if

■ **BELOW: The simple lines of the falling block action as adopted in the Martini-Henry, are shown to good effect by this late version. Note the lever-like cocked indicator above the trigger guard.**

30,000 Turks could fight off 100,000 Russians, who knew what a more sophisticated enemy – resurgent and very much revanchist France, for example – might do. . ?

THE FIRST MAUSER REPEATERS

In Oberndorf-am-Neckar, in 1877 and 1878, Paul Mauser designed a series of magazines for mounting alongside the

■BELOW: In extremis the tactics of the colonial wars were the same as they had always been: hold firm. These British troops at Abu Klea, in 1885, seem to be armed with Enfield-Sniders.

insertion slot of the M/71, some of them in the form of simple boxes, and some U-shaped, in an attempt to transform the existing rifle into a repeater at very minimal cost, but all were ultimately rejected by the commission in Spandau. His own preferred candidate for the Serbian contract awarded in 1878 was for a repeater with a tubular magazine below the barrel – which the Serbs rejected in favour of the (much cheaper) single-shot rifle – so he himself had perhaps begun work on the concept as early as 1875 or 1876. Despite the design being turned down by the Serbs, Mauser made some tubular-magazine repeaters anyway, and

exhibited them at the Württemberg State Trade Fair in Stuttgart in 1881, where Kaiser Wilhelm himself spent some considerable time examining them. The following year, Prussia ordered 2000, and issued them to four infantry battalions for testing purposes.

MODIFICATIONS

The repeater rifles were said to be exactly like the M/71 save for the magazine and feed train, and as far as the soldiers who handled them were concerned, they were. But in fact, Paul Mauser had re-designed virtually every individual part entirely, while sticking as

close to the original as possible to minimise re-tooling costs.

As a result of the 1882-83 trials, Mauser made a few further changes to the design. He shortened the overall length of the magazine (and of the barrel and stock correspondingly), reducing the capacity from nine rounds to eight; this both lightened the rifle and improved its balance somewhat (and even went some way towards ameliorating the problem of the centre of balance shifting as the magazine was emptied, which we touched on earlier).He also had to re-design the M/71 round, for the decidedly pointed projectile in the original had, on a

number of occasions during the trials, set off the cartridge ahead of it in the magazine, and he also took the opportunity to rework the primer seat.

The problem of sharply-pointed bullets impacting on the primer of the round ahead was to become a perennial one in the tubular-magazine rifle, particularly when jacketed spitzer bullets became more popular, and was only solved definitively by Remington who actually rifled the magazine tube – in a manner of speaking; that is, it was fabricated with paired spiral ribs in it, which acted as a cartridge guide, ensuring that the rounds would not lie precisely in a straight line, but that each would be angled in relation to its neighbours, so that bullet nose and primer never came into contact. Lastly, Mauser also reduced the depth of the rifling from .3mm to .15mm, and was to reduce it even further in subsequent rifles.

REFINING IT

The biggest change, of course, lay in the bed of the receiver, in the feed tray. Where before there had been a solid receptacle for the cartridge, now there was a very complex tapered cartridge carrier, pivoted near the rear, which tipped down at the front to allow it to pick up a round from the magazine, and which was brought up through the horizontal position to adopt a slightly nose-up attitude by the action of the bolt, (being guided by the lengthened ejector rail) as it extracted and then ejected the spent cartridge case. The bolt face could then engage the head of the fresh cartridge as it travelled forwards again (the carrier simultaneously dropping back), pushing the new round home as it went. The mechanism was further complicated by the requirement to lock off the cartridge carrier at will, effectively closing off the magazine and turning the rifle from a repeater back into a single-shot weapon. This was accomplished by a lever on the left hand side of the receiver, which locked it permanently in the charging position, where it formed a flat floor to the receiver. This locking procedure could only be carried out with the bolt drawn fully back and the carrier in the raised position, and not a few infantrymen broke the mechanism by trying to shift the change lever with the bolt closed.

Among the other significant modifications Mauser made to the original M/71 design was to link the

cocking piece and the firing pin, as suggested by Wind and outlined above. He tried to solve the problem of the rifle pulling to the right by modifying the bolt so that it locked on both sides, near the tail, but this 'double resistance' device, as he called it, was little more than a makeshift arrangement (although it was also to appear in the essentially similar rifle Mauser began supplying to the Turks the following year). The accepted method of compensating for the rifle's tendency to pull to the right was to set the foresight off from the line of the bore; M/71-84 rifles left the various factories with their sights offset to the right by 0.6mm, but battalion armourers were permitted to double that offset in extreme cases, which meant regularly.

The Mauser rifles of the period were by no means alone in pulling to one side or the other. The rifling alone produced a certain deviation, and asymmetrical bolt locking systems did too; the usual method of compensating for it was to provide a means of adjusting the backsight to one side or the other, generally by mounting it in a dovetail slot, but as a rifleman came to know his personal weapon, the degree of compensation he applied at different ranges by simply aiming off was probably more satisfactory.

RIVAL DESIGNS

In all, some 950,000 M/71-84 rifles were produced in the four Prussian state rifle factories at a nominal cost of 43 Marks (though that did not include the cost of tooling, which effectively increased it to

■OVER: The Henry under-lever-action rifles shown here were all produced in New Haven, Connecticut, between 1860 and 1866, when Benjamin Tyler Henry broke with Oliver Winchester and was replaced by Nelson King as superintendent and designer-in-chief. Note the very slight variations in butt-stock design, the different lengths of barrel (and, of course, magazine) and the use of both brass and iron for the receiver frame. The engraving on some of the rifles shown here is the 'factory standard' type, available for a premium of just a few dollars more over the price of the plain versions; the specially prepared presentation pieces were very much more ornate, as might be expected. All are, of course, in the original .44in rim-fire calibre which was superseded in the rather more famous Model 1873.

HENRY RIFLES

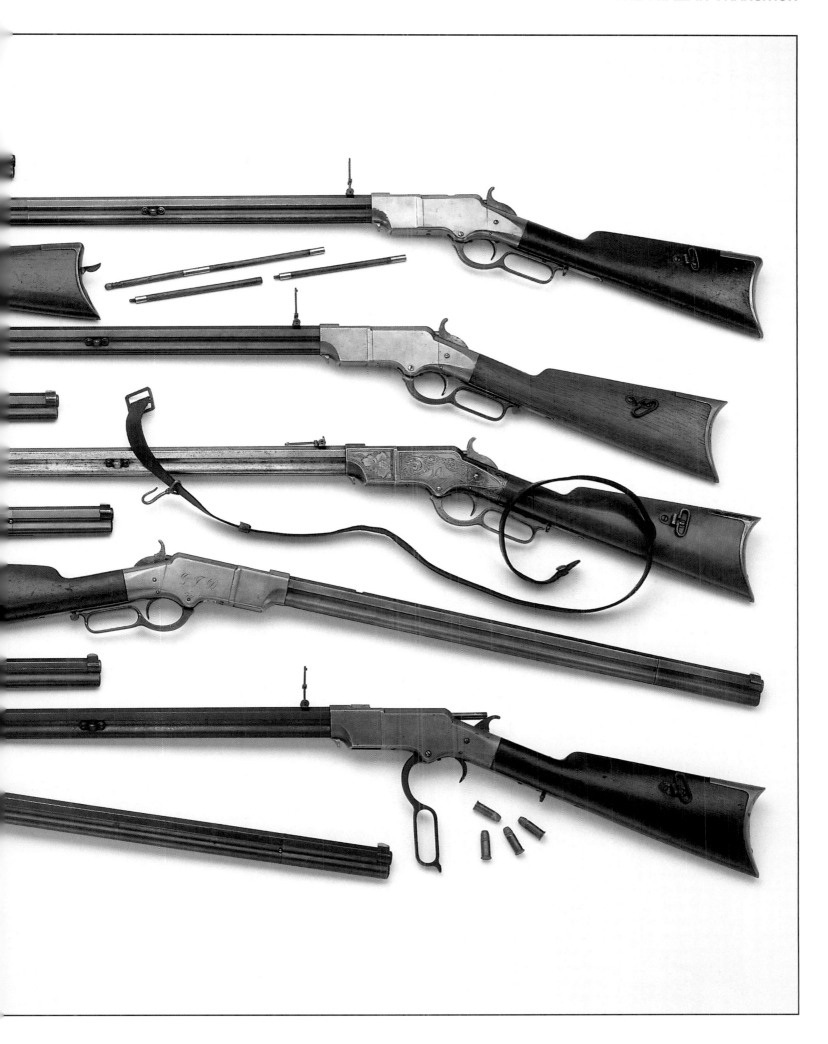

55 Marks, approximately £2/15/-Sterling [£2.75] or US$13.50), and this time Mauser Brothers did actually profit, the patent law in the Reich having been revised in 1878: they received three Marks for each of the first 100,000 rifles, and one Mark for each thereafter. They (actually, just Paul; Wilhelm died in January 1883) had been hoping for a major production order for the Oberndorf factory, which was already tooled up to produce the 'new' rifle, but this was not to be, even though production there could have commenced straightaway (Mauser Brothers finally produced 19,000 M/71-84 rifles for the state of Württemberg, and was to make further good use of the tooling; production of the almost identical 9.5mm-calibre M/87 for Turkey started in Oberndorf early in the following year. This marked the start of the Mauser company's real success, as we shall see, though Paul himself was not to profit from it financially to any great extent).

EQUIPPING THE PRUSSIAN ARMY

In the event, deliveries to the infantry regiments, starting with those in the disputed 'Imperial Territories' (Alsace and Lorraine) began in 1886 and were concluded by the end of the following year. But that same year, France – far and away Germany's most dangerous enemy following events in 1871 and the capture and imprisonment of her emperor (and the cream of her officer corps), the despoliation of her heartland, the permanent loss of the key frontier industrial provinces of Alsace and Lorraine, and the swingeing 'reparations' exacted (for France, of course, had started the war on the flimsy pretext that she could not accept a German prince, Leopold of Hohenzollern, on the throne of Spain. . .) – introduced the 8mm Lebel rifle, and in 1889 Great Britain – equally, Germany's most dangerous rival, particularly in Africa, where the race to develop new colonies was fast and furious – brought in the .303in Lee-Metford, and rendered the 11mm Mauser obsolete. By 1892 the tubular magazine rifles had been withdrawn from all front-line units and replaced by the unsatisfactory 7.92mm 88 rifle; the bulk of them were later sold off for four Marks each, though some were reserved for the use of native troops in the German colonies.

MAGAZINE DEVELOPMENT

The tubular magazine had profound disadvantages, the most important of which was the inherent weakness of a helical coil spring which was forced to act through a compression cycle which, in the case of the M/71-84, was 612mm (24in) long from a full magazine to an empty one. There was also the problem of the shift in the rifle's centre of balance as the ammunition was used up.

Rifle designers everywhere experimented with rival systems. Benjamin Berkeley Hotchkiss (then still working in his native USA, but soon to emigrate to France and virtually take over the machine gun market there) came up with a bolt-action rifle which used a spring-loaded tube in the butt, like the Spencer had employed, and had it accepted by the US Army in November 1877, but only for extended trials.

HOPPER/INSERTION MAGAZINES

The Chaffee-Reece carbine, which was also adopted for trials at about that time, was a bolt-action weapon with its cartridges in a butt magazine too, but this time they were housed between twin inclined racks, each with rounded indentations which conformed to the profile of the cases, within which the rounds lay, and which moved alternately in a shuffling motion, initiated by the opening of the bolt, which caused the entire column of cartridges to advance and present a fresh one to the breech each time. This at least solved the problem of the over-long spring, but created others, and the experiment was short-lived.

Hopper magazines and the very similar insertion magazines (the former fed cartridges downwards under the force of gravity; the latter upwards, assisted by a spring – both were side-

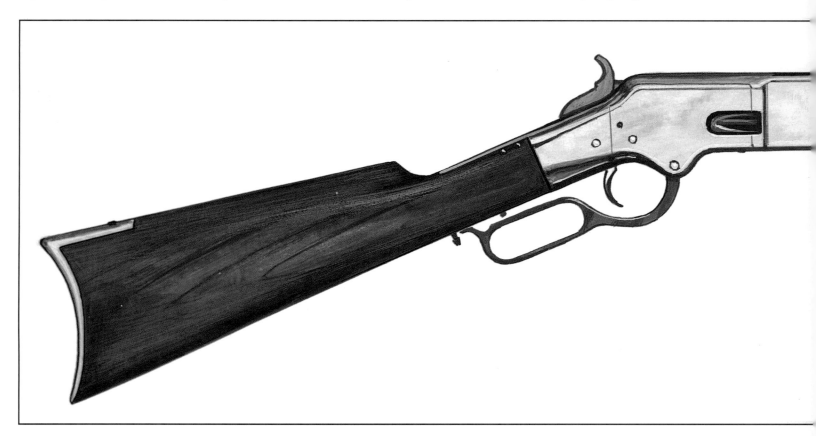

mounted and presented the fresh cartridge in much the same way as it was offered up to the receiver of a single-shot rifle manually) were briefly popular, too, though a truly successful one was never produced, for they seemed to offer a cheap and easy way of converting existing single-shot rifles to repetitive action while still allowing them to be loaded with single rounds at will, since it was easy to slide them downwards out of the way.

The British in particular were struck with them (largely, one suspects, because there was no other satisfactory way to convert a falling block action rifle like the Martini to fire repetitively) and even tried out a variety of completely new falling block action rifles with hopper magazines at a time when the rest of Europe's armies had all adopted the bolt-action.

ROTARY/SPOOL MAGAZINES

Rotary or spool magazines were suggested too, chiefly by Austrians or Germans – Mannlicher, Schönauer, and Schulhof all produced such designs, which utilise a device similar in character to a revolver pistol's cylinder, but with the rounds lying in troughs, accessible from the side, rather than in enclosed chambers accessible from the rear. Their prime virtue lies in the degree of protection they offer to unfired rounds,

but against that must be set their complicated nature.

Eventually, in 1903, after a very long gestation period indeed, a rifle which utilised one – designed in collaboration by Schönauer and Mannlicher, with a turn-down bolt-action designed by the latter – was accepted by Greece as its official service rifle, in 6.5mm (.25in) calibre. Apart from the self-loading Johnson rifle (qv), accepted in limited numbers by Dutch colonial infantry and the US Marine Corps, the Greek M1903 was the only rotary-magazine rifle to be taken into general military service, though the action was popular in sporting rifles in the early twentieth century and enjoyed a long period of popularity in the original Savage Model 99. More recently, it was revived for the 10-shot small-bore autoloader Ruger produced as the 10/22 and by Steyr-Mannlicher in its SSG69 sniper and competition rifle.

THE BOX MAGAZINE

An even more bizarre form of magazine, and a unique one, found its way into a rifle developed by a captain in the Royal Norwegian Artillery, Ole Krag, and Erik Jorgensen, an engineer at the Norwegian Royal Arms Factory. Curiously, the Krag rifle was eventually to be accepted, albeit for a brief period, by the US Army (and also by those of Norway and Denmark),

but we will reserve a more detailed description of that weapon for the next chapter.

On the whole, there was little doubt that the best solution to the problem of how to feed rounds to the breech simply and reliably was a box magazine which sat directly beneath the bolt, within which the cartridges were held one atop the other, retained by inward-curving lips (or sometimes by springs) against the upwards pressure of a multiple leaf spring (a concertina spring, as it was sometimes called), a 'C' spring or, in some

■OVER: This array of classic Winchester under-lever-action rifles includes both Model 1873s and Model 1876s (on the left) together with later Model 1886s (on the right) in a variety of calibres and barrel and magazine lengths. Note, once again, the variation in butt-stock profiles and, in particular, the very different bolt and locking-lever form which was introduced in the later rifles, just visible in the two at the lower right which are half-open (compare this with the bolt of the Model '73 located at the top left). The rifle at the lower left is of especial interest, since it is 'One of One Thousand', and is equipped with a custom-made stock and flip-up aperture backsight as well as a long, extra-heavy octagonal barrel.

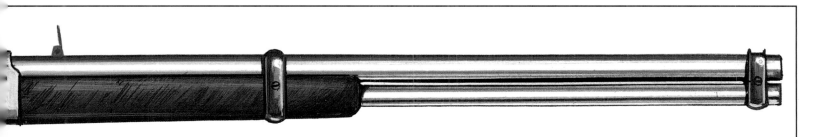

Winchester Model 1866

Calibre: .44in (rim-fire) (11.2mm)
Weight: 4.2kg (9lb 4oz)
Length: 1150mm (45.25in)
Barrel Length: 585mm (23in)
Effective range: 400m (1320 feet)
Configuration: 13-round tubular magazine, under-lever action
Muzzle velocity: 400mps (1320fps)
Country of origin: United States

WINCHESTER RIFLES

■ABOVE: The Vetterli rifle in 10.4mm calibre was taken up by the Swiss Army in 1868. The first version was improved, and was superseded by the Model 1871, shown here.

early forms, a hinged lever which was kept under tension by a coiled volute spring, and from which they could be successively stripped by the forwards action of the bolt.

JAMES PARIS LEE

Such a device was first suggested in the early 1860s (at least, by his own later accounts) by a Scots watchmaker who had emigrated to Canada and subsequently moved to the USA, James Paris Lee. Lee's first (partially) successful invention in the field of firearms had been a conversion of the Springfield muzzle-loader to rival that put forward by Allin and eventually adopted; from then on, he committed himself to the design of rifles full time, much of his work being undertaken first in conjunction with the Sharps Rifle Co. and later, after the demise of Sharps, at the Remington factory at Ilion, New York.

James Paris Lee's most important contribution was a modified bolt-action, characterised by its rear locking lugs. It

was this action which finally convinced the British to abandon the Martini falling block and fall in line with the rest of Europe, but not until the late 1880s. The box magazine and revised bolt-action Lee devised, and for which he had secured patents in 1877, was first adopted by the Chinese, and then by the US Navy, in 1879. Lee was a very important figure indeed in the field at the time, and the basic action he devised was to remain in use in the British Army's service rifle until well into the second half of the twentieth century; we shall have cause to return to him at length later.

FERDINAND MANNLICHER

Meanwhile – and, apparently, quite independently – Ferdinand Ritter von Mannlicher, a minor aristocrat from Mainz in Germany who had moved to Vienna at an early age and thereafter became more Austrian than the Austrians, and who was seduced into the world of firearms after a visit to the Philadelphia Exhibition in 1876, was also working on the problem in association with Werndl at Steyr. In the process he produced a huge number (some say as many as 150, though on the surface that sounds incredible, no matter how prolific Mannlicher was) of variations on the

themes of breech design and magazine format, and eventually came up with a very similar system to Lee's, employing a bolt-action and an under-bolt box magazine, in 1881. Some of Mannlicher's later bolt-actions, and the ones for which he is best known, such as that of the Austrian M1895, were straight-pull rather than turn-down like Mauser's, and employed a rotary-lug locking system which was initiated by a helical guideway.

SCHMIDT'S SYSTEM

Other designers, too, produced straight-pull designs, notably Schmidt, who also used a (rather different) rotary locking system in the 7.5mm rifle he produced for the Swiss Federal Army as the M1889; Ross, who used a modified form of the Mannlicher system in the .303in-calibre rifle he designed, with which the Canadian Army went to war in 1914 (and replaced soon after), and Lee, whose cam-locked straight-pull rifle in .236in-calibre of 1895 was adopted by the US Navy and soon discarded.

Despite their basic weaknesses, straight-pull actions had a good few supporters during this period, and we will look at them in more detail in the next chapter, but none was as successful

Mauser later came up with a (rather better) type of charger, too (and a similar device was also used eventually to load the Lee magazines, and then became universal), but in this case the rounds were transferred from it to the magazine by stripping them out – pressing them downwards into the body of the magazine with the thumb; in Mannlicher's version, the entire clip was placed in the magazine and simply fell through the (open) base when it was empty (later versions, as introduced in Germany just after the start of World War I, popped up when they were empty, thus functioning as a hold-open device and giving the rifleman a positive visual sign that his weapon needed reloading; this modification was made as a result of the need to keep dirt out of the magazine and feedway, which was accomplished by fitting a bottom plate and a spring which acted on the clip).

Mannlicher's clip was fractionally quicker in operation than Mauser or Lee's chargers. Though what might be described as an inveterate inventor, Mannlicher knew a good design by another when he saw it; when he devised his rotary magazine, he set it up to employ Mauser's charger rather than setting out to make up an appropriate one of his own.

MAGAZINE CUT-OFFS

One tactical military requirement exerted what today seems to be very untoward influence indeed on the selection of magazine repeater rifles by the European armies in the 1880s: the question of whether or not they could function as single-shot rifles with the magazines fully charged. As we have seen, the Mauser M/71-84 could function thus thanks to the cut-off lever which locked the cartridge carrier in the raised position, and most other rifles of the same period incorporated similar devices or, like the various hopper and insertion magazine rifles which were submitted for trials, had magazines which could be slid or swung out of the way so that they could not feed a cartridge to the breech. The reason for this was that same old fear of poorly-disciplined troops firing off all their ammunition in a frenzy and then being left defenceless which had so exercised Brigadier General Ripley during the early years of the civil war in the USA. It was still around in the 1880s and 1890s, and forced rifle designers to incorporate unnecessary complications

into the designs they produced. It was, however, impossible to incorporate such a device into a rifle which used the Mannlicher loading system, and those countries which wished to adopt that had to forego the restriction. Austria did, and so did Germany, in a short-lived and generally near-disastrous departure from Paul Mauser's designs, and slowly it became clear that the pessimists' fears were ill-founded; eventually, the requirement was shelved, though as late as 1893, when the US Army selected the Krag-Jorgensen, it was still a factor. Soon enough, of course, the world's armies would do a complete volte face, and, from being a vice, the ability to sustain a high rate of fire would suddenly became a virtue – but for the moment it was strictly taboo.

OTHER BOX MAGAZINES

The remaining variations in the design of the different types of box magazine were minor. Some, like Lee's, were removable; others, like Mannlicher's, were not, while Mauser produced both types, and some of his fixed magazines had removable bottom plates to facilitate cleaning. Some carried their cartridges in a single column, others carried them in two staggered columns. Some were contained entirely within the rifle's stock, others protruded below it, invariably just in front of the trigger guard. In practice, the variations were of minor importance, and made no real difference to the way in which the rifles functioned, just as most different types of turn-down bolt-action actually had little effect on the riflemen who used one or the other (though some did, and the straight-pull bolt-action was quite different again).

AMERICA LAGS BEHIND

The basic principle was the important thing, and the basic principle of the bolt-action repeating rifle with a box magazine was sufficiently better than the available alternatives that it soon became almost universally accepted for military use throughout the advanced industrial world (and especially during colonial campaigns against ill-armed and poorly equipped indigenous forces). Curiously, the laggard was a nation we think of today as dictating technological progress and leading very much from the front – the United States of America – where a box-magazine rifle was not introduced for general military service until the first years of the twentieth century.

even as Mannlicher's, which was supplanted in the Austro-Hungarian Army in 1914.

Mannlicher's influence had all but disappeared by the time the twentieth century was half-way through (though his name still lives on – the successor to Werndl's company is today known as Steyr Mannlicher AG), but during the 1880s it was very much to the fore, and rifles he designed were in use through World War I and beyond. Mannlicher's M/86 was the last new big-bore black powder rifle to be adopted by any army.

MANNLICHER'S CLIP

Mannlicher's various types of bolt-actions and magazines were workmanlike designs, in the main, and were very often beautifully executed, and as a result were very reliable. As a result they were widely popular, and the two-piece firing pin he devised was much easier (and cheaper) to replace than that of the Mauser if it broke – a not entirely uncommon occurrence. However, the most influential contribution he made to the technology of the day was probably the invention of the clip, which allowed the box magazine to be loaded in one action, instead of each round being inserted separately.

CHAPTER 3

THE MILITARY BOLT-ACTION RIFLE REACHES THE PEAK OF ITS DEVELOPMENT

By the beginning of the twentieth century, warfare had become mostly mechanised and the battlefields were ruled by rapid, accurate long-range fire, thanks to the improved nature of infantry rifles, as well as to the introduction of machine guns sharing their ammunition.

Though the reasons for switching over from single-shot to repeating rifles were compelling by the early 1880s, most of the world's armies took their time about selecting new weapons (while most civilians either continued to rely on low-cost army surplus stock or bought Winchesters if they could afford them). We have seen how Germany rushed a modified, repeater version of her single-shot service rifle into production, and achieved very little by the exercise save for the unnecessary expenditure of the best part of 50 million Marks. Of course, there was no way anyone could have known, but the delay in choosing new service rifles was actually to prove to be a very sound move even if it did come about accidentally and often by reason of turgid bureaucracy, for there was a development nearing completion which would render all the large-calibre black powder weapons obsolete overnight.

During the 1860s and 1870s in particular, there had been considerable attention paid to the possibilities of

■LEFT: The Canadian troops shown here at the Second Battle of Ypres, in April/May 1915, were thrown hurriedly into the fray and are armed with SMLE rifles and a Vickers machine gun.

down-sizing rifles, for precisely the same reasons the American rifle had been reduced in calibre a century earlier – to allow the rifleman to carry more ammunition without increasing his overall load. This was a perennial activity, and was to be just as attractive a century later.

SMALLER CALIBRES

Simple theoretical calculation, which experimentation backed up, demonstrated that the minimum calibre to which a rifle bullet propelled by black powder could be reduced and still be effective, in military terms, was of the order of 9mm (.35in). The calculations were based on a simple law of physics: the kinetic energy available within a projectile is the product of its mass times its velocity. Reduce the mass and one is compelled to increase the velocity proportionally to produce the same sort of hitting power, and there is a finite limit to the weight of black powder one can use in a cartridge and still keep the recoil manageable. And maintaining the mass by reducing the diameter of the projectile while increasing its length wasn't an option either, for that demanded that it be made to spin proportionally faster in flight in order to maintain its directional stability, and that meant a heavier charge to overcome the greater resistance of the steeper rifling, which led, once again, to heavier recoil. What was needed was a new propellant; one which produced a more controlled and even explosion than black powder in order to impart a sustained push rather than a jolt to the projectile.

NEW PROPELLANTS

The first new explosive to be discovered since the Dark Ages was the notoriously unstable nitro-glycerine – which will explode if dropped or even shaken – invented by an Italian chemist named Sobrero in 1846. Almost 20 years later, a Swede, Alfred Nobel, solved some of the problems of handling nitro-glycerine when he discovered that an 'infusorial earth' named *kieselguhr* or diatomite would absorb three to four times its own weight of it, creating dynamite and a vast personal fortune in the process.

Earlier, in 1838, Thèophile Pelouze had produced a highly inflammable material by treating cotton with concentrated nitric acid, a process which led eventually to the discovery of nitro-cellulose. Another chemist, a Swiss, Johann Christian Schönbein, introduced sulphuric acid into the process, producing what became known as gun-cotton, also in 1846. Paul Vieille synthesised the first practical propellant from this when he gelatinized it with a mixture of alcohol and ether to make the smokeless 'Poudre B' (the B was for General Boulanger, the right-wing self-styled saviour of France who was that year appointed Minister for War, and who was a leading advocate of seeking revenge on Germany for the events of 1871), but it was left to Nobel to show how the two lines of research could be combined (quite literally) by mixing the nitrated cotton with nitro-glycerine. These new compounds, which, like gunpowder, are progressive explosives (as distinct from high explosives; their rate of combustion can be controlled to some extent, by varying the physical form in which they are presented, for example); form the basis of modern smokeless propellants.

SMOKELESS POWDER

By virtue of the fact that it produced roughly three times more gas than black powder, Vieille's 'Poudre B' generated considerably greater propulsive force. It had its drawbacks, chief among which was the higher temperature at which it

burned, which led to reduced barrel life, and a need for a rather stronger primer charge to set it off, but it did what was required of it by raising muzzle velocity while actually reducing recoil, thanks to its burning more slowly and evenly than black powder. Its performance was later tempered still further, oddly enough by combining nitro-cellulose with an even more volatile explosive, nitro-glycerine, together with a mineral jelly and retardants such as graphite.

Even before the addition of retarding agents, it was discovered that the combustion period of these low-explosive compounds could be controlled by varying the shape and size of the granules, pellets, or flakes into which they were formed (and also by piercing the former through, to form tubes or beads, which enlarged the surface area and hastened combustion slightly). This meant that the rate at which the explosive was converted to gas could be controlled, and the ideal combustion profile was quickly attained; it should start off slowly to free the projectile from the cartridge case and start it in the rifling, and build up to a maximum just before it leaves the barrel. The result was a 50 per cent increase, on average, in muzzle velocity, with all that implied for range and accuracy (for the faster the bullet went, the less time gravity and other influences had in which to work, of course), without a concomitant increase in disabling recoil. The new propellant had a second attribute which was also very welcome: it produced next to no smoke. Thus, not only did it hardly foul the rifle's barrel at all, neither did it give away the firer's position as surely as setting off a flare or waving a flag (and it left his view, and hence his aim, unobscured too). This latter factor was to be significant in the wars of the period at the very end of the nineteenth century, particularly so where one side used the new propellant and the other did not.

THE 8MM LEBEL RIFLE

The French certainly lost no time in exploiting Vieille's discovery, and in 1886 introduced the Lebel rifle in 8mm x 50R (for rimmed) calibre which employed a 2.98g (46 grain) charge and a 12.8g (198 grain) projectile. Its muzzle velocity was stunning in comparison with anything which had gone before – over 700 metres (2300ft) per second, twice the speed of sound. In point of fact, except for the ammunition it fired, the rifle was already obsolescent; a design which betrayed the

■RIGHT: A French colonial infantryman of the late 1880s, with the 8mm M1886 Lebel rifle which at once rendered the rifles of all other nations obsolete.

haste with which it was developed through its employment of the tubular Kropatschek-type magazine and cartridge feed at a point when most other designers had moved on from there to vertical box magazines. It was little more than a re-barrelled version of the large-calibre tubular-magazine Gras-Kropatschek rifle which the French had adopted eight years earlier (though only for marine infantry regiments) as the M1878. Nonetheless, obsolescent or not in that respect, it was still effectively way out in front of anything France's hated neighbours to the east could field. An example fell into the hands of the Germans early in 1887, thanks to a deserter from the French Army who obtained 20,000 Marks for the rifle he stole when he absconded, and this sent them into a frenzy, for clearly the M/71-84 rifles, which were even then only beginning to reach front-line units, were already obsolete.

THE NEW GUNPOWDER PLOT

The composition of 'Poudre B' was a closely guarded secret, of course, and no sooner had it been demonstrated than chemists all over the world worked, sometimes quite literally, night and day to replicate it. Some succeeded rapidly enough; others did not do so well (one of these, curiously, was the USA), despite the initial steps in the process being well enough known, and we can chart their progress fairly accurately by the dates on which various nations' armies joined the 'Small Calibre Club', as we might think of it.

Thanks largely to one man, Max Duttenhofer of Rottweil-am-Neckar, just downstream from Oberndorf, Germany was one of the first to join – and could, indeed, have beaten the French to it, had Duttenhofer himself not taken a wrong turning very early on in his experimentation. By about 1880, he had been producing a type of black (actually, brown) powder for naval artillery using partially-charred buckthorn wood in place of normal charcoal, a development he kept very secret. In 1883, quite independently of Paul Vieille but almost simultaneously, he began experimenting with nitro-cellulose, but where Vieille

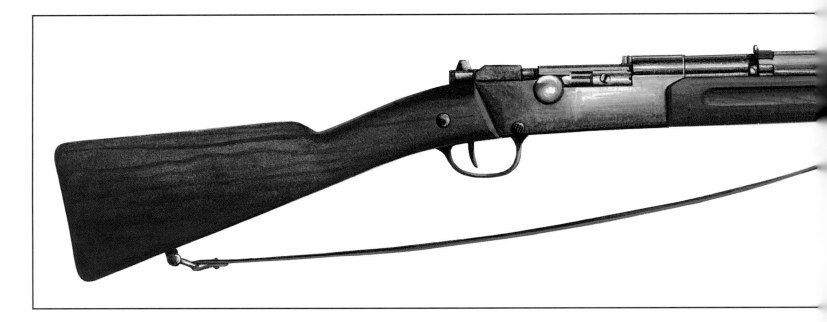

used cotton, Duttenhofer persisted with charred buckthorn, sometimes with disastrous results.

The resulting explosive was unpredictable (the workmen who test-fired the guns charged with it would do so only at the end of a long string), but when it worked, it fulfilled expectations – an 11mm Mauser M/71 round charged with 5g (77 grain) of ordinary black powder and a 25g (386 grain) soft lead projectile produced a muzzle velocity of 430 metres (1410ft) per second, while the same round charged with 3.5g (54 grain) of 'Rottweil Cellulose Powder' produced 525 metres (1720ft) per second with reduced chamber gas pressure and less recoil. A 9mm-calibre, 15.5g (239 grain) test round fired from a specially barrelled rifle, propelled by 3g (46 grain) of the new powder, achieved 607 metres (1990ft) per second. However, the results actually varied so much from one test shot to the next that there was clearly something very wrong with the process; it was, it transpired, the variable cellulose content of the buckthorn wood. (Vieille's cotton, which is very much higher in cellulose and more homogeneous to start with, produced much more predictable results; his powder was to be useable, Duttenhofer's was not.)

GEWEHRBLATTPULVER 88
Duttenhofer kept the Prussian Rifle Testing Commission in Spandau informed of his results, and its members showed considerable enthusiasm initially, but in the light of repeated failures and not a few instances of burst barrels, its support was withdrawn and experimentation ceased. But Duttenhofer's contribution

was not finished yet; when the purloined Lebel rifle, together with a small supply of the new cartridges for it, arrived in Germany in the spring of 1887, chemists immediately submitted the propellant to qualitative and quantitative chemical analysis in an attempt to determine exactly how it was made up. They failed, because they hadn't a large enough sample, and eventually, Max Duttenhofer's brother Carl was asked if he could procure more (like Wilhelm Mauser, he was the businessman of the two). Max did, in a very roundabout way (by way, in fact, of Russia, at a cost of 500 Marks per kilogramme), believing that his assistance would result in a manufacturing contract eventually. Such a contract was indeed forthcoming, in December that year, and what a contract it was – Duttenhofer was to deliver 2500 tonnes of his unreliable wood-based explosive over the following 15 years at a price of 2500 Marks per tonne.

But there was a get-out clause: the German War Ministry had the right to cancel its order if the propellant proved unsatisfactory in any way. . . and, of course, it did just that as soon as the government's chemists found out Vieille's secret. It all turned out well for the Rottweiler in the end. He had received one and a half million Marks for turning over the details of his process to the German Government, and a further two million Marks advance on the manufacturing contract. Now he was given a new contract to manufacture the replicated Vieille powder, which was officially adopted in April 1889. *Gewehrblattpulver* (rifle flake powder) 88, as the new propellant was known (one of

Vieille's secrets lay in his having formed the explosive into flakes, around two millimetres in diameter and less than half a millimetre thick), lived up to expectations; an 8mm (.32in) bullet weighing 14.7g (227 grain), propelled by 2.75g (42 grain) of it, had a muzzle velocity of 620 metres (2034ft) per second and thus produced considerably more energy than the previous 11mm M/71 round while giving a much flatter trajectory and producing virtually no smoke or residue.

Then came the task of developing a smaller-calibre weapon to make use of the new propellant's attributes. Initially, the Germans hoped that they could solve their problem at a stroke by adopting the same solution as the French, and either re-barrelling the existing rifles or, better still, fitting them with reduction tubes as the Americans had with the trapdoor Springfields, but it soon became clear that the locking mechanism of the M/71 – which, we may recall, was no more sophisticated than that of the Dreyse needle-gun – just couldn't cope with the additional pressure. Instead, they had to look for a completely different solution, and that meant a new rifle.

THE EXPLODING RIFLE
The tale which was to unfold over the next two years almost beggars belief. In other circumstances, one might dismiss it as an aberration, but it must be seen in context: we are describing the procurement of the most basic weapon of war by a nation with enormous ambitions, overbearing arrogance, and gigantic pride, all of which were clearly manifest in the domination of the state

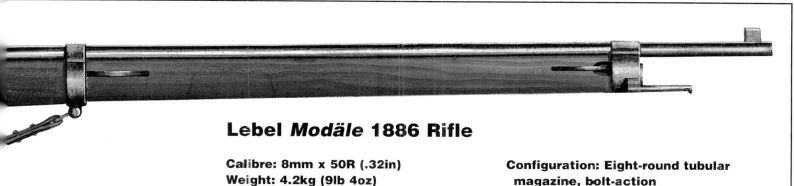

Lebel *Modäle* 1886 Rifle

Calibre: 8mm x 50R (.32in)
Weight: 4.2kg (9lb 4oz)
Length: 1285mm (50.5in)
Barrel length: 800mm (31.5in)
Effective range: 800m (2600ft)

**Configuration: Eight-round tubular
 magazine, bolt-action**
Muzzle velocity: 700mps (2300fps)
Country of origin: France

by the army, which had suddenly found itself to be hugely deficient vis-à-vis its neighbour and worst enemy, a country which only a decade and a half before it had humiliated and brought close to ruination. There was enormous pressure from the War Ministry (much of it applied from even higher up, by Bismarck, who was the real power in the land) to get the new rifle into production and issued to the troops as quickly as possible, and this was to backfire, both

■ABOVE: A French honour guard bearing their long barrelled Lebel 8mm rifles to their inspecting Allied dignitaries, who include President Woodrow Wilson (right) and British Field Marshal Haig (centre).

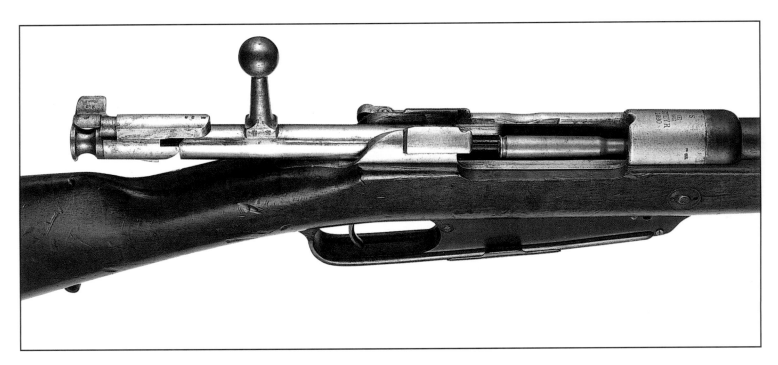

■ **ABOVE: The German *Infanteriegewehr* 88 was poorly designed; the entire stock had to be re-barrelled (as this has been – note the 'S' incised into the breech case, indicating *spitzer*).**

literally and metaphorically, in the worst possible way.

MAUSER BY-PASSED

The obvious place to look for a new rifle was probably Oberndorf, but this time the members of the Prussian Rifle Testing Commission, clearly under the influence of hubris, took matters into their own hands. A limited competition was announced in November 1887, and the commission, in typical committee fashion, combined features from a number of the rifles submitted. But where similar efforts had failed before

(and certainly have failed since) due to an incompatibility between the various disparate components, this time the shortcomings were more profound, and existed within the separate components themselves (though that is not to say that every element of the decision was flawed), even before they were haphazardly brought together.

The bolt the commission chose was a design conceived by a gunsmith called Schlegelmilch from the Spandau arsenal; it was based on that of the Mauser M/71 but with the guide rib and set screw-and-washer bolt stop deleted and replaced by a spring-loaded bolt stop which was located in the receiver, and two symmetrical locking lugs behind the bolt head. This was combined with a barrel with steeper rifling – one turn in 240mm (nine and a half inches), a profile which

was widely accepted thereafter – in a nominal 7.92mm (.31in) calibre measured across the lands, with the rifling just 0.1mm deep and an early Mannlicher type clip-loading box magazine, open at its base.

One late modification to the specification was made: it was decided to adopt a rimless cartridge, as proposed by Rubin in Switzerland the previous August, with a hard lead bullet (that is, lead tempered, in this case, with five per cent antimony; tin and zinc were also used for the same purpose) with a cupro-nickel plated steel jacket of 8mm (.32in) nominal calibre (actually, it was 8.1mm in diameter initially), which necessitated a re-design of the extractor and ejector in the bolt head. Although there were many doubts expressed at the time, the M88 round which resulted was to enjoy a very

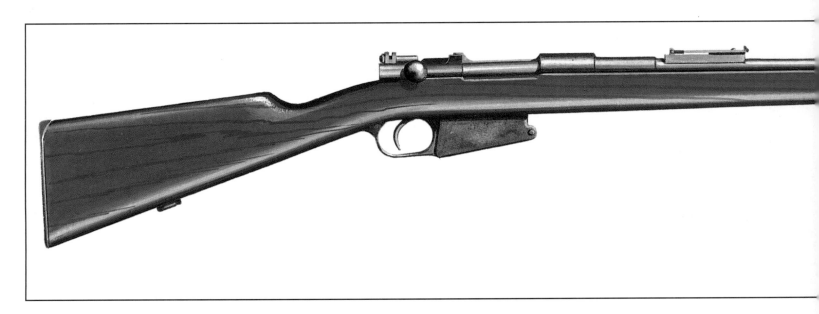

long life, albeit with some modification (particularly to the shape and form of the bullet itself), first in 1903 and then again in 1934, becoming widely but erroneously known as the 7.92mm Mauser cartridge in the process. By way of comparison, the gross weight of an 88 round was 27.3g (421 grain) compared with the 43.4g (670 grain) of the 11mm M71/84 round, so the requirement to save weight was handsomely met.

DELAYS AND DOUBLE-DEALING

Deliveries of the machine tools required to build the new rifles, which were to be made by Ludwig Loewe & Co., were to have commenced late in 1888, and the state arsenals at Spandau, Danzig, and Erfurt were supposed to come on-stream, in that order, in the spring of the following year, to be followed by Amberg in mid-summer, by which time total production was to have reached 2200 each day. But long before production even began, War Ministry officials concluded that such a rate was simply too slow; they decided to give production contracts to civilian manufacturers too, and, Mauser being occupied with a large order for Turkey, selected Ludwig Loewe & Co. (which by this time owned Mauser Brothers anyway), and gave it a contract for 300,000 rifles (with another, for a further 125,000, to follow). The result was something of a fiasco. Instead of concentrating on producing machinery for the state arsenals, the Loewe factory in Berlin-Martinikenfelde was largely turned over to rifle production itself, and the deliveries of machine tools were reduced to a trickle. To compensate for that in turn, Werndl's factory in Steyr was also commissioned to produce

300,000 rifles, in a contract signed in early 1889; but production there had barely started when, on 31 October, it was halted by order of an Austrian judge, for it transpired that a patent had been unknowingly violated (for the barrel jacket; a non-essential but then-fashionable component which had been included in the specification at the suggestion of the apparently innocent Ludwig Loewe & Co., which was part of a consortium which held the patent for it. The purpose of the barrel jacket was supposedly to isolate the barrel itself from the woodwork of the fore-stock which, if it were to warp, would throw the barrel out of alignment; in fact, the barrel jacket was to act as little more than a rust-trap). The problem did not arise in Germany; the state factories were immune, and Loewe, of course, didn't have to pay licensing fees to itself. Werndl, with many hundreds of thousands of Marks invested in tooling and a contract with severe penalty clauses to meet, had to cave in. Production resumed quickly enough, though only at the cost of 175,000 Marks in unexpected licensing fees.

AN EXPLOSIVE SITUATION

By the end of 1889 the old Prussian rifle factories had delivered 270,000 *Infanteriegewehr* 88 (the old designation formula had been dropped), and the following year they produced a further 660,000; in addition the Bavarian State Factory at Amberg, Loewe, and Werndl delivered a total of 970,000 more, bringing the grand total to 1,900,000, or roughly two rifles for each German soldier. By the end of July 1890 all the Reich's active infantry units had received

new rifles, and on 6 August, the first official acknowledgement of the fact that they were fatally flawed was issued.

Over the next six years, literally thousands (perhaps even tens of thousands) of rifles exploded when they were fired, severely wounding many soldiers in the process, and there was not just one major fault, but at least three, and some minor ones, too. Firstly, it was possible to attempt to chamber a second round if one had been loaded but the bolt had not been pushed all the way home so that its extractor hook did not engage the head channel; this resulted in the tip of the second projectile being driven directly into the primer cap of the round already loaded, igniting it with the bolt open, with predictable results. A number of modifications were suggested to cure this, but none of them worked, and it was left to drill and discipline to prevent accidents.

Secondly, there were numerous manufacturing defects in the new 88 cartridge which often led to cases ripping; if the tear occurred on the wall of the case, there was no serious problem (though extraction was often compromised), but cracks also occurred in the head of the case, and then gases at temperatures in excess of 1000 degrees Celsius, and at considerable pressure, found their way back through the leading groove of the left locking lug and hit the rifleman directly in the face. This time the fault could be cured, and was, by re-engineering the bolt and adding a gas shield to the firing pin nut, but this was not finally accomplished until 1894.

Thirdly – and this was the most important weakness of all – the barrels of 88 rifles frequently ruptured or burst catastrophically. Initially it was supposed that this was due to the barrels themselves being too thin, particularly towards the breech, and they were thickened accordingly – but that didn't stop the bursting. It was to be five years before it was discovered that the cause was a poor match between the dimensions of the barrels and those of the bullets fired through them, caused by a misunderstanding of the behaviour of the new jacketed ammunition. The designers had supposed that the new projectiles would not be subject to the very small degree of expansion which soft lead bullets underwent as they took the rifling, and had specified that they should be slightly over-size (all previous rifles had had barrels whose bore

Belgian Mauser, M/89

Calibre: 7.65mm x 53 (.301in)
Weight: 4.0kg (8lb 13oz)
Length: 1275mm (50in)
Barrel length: 780mm (30.75in)
Effective range: Over 1000m
(3250 feet)

Configuration: Five-round fixed box
magazine, bolt-action
Muzzle velocity: 620mps (2015fps)
Country of origin: Belgium

dimensions were exactly that of the projectiles they were to fire). As a result, the projectiles were too tight a fit, which led to nickel from the jackets being deposited in the barrel, which in turn made matters worse still.

Lastly, the Mannlicher-system magazine, which was open at the bottom to allow the empty clip to fall out, allowed mud and dust into the cartridge storage area, contaminating the rounds there and causing frequent jams. Almost incredibly, this was not rectified after training exercises had shown it up, and was not cured until World War I was already four months old, in December

■ BELOW: An original Norwegian model Krag-Jorgensen rifle with the front-hinged magazine cover. Perhaps an odd choice for the US Army, which adopted it with some modifications in 1892.

1914, when a simple plate to close off the aperture was issued and fitted locally by armourers. Now, of course, the empty clip could not simply drop out, and a further modification involving a spring-assisted platform, which pushed the clip up and out of the magazine as soon as the bolt opened when no more cartridges were present, was introduced, though as we have noted, this had the extra benefit of functioning as a hold-open device to indicate that it was time to reload.

MODIFICATIONS TO THE 88 RIFLE
The most important fault was finally rectified definitively by increasing the depth of the rifling to 0.15mm (from 0.1mm; this modification was made in 1896, and the rifles so altered were marked with a Z on the head of the breech case). In the meantime, in 1893 all the 88 rifles in Germany were

progressively returned to artillery depots (where the armourers' workshops were located) and exchanged for unissued examples; 50 per cent of those sent in had to be re-barrelled before they could be returned to stock. In 1897 the process was repeated, with similar results. That same year, cleaning with oiled patches was introduced for the first time – before that, only boiling water had been used.

The 88 rifle series underwent two modifications, and both took place after it had actually been superseded as a front-line weapon – they were made not so much to improve the weapon (though both did) as to introduce an element of standardisation with its much better replacement, the Paul Mauser-designed *Infanteriegewehr* 98. Firstly, in 1903 the 88 bullet was altered to marginally increase its diameter (from 8.1mm to 8.22mm), and at the same time its profile

was changed to the now-familiar pointed '*spitzer*' form and a more powerful charge was introduced (see below for a more comprehensive description of the new cartridge). The rifles which were to fire the new 88S round had to be re-barrelled (again!), with the deeper rifling and a wider chamber (sound existing barrels were reused, of course, after modification). The rear sights were changed, too, to reflect the new round's characteristics; 88 rifles thus modified were stamped with an S on the head of the breech case. Then, in 1905, the Mannlicher clip was abandoned, to be replaced by the simpler Mauser charger. This necessitated machining a pair of grooves into the receiver bridge (and introducing a small cut-out in the head of the breech case, so that the longer pointed rounds could pass through); cutting out a 'thumb slot' in the left wall of the receiver, so that the cartridges could be stripped out of the charger more easily; introducing a false rear plate to the magazine, to take up the space formally occupied by the clip; and fabricating and fitting a device at the left rear of the magazine well to hold the cartridges in against the pressure of the spring-loaded magazine floor plate when the bolt was pulled all the way back. Rifles modified under this programme were known as 88/05. Some 200,000 rifles

were modified in this way in 1906 and 1907, at a cost of eight Marks each; later, in 1915 and 1916, faced with losses of war *matériel* much greater than had been envisaged, older 88 rifles still in storage were brought out and hastily, often crudely, modified in the same way; these were known as 88/14 rifles. However, many had been sold off, for just two Marks each; we may recall that redundant, obsolete M/71-84 rifles had been sold for twice that. Only in 1917 did sufficient supplies of 98 rifles become available to allow them to be withdrawn, and the following year those that remained were sent to Turkey, Germany's by-then hard-pressed ally.

THE FIRST BRITISH REPEATER

The British began officially considering rival magazine rifles to supplant the single-shot Martini-Henry in 1879, when the War Office's Machine Gun Committee was asked to compare a selection of available weapons with the Martini-Henry rifle and then examine the broader question of whether one should be taken into service. They started work in March 1880, a sergeant and three men of the Royal Welch Fusiliers being provided to carry out firing trials, which were conducted at Woolwich. The weapons they considered included the Kropatschek tubular-magazine rifle from Austria, the

■ABOVE: The Mannlicher-Carcano rifle the Italians adopted in 6.5mm calibre in 1891 had a bolt that was a free adaptation of the Mauser M/89 design with a new sleeve safety feature.

American Hotchkiss, the Winchester '76, the tubular-magazine Vetterli, and a turn-down bolt-action, box-magazine rifle from James Lee. All were in 11.4mm (.45in) calibre, chambered for the solid-drawn 'Gardner-Gatling' cartridge (the British Army was still issuing fabricated, wound cartridges to its infantrymen, but had switched over to the solid-drawn type for the Gardner and Gatling hand-cranked multi-barrelled machine guns which were then in service; they were loaded with 5.5g (85 grain) of black powder and fired a 31g (480 grain) bullet or as close to it as was available. The tubular-magazine rifles were eliminated almost immediately, after one of the testing party was injured when a round went off in the magazine of a Winchester, which left the field rather narrow; to provide more comparators Mauser M/71s were obtained from Germany, though there was certainly never any intention that they should be adopted. The Lee rifle emerged as the winner, but the committee was not convinced. It reported in 1881 that there was no justification for procuring a new service rifle.

The Royal Navy – which still saw itself as having close-quarters battles to fight at sea, and whose men were frequently employed on land in both the artillery and infantry roles – dissented. It wanted a rifle capable of rapid fire and favoured the Lee (the Welsh infantrymen conducting the test-firings had been able to get off 20 rounds in 53 seconds with it, after only cursory drilling; we may recall that it took an expert instructor to put up the same performance with a Martini-Henry. Later, experts with the new rifle would put up even better performances), and the following year a sub-committee, which soon evolved into a new Committee on Small Arms, with a brief widened to

Burton hopper magazine, and thereafter was known as the Lee-Burton.

EXTENDED TRIALS

The Lee rifles, one with the original box magazine and one with the hopper, were among the top three contenders, it turned out, along with the Owen Jones, which the Royal Navy later tested independently and rejected. No definitive decision was reached then and deliberations continued; as time went on, new rifles and existing types with new modifications continued to be submitted for trial, (the total number was to reach 42 in all), and still no decision was made. And then, in 1886, came rumours of the

of several of the committee members), now in .402in (10.2mm) calibre.

But in December 1886, two things happened to give them pause. Firstly, they were able to examine a prototype Schmidt-Rubin rifle in nominally 7.5mm calibre, which fired jacketed, smokeless ammunition which proved most satisfactory in terms of accuracy, range, penetration, and effect (they didn't like the straight-pull bolt-action, but that was irrelevant since the rifle itself wasn't under consideration). And secondly, Lee came up with an improvement to his removable magazine, which effectively ruled out the Lee-Burton; previously the magazine had had to be detached from

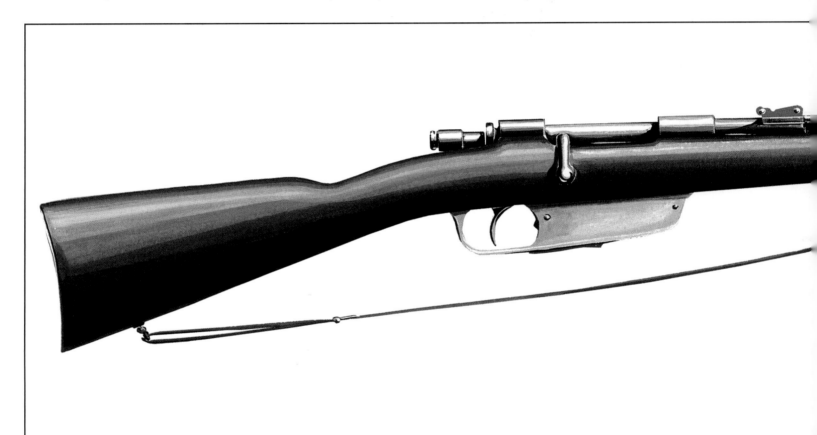

include pistols and other individual weapons, was formed to consider it again, alongside new submissions which included Mannlicher, Schulhof, and Chafee-Reece bolt-action rifles, as well as a new falling block-action rifle equipped with a hopper magazine, the American Owen Jones. The Lee rifles provided this time were chambered for the Springfield .45in cartridge which had very different ballistic properties to the round the British Army used, and after an initial test firing these were sent to Enfield to be fitted with Henry barrels chambered for the Gatling cartridge; one was also fitted with a locally-developed Bethel-

impending switch to 8mm calibre and smokeless powder in France.

Just months earlier, the committee – which had by now been meeting on and off for the best part of five years – had been ordered to speed up its work; as a result many border-line submissions were rejected out of hand.

The decision still lay between the box-magazine Lee and the hopper-magazine Lee-Burton, essentially similar weapons apart from their magazines (both had Lee's bolt-action, and rifling and a cartridge entry system designed by William Ellis Metford, a respected figure in the field at the time, and a close friend

the rifle to be loaded, but the revised version could be charged in situ via the receiver. A simple plate which pivoted on a vertical pin, which depressed the cartridges in the magazine, served as a cut-off, allowing 'more economic' single-shot firing.

THE LEE RIFLE

On 22 December 1888 the Rifle, Magazine, Mark I in .303in (7.7mm) calibre was officially adopted as the British Army's new rifle, and a new cartridge, the Cartridge, .303 Mk I Ball, loaded (for the time being) with 4.85g (75 grain) of compressed black powder and a

13.93g (215 grain) round-nosed bullet, which gave a muzzle velocity of 670 metres (2200ft) per second at the cost of very severe recoil, was provided to go with it. It was three years before the Mark VI cartridge became available, the first to be filled with cordite, as the British called their version of the 'new' propellant (it was actually an advance over the Vieille flake powder, being a mixture of nitro-cellulose and nitro-glycerine with a mineral jelly retardant; it was formed into strands, and it was its resemblance to short lengths of string which gave it its name). The performance of the rifle loaded with them dropped somewhat – the muzzle velocity was

NATO round, over four decades later. Existing rifles were modified, which meant altering their sights and making very small modifications to their magazines.

The cartridge for which the prototype Schmidt-Rubin rifle was chambered was rimless, of course, and the committee fought hard to retain this form for the new British cartridge, reasoning that it was both basically sounder and stronger than a rimmed round, that rimmed rounds occupied more space in the magazine than rimless rounds (and that closer attention had to be paid to the way in which magazines were charged with them; each round has to lie with its rim

his family firm was already well respected, and was still very much in business a century later), which caused the new round to be specified with a rimmed case, and that was to cause many problems in the future, not so much in the rifle as in other applications. The committee's case was not helped by the quality of the ammunition Rubin had furnished for the trials of the Swiss rifle; there were frequent blow-backs caused by manufacturing defects.

METFORD'S CONTRIBUTION
The Lee rifle as adopted was to prove an excellent choice, and most experts rate it as one of the best all-round military bolt-

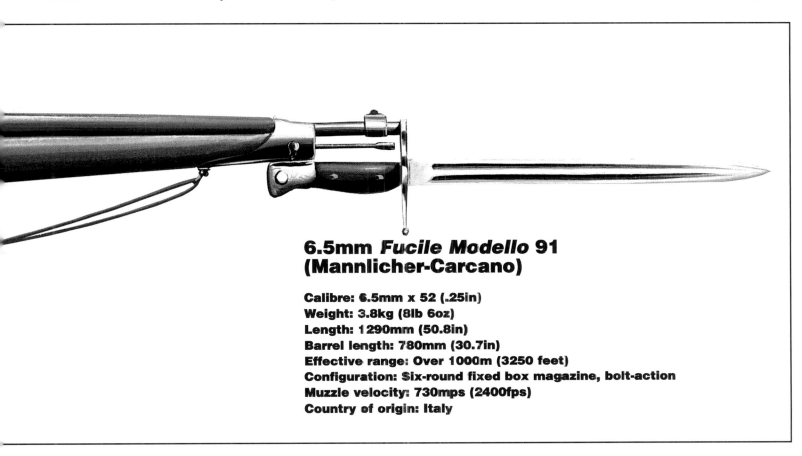

6.5mm *Fucile Modello* 91 (Mannlicher-Carcano)

Calibre: 6.5mm x 52 (.25in)
Weight: 3.8kg (8lb 6oz)
Length: 1290mm (50.8in)
Barrel length: 780mm (30.7in)
Effective range: Over 1000m (3250 feet)
Configuration: Six-round fixed box magazine, bolt-action
Muzzle velocity: 730mps (2400fps)
Country of origin: Italy

reduced to 630 metres (2065ft) per second – but they were much easier on the shoulder, and that was a considerable factor in battle; it was proved very clearly that even the toughest infantryman started to flinch after he had fired 30 or so rounds, and by the time he had fired 50, his aim was totally unreliable. The Mark VI round was superseded by the Mark VII – with a pointed 11.34g (174 grain) bullet and a propellant load of 2.4g (37 grain) of modified cordite, which gave a muzzle velocity of 740 metres (2425ft) per second – in November 1910 and that round continued unchanged thereafter until it was superseded by the 7.62mm

in front of that of the round to be fed after it) and that rimless rounds presented fewer problems in the belt-fed machine guns which were just coming into service where the use of a rimmed round caused complications in the feedpath (Hiram Maxim submitted his first such gun for official testing by the British Army in March 1887, and deliveries started the following year).

It was the objection of the then Superintendent of the Royal Small Arms Factory at Enfield, John Rigby (incidentally, the first man to hold that position who came from a gunmaking, rather than from a military, background;

action rifles ever produced (Metford's name appeared, somewhat belatedly, in the official designation from 1891 to 1895, when his seven-groove rifling system was dropped in favour of one developed at Enfield which had just five grooves. Metford's rifling, which had no sharp shoulders to the lands but made the transition in smooth curves instead, was designed to take a minimum of fouling from black powder; once the changeover to cordite had been completed, this was no longer an issue, and more efficient sharply-angled rifling – which was also cheaper to produce – could be used instead.

The bolt-action itself, with its rear locking lug and symmetrically-opposed rib, the rear surface of which functioned as a second locking lug, was to prove strong enough to cope with considerably more powerful propellant loads than had initially been envisaged, and that was a most important factor in subsequent decisions not to abandon the design, despite the fact that bolt-actions whose locking lugs were located immediately behind the bolt head were widely held to be more satisfactory; perfectionists argued later that the Mauser three-lug system was more secure, but Lee's was certainly more effective on the battlefield in the hands of less-than-skilled conscripts and war-service volunteers. The doubters tried long and hard to vilify the Lee-Enfield rifle, particularly when it was re-introduced in its shortened form (and many who didn't know a rifle bolt from that on their outhouse door jumped on the bandwagon), but were ultimately to fail.

THE LEE'S MODIFICATIONS

The Lee-Enfield rifle underwent a considerable number of further modifications over the next half-century and more – some, like the changeover from the eight-round in-line magazine to the wider but shorter 10-round staggered-column version, which took place in 1894, or the improvements required to upgrade it to cordite ammunition in the following year, were aimed at improving it as a weapon; others at making it easier to produce – as well as two rather more major changes which altered its appearance considerably, though not its basic nature. Most significantly, it was reduced in length by lopping 125mm (five inches) off the barrel) in 1903, at which point the cleaning rod was deleted too, and the design of the fore-end was changed to accommodate a protector for the foresight (the trigger mechanism was modified from single- to two-stage operation and a pair of charger guides for clip loading, the left hand in the receiver, the right hand on the bolt head, were also added, though neither of these modifications changed the rifle's appearance) at which point it became the Rifle, Short, Magazine, Lee-Enfield Mark 1, widely known as the SMLE.

In 1941 the design of the bolt and receiver were changed quite radically to make field-stripping easier, and the form of the muzzle and fore-end were altered

again, to allow a handle-less bayonet to be fitted by a push-and-twist action (what we know as a 'bayonet' fitting) in place of the original knife bayonet with a haft, which was located by a muzzle-ring in its guard and fixed on a dovetail lug below the fore-end which located in a groove in the haft.

THE LEE-ENFIELD

Known by now more simply, as the Rifle, Number 4 (having gone through a bewildering series of designations in the meantime – at least two dozen, each one representing a different stage of modification, however small), it was superseded for general service with the British Army only in the 1950s, by a modified version of the FN FAL (*Fusil Automatique Léger* – Light Automatic Rifle) with its capacity for fully-automatic fire deleted, as the L1A1 SLR (Self-Loading Rifle), chambered for the 7.62mm x 51 NATO round. But it continued in limited service (re-chambered for the rimless NATO round) as the L42A1 sniper rifle (with telescopic sights) and the L39A1 competition rifle (with aperture sights) until the mid-1980s.

In its L42 form, the Lee rifle managed to set a record which is unlikely to be broken – over 100 years of continuous military service. It was finally declared

obsolete in April 1992, almost 105 years after the first Lee-system rifles had been accepted for service with the British Army. As the twentieth century drew to a close, it was still in use by police forces in the United Kingdom and elsewhere under the name Enfield Enforcer, fitted with a variable x4 to x10 Pecar telescopic sight and a modified butt-stock with cheek-rest, pistol grip and recoil pad, its robust nature making up for its lack of some advanced features.

While the British Army was completing its selection process for a new rifle and the German factories were gearing up for production of the 88, all across Europe firearms designers were busy producing prototype small-calibre rifles to take advantage of the new propellant; most of them never got past that stage. One which did, and which was to find a surprisingly large market, was the brainchild of Captain Ole Krag of the Royal Norwegian Artillery and Erik Jorgensen of the Norwegian State Arsenal.

THE KRAG-JORGENSEN RIFLE

It had a conventional enough turn-down bolt-action with a single locking lug at the front of the bolt, and the bolt handle acted as an auxiliary lock, being located in a recess in the receiver in much the same fashion as the long-outdated Dreyse

6.5mm Moschetto M/91 *Per Cavalleria*

Calibre: 6.5mm x 52 (.25in)
Weight: 3.0kg (6lb 10oz)
Length: 920mm (36.2in)
Barrel length: 610mm (24in)
Effective range: Circa 600m (1950ft)
Configuration: Six-round fixed box magazine, bolt-action
Muzzle velocity: 700mps (2275fps)
Country of origin: Italy

needle-gun. This was criticised at the time as being insufficiently strong, but it was actually substantial and safe enough for the 8mm x 58R m/89 round for which it was designed (the two were developed in parallel – a common procedure and the main reason why we have such a wide variety of really very similar ammunition types; conservative as they are, gun designers would rather develop and specify a new cartridge than take up one which they know only imperfectly), which

produced a muzzle velocity of just over 600 metres (1970ft) per second firing a comparatively heavy 15.4g (237 grain) bullet with a light 2.2g (34 grain) charge.

The Krag-Jorgensen rifle's oddest feature was its magazine, which was in effect an internal tray set below the bolt, holding three rounds horizontally and a further two within the portion which turned up and back through 130 degrees to bring them up to the feeding position on the left hand side of the receiver.

Rounds were introduced – simply dropped in, in fact – via a front-hinged trapdoor on the right hand side, above and in front of the trigger guard; a leaf spring and follower were located on the inner face of the door and acted on the

■BELOW: The Mosin-Nagant was first adopted by the Russian Army in 1891 and stayed in service until the 1930s. This is the later version, introduced in 1910, with strengthened magazine ribs.

rounds in the magazine when it was closed. So, the rifle's action was widely held to be insufficiently secure, and the magazine-cum-feedpath was downright idiosyncratic (as well as obsolete, since the rounds had to be hand-loaded, one at a time).

AN ODD DECISION

However, first Denmark adopted it as its general service rifle in 1889, and, three years later, so did the United States Army (in .30in calibre) as the replacement for the venerable trapdoor .45in-70 Springfield, putting it into production for itself. Less surprisingly perhaps, the Norwegian Army adopted it too, this time in 6.5mm calibre, in 1894. Apart from altering the chambering, the latter two also modified the rifles to a small degree – the US Army Krags had trapdoor magazine covers hinged on their lower edges, which were rather more convenient in use, and those produced by the Norwegian State Arsenal (where Krag was by now superintendent) for the use of its own forces had butt-stocks with semi-pistol grips. The Norwegians also produced shortened carbines which were half-stocked with no handguard in front of the rear sight, which was positioned well in front of the breech; they looked more like modern sporting rifles as a result. The Norwegian Army was equipped with Krag rifles until well into the 1930s, when they were replaced by Mauser-pattern arms.

With the benefit of hindsight, the US Army's decision to adopt the Krag-Jorgensen rifle seems distinctly odd.

True, it is said to have had a very smooth bolt-action, and could be loaded with the action closed and a round in the chamber (and thus could be fired at a second's notice, even while being loaded, but so could the Lee-Enfield if one chose to substitute one magazine for another, rather than loading it in situ via the receiver), but that hardly made up for the fact that it had to be charged with single rounds, one by one, at a time when many of its competitors were clip- or charger-loaded, or that it was limited by its single-lug locking system to a 14.25g (220 grain) round with a muzzle velocity of just 610 metres (2000ft) per second. Virtually every American-made rifle of the period in question, from the Henry and the Winchester '66 onwards, has been reproduced in replica during the latter part of the twentieth century; perhaps it is significant that no-one has ever chosen to produce a copy of the service arm with which the US Army fought its first foreign war!

The regular units of the US Army which were employed during the Spanish-American War of 1898 and in the Philippines 'rebellion' which followed were armed with Krag-Jorgensen rifles, and found themselves out-ranged by Spanish troops and Moro warriors armed with 7mm 1893-pattern Mausers, while the US militiamen in the same campaign, who had not yet been refitted and who were armed, as a result, with obsolete .45in-70 Springfields, were hopelessly outclassed. In short order, the US Ordnance Department set out to make good the deficiency and, since the Krag's

design would not stand a heavier propellant load, that meant looking for an entirely new rifle less than a decade after adopting it. This was an entirely necessary decision, but, one can imagine, a difficult one to take given the huge amount of money which had gone into the tooling and production of a weapon which was now reckoned to be next to worthless. The rifle the US Army selected – known officially as the US Rifle, Caliber .30in, M1903, and universally as the Springfield '03 – owed a very considerable debt to Paul Mauser (so much so that the US Government paid him a royalty), and thus we need to backtrack at this point and return to Oberndorf-am-Neckar to trace the developments which had been made there since the mid-1880s.

RIFLES FOR EXPORT

Despite losing many of her Balkan possessions, Turkey – which still extended to the Adriatic Sea through what is now southern Bulgaria, Macedonia, and Albania, and stretched down to the Red Sea and from the Persian Gulf to Egypt in the south – was still a major force in world affairs at this time and an important market for arms of all sorts. In 1886 Paul Mauser participated in an international competition to supply a new repeating rifle to the Turkish Army, and suggested what was really nothing more than the M/71-84, re-chambered for a considerably more powerful black powder 9.5mm round which he had developed himself, cut down by 40mm (one and a half

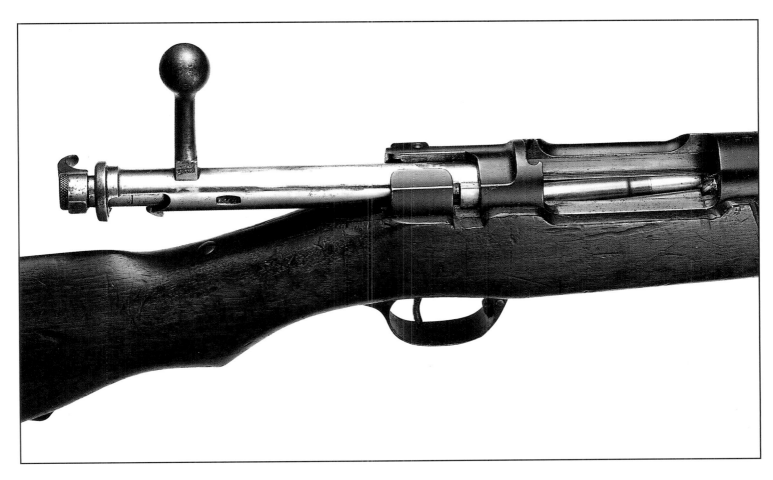

inches) and with the 'doubled resistance' modification to the bolt locking system which he had hastily devised in an effort to prevent the rifle pulling so badly to the right (see above). The only other modification saw the re-installation of a cleaning/unloading rod, housed on the right hand side between the barrel and the magazine tube, which the German War Ministry had deleted. At that time, the Oberndorf factory was engaged in

filling the order for 19,000 M/71-84 rifles it had received from the state government of Württemberg, so was set up to produce the modified rifle almost immediately. There was one small worry – the sheer size of the order: Turkey wanted half a million rifles and a further 50,000 shortened versions for issue to its artillery, and there was no way in the world the Oberndorf factory could produce them in the time available.

ABOVE: The Japanese Arisaka rifles were basically Mauser designs. This is the Meiji 30 Year type, introduced in 1897, chambered for the 6.5mm x 50 round and available as rifle and carbine.

Mauser turned to Ludwig Loewe & Co., which had undergone a change of direction following the death of the eponymous founder just months before, and was now run by his brother Isidor. Isidor was even more keen than Ludwig had been to shift the firm's focus away from general machine tool production (it had long-since stopped making sewing machines) and into the manufacture of armaments, and willingly accepted Mauser's offer of participation. We have already seen Loewe's shadow looming over the scene, but this deal with Mauser marked the start of a new phase in the company's fortunes, and from this point on it was to gather further momentum. Mauser's offer was accepted by the Turkish Government, and on 9 February 1887, a contract to supply 550,000 rifles and carbines was signed. Production started at Oberndorf the same month and was soon running at 500 rifles per day; by the end of the year, the Turkish inspection team who lived on the site in a house specially built for them had already accepted 70,000, and another

Mousqueton d'Artillerie, Modäle 1892 (Berthier)

Calibre: 8mm x 50R (.32in)
Weight: 3.1kg (6lb 13oz)
Length: 940mm (37in)
Barrel length: 445mm (17.5in)
Effective range: 500m (1625ft)
Configuration: Three-round integral box magazine, bolt-action
Muzzle velocity: Circa 600mps (1750fps)
Country of origin: France

Mauser Infanteriegewehr 98

Calibre: 7.92mm x 57 (.31in)
Weight: 4.2kg (9lb 4oz)
Length: 1255mm (49.5in)
Barrel length: 740mm (29.15in)

Effective range: Over 1000m
(3250ft)
Configuration: Five-round integral
box magazine, bolt-action

Muzzle velocity: 640mps
(2100fps); 895mps (2900fps)
with 'S' ammunition
Country of origin: Germany

60,000 had been completed at the Loewe factory in Berlin.

Three days before the year's end, and for reasons which remain not entirely clear, Ludwig Loewe & Co. was able to acquire all the shares in Waffenfabrik Mauser, as the company had become, including Paul Mauser's personal holding. Mauser – who was still only 49

years old – became General Manager and the Württemberger Union Bank, which had played an important part in the commercial management of the company since Wilhelm's death, dropped out of the picture. Ludwig Loewe & Co. had just accepted the order to supply all the tooling for the 88 rifle at this point, and to make way for that, all the residual

production for Turkey was re-assigned to Oberndorf. By 1890, 220,000 M/87s had been delivered, but by that time, Paul Mauser had been at work again and had developed an entirely new rifle, his first in a small calibre and designed to employ nitro-cellulose as a propellant, in response to a competition launched by the Belgian Government. Under a clause

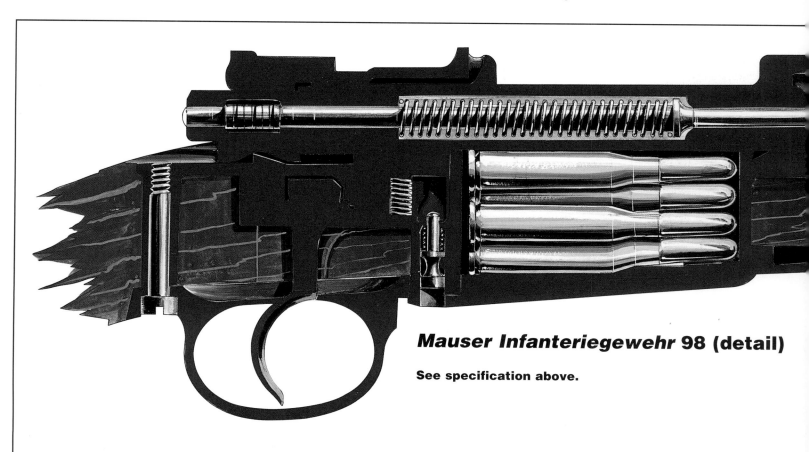

Mauser Infanteriegewehr 98 (detail)

See specification above.

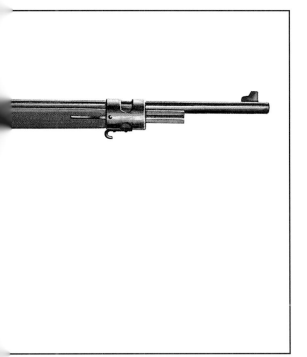

■ **ABOVE: Boer 'commandos' like these, armed with Mauser rifles (these are 'Belgian' M/98s in 7.65mm calibre) employed hit-and-run tactics to give the British Army a very bad time.**

in the contract with the Turks, Mauser was obliged to offer them any new and improved rifle he produced in place of any as-yet undelivered M/87s, and when they saw the new rifle, the Turks promptly insisted he comply.

THE BELGIAN M/89 MAUSER

The rifle Mauser produced for Belgium

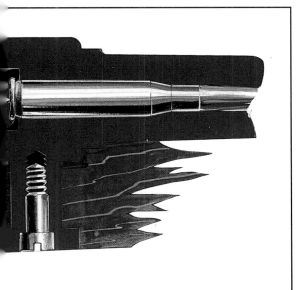

was designed around a new cartridge, the 7.65mm x 53, which was loaded with 2.72g (42 grain) of 'Poudre de Wetteren' (a near-replica of Vieille's 'Poudre B') and a 13.95g (215 grain) nickel-plated, steel-jacketed bullet with a cylindrical body and a rounded head, characteristic of the projectiles of the day, which gave a muzzle velocity of just over 610 metres (2000ft) per second. Like the Rubin cartridges on which it was based, it was rimless.

The box magazines of the first models of the new rifle were loaded, via the receiver, one round at a time. Before the competition date, late in 1888, Mauser responded to Mannlicher's invention of the ammunition charger and devised a clip of his own, which held five rounds. It was placed vertically in a pair of cut-outs in the front of the receiver bridge so that the ammunition could be pushed down into the magazine in a single movement of the thumb, and the right hand side of the receiver ahead of the bridge was cut away to make that action simpler and quicker (the empty charger was then ejected upwards and forwards by the action of closing the bolt).

Compared with the Mannlicher clip frame, as employed by the 88 rifle, the Mauser method had one important advantage, despite being fractionally slower in operation: the magazine could be topped up with individual rounds at any time (we may recall the similar modification which Nelson King had made to the Henry-model Winchester, over two decades earlier). This was the

first time the strip charger-loading box magazine had appeared, and Mauser was to employ it in every rifle he designed from then on; gunmakers all over the world were soon trying to copy the innovation in one form or another. Mauser secured nine foreign patents for the device, in all the important markets, but failed to obtain one at home (though not for the want of trying); once again, the German military establishment acted to protect itself against having to enter into a licensing agreement, to Paul Mauser's cost.

The most significant change in the appearance of the new rifle was the relocation of the bolt handle to the rear of the receiver bridge. This was made possible by Mauser's timely decision to drop the old, discredited method of locking the bolt by means of a camming surface at the root of the handle, and to replace it with a pair of lugs with camming surfaces on the bolt cylinder, right behind the bolt head, which located in grooves in the breech case immediately behind the chamber, one at the top and the other at the bottom, as the bolt was turned through 90 degrees. This arrangement was similar to that suggested by Schlegelmilch and adopted for the 88 rifle, but nonetheless is widely known as the Mauser system to this day.

Unlike the M/71, the M/89's bolt head was an integral part of the bolt cylinder, and not removable. Its front surface was machined out so that the base of the cartridge fitted inside it, and a small spring-loaded extractor located there slipped into the cannelure (the extraction groove) in the cartridge at the very beginning of its forward travel in an attempt to ensure that, unlike the 88 rifle, the M/89 would not chamber two cartridges at once by permitting the bolt to be withdrawn while the cartridge stayed in place – the procedure worked, but not entirely to Mauser's satisfaction; he was to solve the problem definitively in his next all-new design, the 'Spanish' M/93. Also unlike the M/71, the action was cocked by the act of closing the bolt,

BELOW: German troops pictured in China at the time of the joint expedition to put down the Boxer Rebellion in 1900. They are armed with Mauser *Infanteriegewehr* 98 rifles.

not on opening it. This was widely held to be less effective by virtue of the extra pressure required to drive the bolt home and cock the action at the same time, and Mauser reverted to the original method (in an improved form) for his masterpiece, the 98 rifle. The wing-style safety catch Mauser produced for the M/71 was retained, albeit in a slightly modified form. This version of it also locked the bolt in the closed position if it were cocked, preventing it from being opened inadvertently.

MAUSERS FOR EXPORT

The new weapon shared one questionable feature with the 88 rifle: the infamous barrel tube. It is sometimes suggested that Ludwig Loewe & Co. insisted that it be incorporated into the design so that the company could collect its share of the licensing fee, but in fairness, one must point out that the floating barrel which resulted from its use was, theoretically at least, likely to be more accurate, and it

RIGHT: The French Berthier rifle had a three-round integral box magazine and an effective range of 500m (1625ft). It was a rather ordinary and insignificant rifle when compared to its rivals.

did permit both the fore- and backsights to be soldered on without any danger of the process introducing any distortion.

An additional similarity to the 88 rifle was the fact that the M/89 also had a magazine which protruded below the fore-stock, immediately in front of the trigger guard. In this case, however, it was removable for cleaning, and was retained by a simple snap catch inside the trigger guard; the distinctive hump in its front lower part housed the pivot for the sprung lever which acted on the

BELOW RIGHT: The British Army in South Africa at firing practice. The men are armed with the Rifle, Magazine, Lee-Enfield Mark 1, introduced in 1899, the year war began.

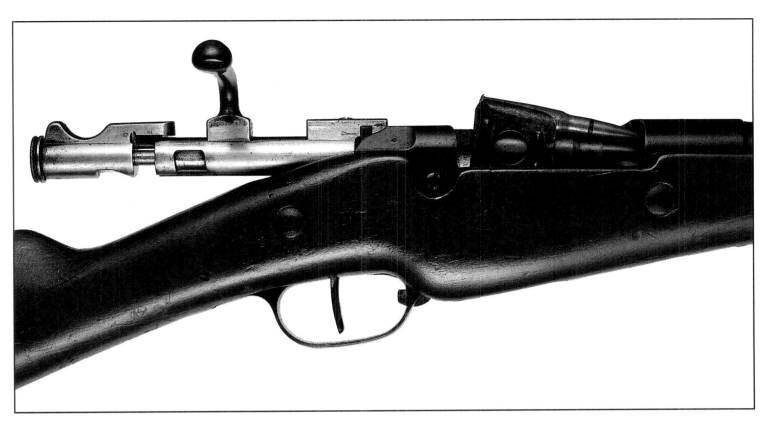

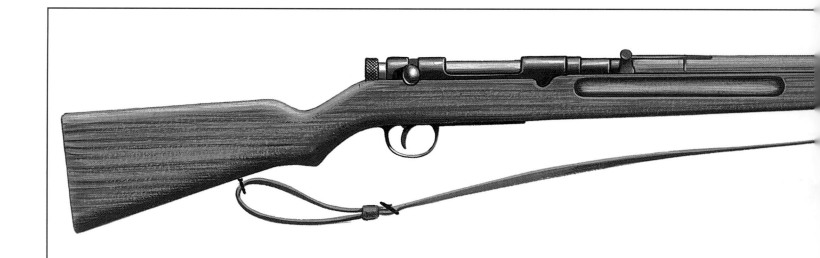

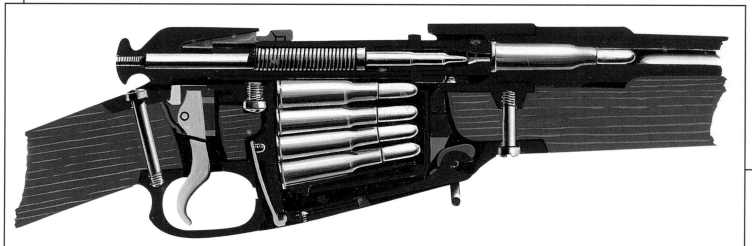

Soviet M1891/30 Rifle

Calibre: 7.62mm x 54R (.30in)	Barrel length: 730mm (28.75in)	box magazine, bolt-action
Weight: 4.35kg (9lb 9oz)	Effective range: Over 1000m (3250ft)	Muzzle velocity: 790mps (2600fps)
Length: 1240mm (48.75in)	Configuration: Five-round integral	Country of origin: Soviet Union

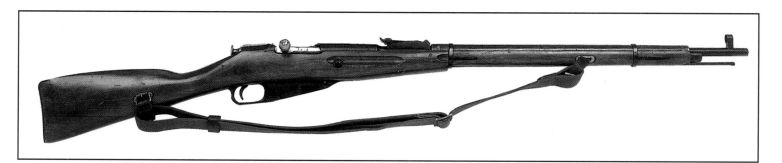

■ABOVE: The Russian M1891 stayed in service with the Red Army after the revolution of 1917, and was revamped twice: this is a shorter carbine model often known as a Dragoon or Cossack.

cartridge follower to maintain pressure on the rounds themselves, a mechanism which Mauser had long favoured but which was to disappear in subsequent designs, to be replaced by a simple

platform supported by a compound leaf spring.

The design found ready favour with the Belgian Government, and was accepted in both rifle and shorter carbine form. Originally, it had been intended that it should be manufactured exclusively at the State Arms Factory in Liège, but in the event – and somewhat surprisingly, it must be said – a newly-established private company, Fabrique

Nationale d'Armes de Guerre (FN), was also given a contract to supply M/89 rifles. More surprisingly still, perhaps, Ludwig Loewe & Co. was permitted to own a half-stake in the new company, which it retained until the end of World War I. A modern factory was constructed in Herstal-lèz-Liège, and by the end of 1889, manufacture was in full swing. M/89 rifles were later made under licence in small numbers in both Great Britain

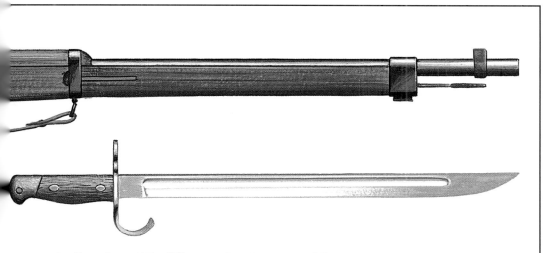

Arisaka Meiji 38th Year Rifle

Calibre: 6.5mm x 50 (.25in)
Weight: 4.3kg (9lb 8oz)
Length: 1275mm (50.25in)
Barrel length: 800mm (31.45in)
Effective range: Over 1000m (3250ft)
Configuration: Five-round integral box magazine, bolt-action
Muzzle velocity: 730mps (2395fps)
Country of origin: Japan

and the United States, while FN went on to become one of the most important arms producers of the twentieth century. Ludwig Loewe & Co., which later transformed itself into Deutsches Waffen und Maschinefabrik (DWM,) and which also held a franchise to manufacture Maxim's machine guns, was to become an even more important and influential enterprise.

The Turkish Government liked the new rifle too, and soon invoked the get-out clause in its contract with Mauser for the M/87 rifle, switching to a slightly modified version of the new weapon for the balance of that order instead. As the M/90, it was produced in slightly modified form – the barrel jacket was deleted, and Mauser devised a simpler and easier solution to the problem of locating the barrel in the stock – he introduced a stepped cylindrical barrel (all his earlier units had been tapered) and secured it at the step to the fore-stock with a ring profiled so as to allow lateral expansion.

Between 1890 and 1893, 280,000 Turkish M/90 Mausers were produced at Obernsdorf. The following year the Argentine Government placed an order for 180,000 identical rifles, which were produced at the Loewe factory in Berlin. Mauser, under its new ownership, had

finally become a force to be reckoned with in the burgeoning field of armaments production.

THE SPANISH MAUSER

Paul Mauser's next design is widely held to be the first perfect bolt-action – that is, it had no inherent flaws or faults, and would work as designed every time, provided that it was kept clean and well maintained. It appeared as the M/93, originally produced for the Spanish Government but was very widely distributed later. Some authorities suggest that by a narrower definition, the action was less than perfect, in particular since it retained the cock-on-closing method adopted for the Belgian M/89, and by that narrower definition, they have a valid point, but the perfectionism was lost on the vast majority of the million-plus men who carried it.

The main sub-assembly still in need of improvement by 1891, when the design was first conceived, was the extractor, for despite the changes made to the M/89's bolt there was an enduring weakness in the way the extractor was located in the cannelure, and while this seldom led to misfeeds, they were known to happen. Mauser corrected it by introducing a long, wide leaf spring, which lay along three-quarters of the length of the bolt

and which finished in a claw fully as wide as the right/lower locking lug on the bolt head (which the spring bridged: the spring travelled in a groove machined within the right hand side of the receiver bridge) and which was of a size and profile corresponding to those of the cannelure in the cartridge case. What had been the lower side of the bolt head when the action was open was flattened, so that the cannelure of the cartridge was forced to locate with the claw from the moment it was picked up out of the magazine. The left/upper locking lug had a longitudinal groove machined into it, so that on the rearwards stroke of the bolt, the ejector would enter it, arrest the extracted cartridge case's progress, and flip it out of the breech.

The most obvious difference in the look of the M/93 rifles and carbines was their apparent lack of a magazine. Mauser realised that the five cartridges contained in it did not need to stand in a single column, but that instead they could be staggered, two towards one side, two towards the other, with the upper side walls ensuring that the topmost round was centralised. This made the cross-sectional profile of the magazine space somewhat wider and shorter but did away with the need for a separate box since it allowed the entire magazine to be contained within the stock and not project from it. It was finished at the bottom by means of a flat plate laying flush with the woodwork, which was secured by a hook at the front and a catch at the rear, just in front of the trigger guard. To this plate, which was removable for cleaning and maintenance, was fastened the bottom arm of a W-shaped composite leaf spring, the top arm being fastened to the magazine platform-cum-cartridge follower. On the left hand side of that platform was a raised longitudinal rib, which controlled the manner in which the cartridges were staggered, and which acted as a hold-open device when the magazine was empty. A pair of longitudinal lips machined into the lower side of the receiver acted as the feed guides.

WORLD BEATER

Mauser also improved the action of the cocking piece and safety catch. The cocking piece gained two short ribs, which located it within the guide attached to the bolt cylinder more precisely, and to assist in this, the forward path of the striker and firing pin

■LEFT: Assault infantrymen of the Wehrmacht in Italy in 1943, armed with the Mauser 98k rifle – essentially the same weapon their fathers had carried in the war of a generation earlier.

Kruger, ordered 37,000 from Germany in 1896 and 1897). The Boer commandos, quick to learn the power of the new weapons, used them from cover, at long range (up to 1200 metres/3935ft), and they were deadly:

'The ground in front of me was literally rising in dust from the bullets, and the din echoing around the hill and the wood below and among the rocks from the incessant fire of the Mausers seemed to blend with every other sound into a long drawn-out hideous roar. Halfway over the terrace I looked round over my shoulder and I confess I was rather horrified at what I saw. S—- was close beside me, and a few men here and there, but the whole ground we had already covered was strewn with bodies, and no more men were coming from over the wall. . .'

(Captain Nugent, 60th Rifles, describing to the correspondent of *The Times* his battalion's advance over open ground towards Boer positions near Dundee, Northern Transvaal, 19/20 October 1899. Nugent was wounded three times during the battle, in each leg and in the lower back; even at that extreme range, he related how a round which hit him in the leg 'moved his whole body as if it had been struck by a club.') In less than 40 years the technology which

was lengthened to 25mm (one inch) – which meant that the cocking piece protruded that far when the action was cocked, providing a ready visual indication to the user of the state the weapon was in.

A modification to the trigger sear – it was formed with two projections which extended into the bolt guide – provided a second safety feature. The rear projection was a true sear, retaining the striker when the action was cocked; when the trigger was pulled, this dropped and allowed the striker to operate, but in the same motion, the safety sear at the front was raised through an opening in the floor of the receiver bridge into the bolt guide and into a slot in the bolt itself. If the bolt was not fully closed and the action locked, the two did not align, and the action was blocked.

MAUSER'S 7MM CARTRIDGE

The Spanish Mauser, as the model was usually known, was chambered for yet another cartridge form which Mauser developed, this time in nominal 7mm calibre, with a case length of 57mm (2.2in), the same as that of the German service round. Firing a 11.2g (173 grain) bullet, 7.25mm in actual diameter, that was propelled by 2.45g (38 grain) of a new formulation of Rottweil flake powder, the new cartridge produced a muzzle velocity of around 700 metres (2300ft) per second.

This new cartridge set a new standard, and for decades afterwards was the chosen service round for many of the world's smaller nations' armies. The

Spanish Government ordered a quarter of a million M/93s, all of which were produced in Berlin, while the ever-present Turks bought a further 200,000, this time chambered for the 7.65mm cartridge developed for the M/90, and these were made at Oberndorf. The rifle was later put into production in Spain at the Government Arms Factory in Ovieda, and from there most of the countries of Latin America were supplied.

It was the Mauser M/93 in the hands of Spanish troops in Cuba which forced the US Army to re-evaluate its Krag-Jorgensen rifles during the short, momentous Spanish-American War of 1898, while the Boers in South Africa used them to very good effect against the British (the leader of the Transvaal, Paul

produced the modern rifle had changed the practice of warfare forever.

STRAIGHT-PULL BOLT-ACTION

The part Paul Mauser was to play in the development of that technology was by no means over yet, but he was not the only successful gun designer in Europe at the time. We have already looked at some of Lee's activities and at Krag's short-lived contribution to the genre, but there were others, too, and first among them were the two exponents of the straight-pull bolt-action, Ferdinand von Mannlicher and Colonel Rudolf Schmidt.

The Swiss stuck to the tubular-magazine Vetterli in 10.4mm (.41in) calibre until 1889, and then switched to the jacketed small-calibre, rimless round filled with smokeless powder which Rubin developed, which was first employed in the box-magazine rifle with its idiosyncratic straight-pull bolt-action Schmidt had designed in 1887, and which entered service with the Swiss Federal Army as the *Repetiergewehr Modell* 1889, in 7.5mm x 54 calibre.

The most noticeable feature of the M1889 was the location of the trigger group, well behind the line of the receiver, and the length of the magazine in front of it, which held 12 rounds in a single column, but its most interesting aspect was the action of the bolt.

MAUSER'S COMPETITORS

'Conventional' (as we may call them, for they have prevailed) turn-down bolt-actions rely, as their description suggests, on the handle of the bolt being employed to turn the body of the cylinder through

(something like) 90 degrees at the completion of the forward charging stroke, seating the lug or lugs in the recesses cut to receive them. Sometimes the engagement surfaces of the lugs and recesses are cut square, but more often, the surfaces which first meet are set at an angle, so that a camming action takes place to ease them together (the same action also serves to ease them apart, of course, and that is an important factor in the primary stage of extraction).

In the Schmidt-Rubin, there was no manual rotation of the bolt; instead, the rotation of the bolt cylinder to achieve locking (and the subsequent opening of the breech) was carried out by the movement of a lug on a secondary operating rod which lay alongside the bolt proper, and to which the handle was connected, in a helical slot in the bolt itself.

The first rearward movement of the handle and rod caused the bolt cylinder to rotate partially and free the locking lugs from their recesses in the receiver bridge, at which point the entire assembly was free to move to the rear, opening the breech and extracting the spent case in the process. Closing the bolt by reversing the procedure cocked the action and stripped the topmost round off the magazine, introduced it into the feedpath and re-locked the action. The firing pin/striker was fitted with a large-diameter ring at its rearmost end, which protruded; this was both cocking piece and safety catch – it allowed the action to be decocked, set to half-cock or brought back to full cock. Turning it through 90 degrees locked the action.

The Schmidt design was noticeably stiffer to operate than contemporary turn-down bolt-actions (its supporters maintained that in practised hands it was quicker, though it is difficult to see how that could be) thanks to its geometry and the mechanical resistance involved in translating a linear motion into a rotative motion by means of a cam acting in a helical guide (and that is what it and the similar Mannlicher and Ross actions did), and it was noticeably less effective at unseating and extracting sticky, tight-fitting cases. It was certainly more susceptible to contamination, too, and it is fairly safe to say that it would not have been found acceptable in conditions of trench warfare; it is probably just as well that the Swiss were never forced to go to war with it.

Though a total of some 350,000 were manufactured in all, the Schmidt-Rubin was not the only rifle in use in the Swiss Federal Army at the time – some cavalry units were issued in 1893 with a turn-down bolt-action Mannlicher carbine which was also chambered for the Rubin 7.5mm round. It had a short life, being superseded by a Schmidt-system carbine in 1905.

In 1896, a modification was introduced to these Mannlicher carbines which shortened the bolt and the receiver somewhat, though the action or throw was still very long indeed in comparison to other service rifles, which did nothing to make it easier to use.

The Schmidt-system rifle and carbine were subsequently reworked from 1911 to take an improved, more powerful cartridge which delivered a muzzle

Mauser Kar98k

Calibre: 7.92mm x 57 (.31in)
Weight: 3.9kg (8lb 9oz)
Length: 1110mm (43.6in)
Barrel length: 600mm (23.6in)
Effective range: Over 1000m (3250ft)
Configuration: Five-round integral box magazine, bolt-action
Muzzle velocity: 745mps (2450fps)
Country of origin: Germany

velocity in the rifle, with its 780mm-
(31in) long barrel, of 790 metres (2590ft)
per second. At the same time the old 12-
round magazine was replaced with one
holding half that number.

The Schmidt-Rubin weapon's worst

fault – its over-long throw – was finally
rectified by re-designing the action to
operate in half its length, although this
did not take place until 1931. The
resulting carbine (the rifle was deleted)
stayed in service until it was replaced by

the self-loading *Sturmgewehr Modell* 57
assault rifle (qv) in 1957.

THE SUCCESSFUL MANNLICHERS
Mannlicher's straight-pull bolt-action,
which was adopted by the Austro-

■ **LEFT: American troops fighting house-to-house with M1917 Enfield rifles on the Argonne sector of the Western Front in 1918. A later generation would find sub-machine guns much better.**

■ **ABOVE: The Springfield-developed M1903 rifle was the only home-developed bolt-action rifle ever issued to American troops, and then only in comparatively small numbers.**

simpler (but intrinsically no more satisfactory) method than that employed by the Swiss, involving interrupted threads rather than lugs in the bolt head (though at that it was certainly more efficient than his earlier attempt in 1885, which was locked by a hinged block which dropped down from the bottom of the back of the bolt to engage a stop in the boltway). It was not adopted elsewhere – though conventional turn-down bolt-action rifles by Mannlicher were, notably by Rumania in 1892 and by the Netherlands in 1895 (both in 6.5mm calibre and with a heavy charge which gave a muzzle velocity of around 730 metres/2395ft per second), and Hungary, after its independence, also produced a rifle with a very similar action. Mannlicher's name is often associated with the rifles adopted by Italy during this period, as well, in fact, as those used later, but the only element of their design actually attributable to him was that of the magazine. Just before the outbreak of World War I, Austria changed over to the Mauser turn-down bolt design championed by its major ally.

THE ROSS AND LEE RIFLES

Across the Atlantic, two further designers were also experimenting with straight-pull designs, with some initial success – James Lee was one, and the other was a Canadian named Charles Ross.

Ross patented his straight-pull action in 1897, and it owed much to Mannlicher's earlier work – a lug on the bolt travelling in a helical track in the receiver translated the direct pull into a rotation, which freed the interrupted threads which locked the bolt. Ross

switched over to locking lugs in 1900, and it was a rifle so equipped, chambered for the .303in Enfield round, which the Canadian Department of Militia and Defence (and the Royal Northwest Mounted Police) adopted as the official service arm in 1902. Ross was nothing if not persistent in his efforts to perfect his design, and he switched back to interrupted threads again in 1910. The rifle was tested by the British on a number of occasions between 1900 and 1912, and was rejected each time as being too fragile for use on active service 'by large bodies of men of average attainment'.

The Canadian Army went to war with the Ross rifle in 1914, but by the following year it had become clear that the troops had lost confidence in it (as many as could were using scavenged Lee-Enfields instead). An official inquiry revealed that there were severe difficulties in extracting (often poor-quality) mass-produced cartridge cases and that, more crucially, the bolt stop tended to deform the rearmost locking screw, making it next to impossible to close the action. The Ross rifle was promptly set aside, and replaced by the Short Magazine Lee-Enfield. Many found their way into store instead of the melting pots (though the Canadian Government managed to sell around 20,000 to the US Army, for training purposes), and not a few were dispatched to Britain in the dark days of 1940, where they were issued to the Home Guard units.

But the chequered career of the Ross rifle was not over yet. The year after it was supplanted, a group of engineers at

Hungarian Army in 1895 for its infantry rifle (and which had been taken up five years earlier for its cavalry carbine) was basically similar in that it, too, translated a straight pull-and-push into a rotary locking motion, though by a rather

the Dominion Rifle Factory in Quebec, where the Ross had been manufactured, began experimenting with a method of turning it into a light machine gun (LMG) at minimal cost, having realised that the straight-pull bolt-action could be actuated by a simple piston as easily – if not more so – as it could by hand.

The barrel was shortened and drilled to take a gas regulator, and a cylinder and piston were added, lying parallel to it, the whole ensemble being enclosed within a tubular guard which extended back to the breech. The piston rod was linked directly to the bolt handle by means of a simple collar, and a buffer was added to absorb excess energy. A 25-round drum magazine, very similar in character to that employed by John Tagliaferro Thompson's famous 'Trench Broom' sub-machine gun, completed the picture. The conversion looked somewhat ungainly, but it worked surprisingly well – and cost just CAN$50, when a Lewis gun, the best of the genre then available, cost 20 times that.

The only real weakness displayed by the Huot LMG (as it was named, after the man who headed the engineering team) was fairly excessive barrel wear – around 8000 rounds was the maximum that could be put through it – though this was by no means a total disability, given its cost. In the event it never saw action,

since the war ended before it could be put into production.

There was one straight-pull bolt-action (though it is probably better described as a travelling block) which did not rely on a helical slot to translate linear movement into rotational, and that was the system devised by James Lee and adopted by the US Navy in 1895 in .286in calibre.

The bolt Lee used for this rifle did not rotate at all (and indeed, was square, not cylindrical in section), locking being achieved by a latch on its right hand side which located directly into a suitably shaped recess in the outside of the receiver. This latch formed the upper portion of a handle which looked similar in every way to the rear-set handle of a rotating bolt; pulling this handle directly to the rear first overcame the resistance of the latching mechanism and then hauled the bolt back up a slightly inclined track, extracting and then ejecting a spent cartridge and exposing the breech. On the return stroke a fresh round was stripped out of the magazine (which was much the same design as those Lee had incorporated in the conventional bolt-action rifles which had been accepted seven years earlier in the United Kingdom, though it was non-detachable, and which seems to have been the first manufactured in the USA to accept clip loading) and chambered,

and the locking latch was re-seated and locking re-established by forcing the handle fully forwards. It was, as one authoritative study of twentieth century military rifles says, not an altogether easy motion to work.

The US Navy acquired 10,000, and never renewed its contract. Winchester, who manufactured them, also secured the rights to produce a sporting rifle utilising the same action, and made 20,000, only 1700 of which were ever sold.

RUSSIAN RIFLES

It was 1890 before Tsarist Russia got around to replacing the heavy-calibre Berdan single-shot bolt-action rifles which had shown up so poorly before the Turks at Plevna, and when it did, it took elements from a design put forward by the Belgian Nagant brothers, Emile and Leon, who were also responsible for a six-shot revolver pistol with a patent gas-seal action which was adopted as the official Russian side-arm in 1895 and which was still in widespread use a half-century later, and combined them with some from a captain of artillery named Sergeii Ivanovich Mosin, though the rifle which resulted bore neither name. It was known as the *3-lineyaya vintovka obr* 1891 (3-line Rifle, 1891 Model), the 'line' being a now-obsolete unit of measure approximating to 25.4mm (one inch). The

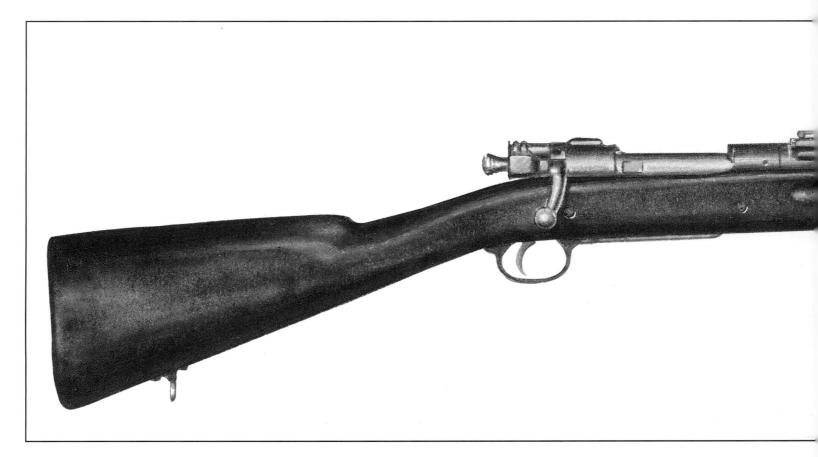

rifles were conventional enough turn-down bolt-action designs, with five-round integral box magazines, and their most impressive feature was the muzzle velocity their relatively heavy 7.62mm rounds achieved – over 800 metres (2625ft) per second. The 1891 design was revamped in 1930 (though shortened carbine and dragoon versions had appeared in the meantime), and again in 1944 (but this time only by the addition of an archaic folding bayonet), and saw service in both World War I and World War II, latterly alongside the self-loading Simonova of 1936 and the rather better Tokareva of 1938.

THE ARISAKA RIFLES
The Industrial Revolution came late to Japan, but when it did, it arrived fully developed, and as a result the Japanese lost little time in catching up with the West. However, as late as 1894, when Japan went to war with China, her army was still armed with tubular-magazine repeater rifles – the 8mm Murata, known, from its year of adoption, as the Meiji 20th year Type – which were already effectively obsolete. A commission was set up under an army officer named Arisaka to devise a replacement, and the result was the Meiji 30th year Type, adopted in 1897 in 6.5mm x 50 calibre. The rifle was clearly derived from Austro-

German roots, with a magazine which was pure Mauser and a bolt which owed a lot to Mannlicher, with its separate head. One distinctive home-grown feature was the pronounced safety lever protruding from the cocking piece. It was replaced, in its turn, in 1905, by the Meiji 38th year Type, which had a bolt very much more like that adopted by Mauser and a receiver-mounted ejector in place of the bolt-mounted version found on the earlier model. The safety catch lever was also replaced. The two designs were both produced as rifles (with 800mm/31.5in barrels) and as carbines (with 470mm/18.5in barrels). The weapons were subsequently re-chambered and re-barrelled for a heavier 11.65g (180 grain) 7.7mm round, still with a muzzle velocity of around 730 metres (2395ft) per second, and it was with modified versions of this rifle, known as the Type 99, that Japan went to war in 1941. Small numbers of Japanese rifles were acquired by Britain during World War I for use in training, though it is extremely doubtful whether any were actually taken into combat. At around the same time, the US Army acquired 280,000 M1891 rifles from Russia, also for training purposes.

FRANCE'S BERTHIER
The French, who had made a giant leap forward with the Lebel M1886, then

proceeded to lose momentum, and soon found themselves armed with weapons which were completely outclassed. In an effort to bring the M1886 up to date, a modification was made to the ammunition, and in 1898 the round-nosed 'Balle M' was replaced by a pointed projectile, the cast-bronze 'Balle D', though this made for serious problems of accidental detonation when bullet tip met primer cap within the tubular magazine.

In the meantime, in 1892 a rather different design for a cavalry carbine, still with the Gras-designed bolt-action which had been used in the M1886, but now with a three-round-capacity box magazine in the Mannlicher style, was adopted in small numbers. Over the following 40-odd years, this weapon – which is generally known by the name of the man who headed the commission which approved it, a talented designer named André Berthier – was modified successively. The most important change was the switch in 1916 to a larger-capacity five-round Mauser-style magazine, but the longer-barrelled rifle version, introduced in 1902, was also reduced in length from a rather unmanageable 1300mm (51in) to 1085mm (42.7in) in 1934, at the same time that the by-then old fashioned 8mm cartridge was discarded, and the rifles were re-chambered for a 7.5mm round.

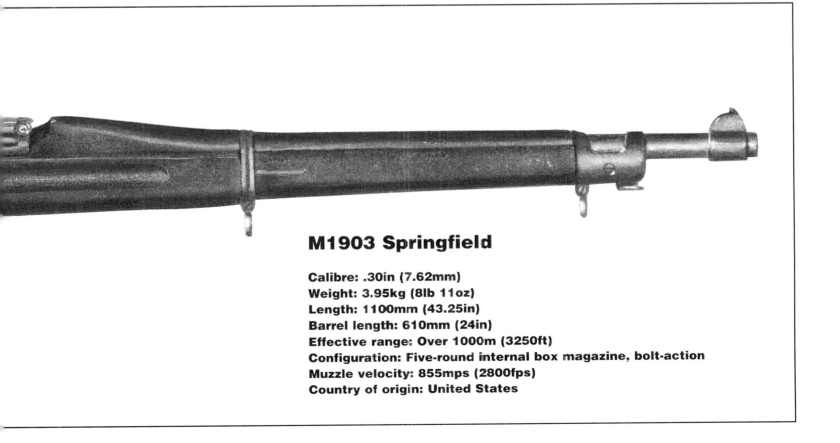

M1903 Springfield

Calibre: .30in (7.62mm)
Weight: 3.95kg (8lb 11oz)
Length: 1100mm (43.25in)
Barrel length: 610mm (24in)
Effective range: Over 1000m (3250ft)
Configuration: Five-round internal box magazine, bolt-action
Muzzle velocity: 855mps (2800fps)
Country of origin: United States

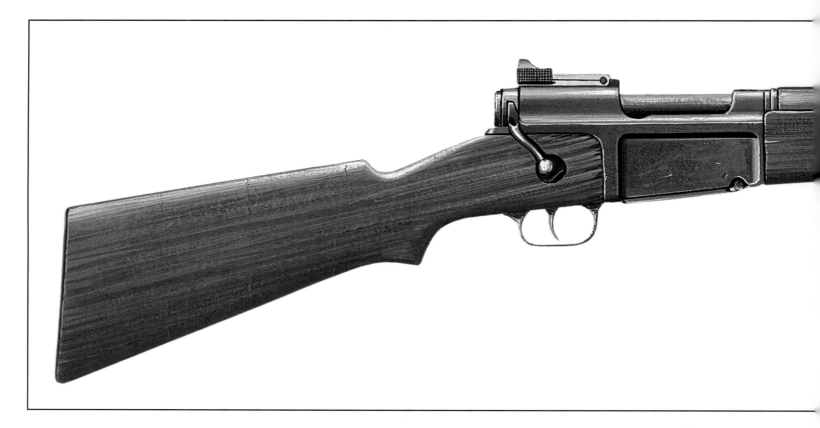

Even so, the Berthier never replaced the Lebel; both were finally superseded (though only in theory) in 1936, but were still to be found in the hands of reservists at the outbreak of World War II.

MAS36: THE LAST BOLT-ACTION
The rifle which appeared in 1936, the Fusil MAS36 (for 'Manufacture d'Armes de Saint Etienne') was developed to utilise a rimless cartridge in 7.5mm nominal calibre which the French had introduced to replace the obsolete rimmed 8mm round, the form of which defied the development of an adequate automatic weapon. A light machine gun which chambered the new round, which was based on the 7.92mm 88S cartridge, was developed first, and then came a new rifle. The MAS36's bolt-action is considered to have been modelled on the Mauser, but there was one vital difference – the twin locking lugs were located towards the rear of the bolt, and engaged recesses in the receiver bridge, rather than in the breech case, which permitted a somewhat shorter bolt stroke at the expense of ultimate strength. Unwilling to place the bolt handle in front of the locking lugs, the designers had no choice but to place it at the very rear of the cylinder and then turn it forwards to bring it into a more convenient position above the trigger. The result was clumsy and unpopular. Like the rifles which preceded it, the MAS36

had no safety catch. Its one real distinction was its position in the chronology of the military bolt-action rifle: it was to be the last new design ever adopted by a major power. A short-barrelled version with a folding hollow aluminium stock was also produced, in small numbers, for use by parachutists. By the time war broke out again in Europe, in 1939, the MAS36 had been issued to all the French Army's infantry battalions.

MAUSER'S 88/97 RIFLE
But whatever else was happening in the world's armouries, all eyes were still, if only metaphorically, on Oberndorf-am-Neckar; those of the commission at Spandau certainly were, and finally, in 1894, Mauser was asked to produce modifications to improve the 88 rifle which by that time had become completely discredited. He reworked a bolt mechanism from the improved M/93, adding a third 'emergency' locking lug to the rear, which served the dual purpose of blocking any escape of propellant gas from a ripped case or a penetrated primer – a regrettably common occurrence, which led to the re-design of the 88 cartridge and the introduction of the 88n/A (*neuer Art*) in 1895 – via the groove cut in the bolt for the 'safety' sear, also making a small modification to the striker head and bolt so that the action was cocked on the first movement of the

bolt handle. He also re-designed the magazine and introduced his own method of loading from a charger strip. Upon the personal intervention of Kaiser Wilhelm II, a new type of rear sight, designed by the Director of the Prussian State Ammunition Factory at Spandau, Lieutenant-Colonel Lange, was also introduced (a considerable amount of attention had – necessarily – been paid to the design of rear sights over the previous decade, as the effective range of rifles got longer and longer).

Mauser was ordered to produce 2000 examples of the modified weapon (in two slightly different forms; the variation concerned the way the action was mated to the stock) and early in the summer of 1895, trials involving four infantry battalions commenced. They were declared a success, and the modified rifle, designated the 88/97, was ordered into (limited) production, at Erfurt only, where some 130 a day were to be made.

The 88/97 rifle was also used as a testbed for smaller-calibre rounds than the 7.92mm 88. As the 'new' nitro propellants improved (and it's worth bearing in mind just how recently they had been introduced) and muzzle velocities increased, the ballisticians' dreams of flat trajectories out to 1000 metres (3280ft) and more, with all that meant for effective accuracy, became more and more attainable, but only at the cost of reducing the weight and the

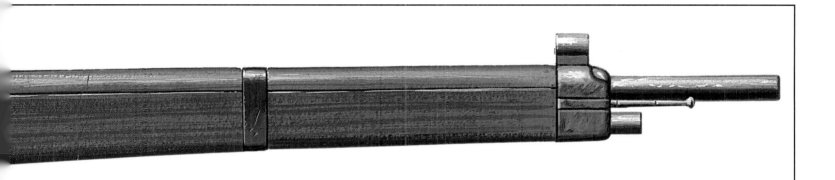

Fusil MAS36

Calibre: 7.5mm x 54 (.29in)
Weight: 3.8kg (8lb 6oz)
Length: 1020mm (40.15in)
Barrel length: 575mm (22.6in)
Effective range: Over 1000m (3250ft)
Configuration: Five-round integral box magazine, bolt-action
Muzzle velocity: 825mps (2700fps)
Country of origin: France

calibre of the bullet. Here they clashed with the military establishment, which still insisted (erroneously, and in defiance of the physical law which tells us that energy is derived from the relationship between mass and velocity, a fact which had been well understood for over two centuries) that a bullet had to be big in order to be sure to inflict a disabling wound. Nonetheless, over 2000 88/97 rifles were produced in 6mm x 59 calibre, the new cartridge being charged with 2.25g (34.7 grain) of Duttenhofer's best powder yet, the Rottweil M91/93 flake, and loaded with a jacketed 8.7g (134 grain) round-nosed bullet, some 32mm (one and a quarter inches) in length – the 14.7g (227 grain) 88 bullet was just one millimetre longer – and produced a muzzle velocity of 800 metres (2625ft) per second, almost 200 metres (655ft) per second faster than the 88n/A round. It is suggested that these tests were the cause of the decision not to put the 7.92mm 88/97 rifle into full production, but in view of the decision to adopt the larger calibre for the next generation of German service rifles, that seems unlikely; more probably, innate conservatism, coupled with the fact that there were vast stocks of 88 ammunition on hand, won the day.

MAUSER TRIUMPHANT – THE 98
Having got its collective fingers severely burned with the 88 rifle, the Prussian War Ministry was considerably more

cautious when it came to identifying a replacement, even though there wasn't really anywhere else to go but Oberndorf (though the unification of the Reich was completed in 1871, each of the major states still maintained a degree of autonomy. They took their lead from Prussia but retained the right to set policy in some areas; this included the selection of weapons for their armies, for

■ **ABOVE: British troops armed with SMLE rifles wait to go 'over the top'. Judging by their equipment it is probably some time near the end of World War I.**

example, and could – but did not – have resulted in a nightmare of proliferation).

On 5 April 1898 Kaiser Wilhelm II designated a new rifle, the 98, for prototype testing. As we have seen, it was to be chambered for the tried and tested (and not altogether satisfactory) 88n/A 7.92mm x 57 round, and its action and barrel were to be that of the 88/97, with the three lug bolt and five-round integral magazine and four-groove, .015mm deep rifling with one full twist in 240mm (9.45in) in a barrel 740mm (29in) long. The only meaningful modification saw the rib in the magazine platform modified so that it no longer functioned as a magazine hold-open device. The barrel

was shortened to carbine length in 1904, in keeping with a general revision (the Lee-Enfield and the Springfield set the tone, the former being shortened to become a 'universal' rifle, suitable for both infantry and cavalry, and the latter being designed to fulfil both roles) at which time the awkward straight bolt handle was replaced by one which was turned down through 90 degrees, with a recess cut into the stock beneath it, to make it easier to grip. At that point the *Infanteriegewehr Modell* 1898 became the

operate smoothly and rapidly (only the French MAS36 had a worse one). Bending it down through 90 degrees prevented it catching in clothing, but did nothing to improve the action.

That caveat apart, the Kar98k served the soldiers of the Wehrmacht and the Waffen-SS admirably. Was it a better rifle than the Lee-Enfield in its 1940 form, as the Rifle, Number 4? That particular argument still rages, and probably always will. Suffice to say that both were excellent; truly great rifles. And was

Short Magazine Lee-Enfield Mark III

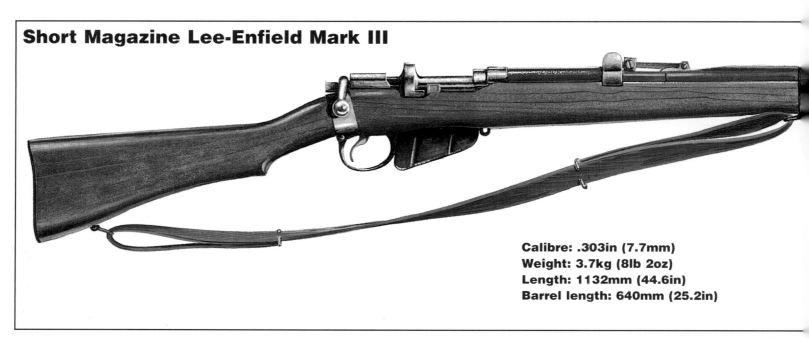

Calibre: .303in (7.7mm)
Weight: 3.7kg (8lb 2oz)
Length: 1132mm (44.6in)
Barrel length: 640mm (25.2in)

tube disappeared, and the stock gained a semi-pistol grip (a first for a Mauser rifle). It retained a cleaning rod (though it was cut down to 395mm (15.5in); it was threaded, and three were joined together in use) which was located in the bayonet fitting, the bayonet haft being drilled out to accommodate it; the rod also served as the mounting for a muzzle protector cap. After a short troop test with three battalions of infantry, which commenced in February 1899, the new rifle was accepted for general service without a murmur of dissent, and went into production at Obernsdorf (this was the first time Mauser had ever been awarded a major production contract, we may note) and at the Prussian and Bavarian state rifle factories too, though Bavaria didn't fall into step until 1903. The very first of them were issued to the Imperial Navy and to the East Asian Expeditionary Corps which took part in the multi-national punitive campaign against the rebellious Boxers in China.

The 98 rifle was to be only slightly modified in the course of a long life. It

Karabiner Modell 1898, and widely known as the Kar98. Later, in 1935, its stock was shortened too, so that the overall length was reduced by some 140mm (five and a half inches) to 1110mm (43.7in), and it became the Kar98k (for '*kurz*' – short).

THE MAUSER KAR98K
The Kar98k rifle/carbine was to stay in service with the German Army until the end of World War II, almost 50 years after it was first adopted. Inevitably, it was to be compared with the Lee-Enfield which preceded it into service, and with the Springfield '03, which resembled it in more ways than one; and, like those two, it is widely held to be one of the best military bolt-action rifles ever devised. In truth, however, it was not until the development of the 88S round, with its lighter, pointed bullet, that it really came into its own. If it had a major defect it was the positioning of the bolt handle (horizontal in the closed position, like all the previous Mausers), which, because it was placed so far back, was difficult to

either of them better or worse than the later semi-automatic M1 Garand, with its much greater rate of fire? In this argument different ground rules apply, but on balance, since firepower alone had come to have an overwhelming importance, and skill-at-arms was diluted by the huge influx of for-the-duration volunteers and conscripts, the Garand has to be perceived as a much more effective tool for the job at hand. It certainly wasn't as accurate as any of the 'big three' bolt-action rifles at extreme range (and the Springfield stayed the arm of choice of US Army and Marine snipers long after it had been supplanted by the Garand) but there was no real requirement for such accuracy within the rank and file of the soldiery.

THE SPITZER BULLET
Research into new forms of rifle bullet in Germany began to show, by early 1898, that a lighter projectile with a pronounced point would be more effective at high velocity than the rounded cylindro-ogival form which had been in

use for so many years (the French had already come to the same conclusion, and introduced the pointed 'Balle D', which was made of bronze rather than lead, that same year). The conservatives took a deal of convincing, in part due to deficiencies in the original propellant, newly introduced by the Royal Gunpowder Factory at Spandau and known as Type 436, formed into square flakes a little over 1.5mm across and around four-tenths of a millimetre thick. With this as its propellant the new 9.8g

Effective range: Over 1000m (3250ft)
Configuration: 10-round detachable box magazine, bolt-action
Muzzle velocity: 670mps (2300fps)
Country of origin: United Kingdom

(151 grain) S bullet (the original, we may recall, weighed 14.7g/227 grain; the weight saving was made by shortening it by a little over three millimetres as well as by drastic re-profiling) produced inferior results: its muzzle velocity was only very little higher than the old 88 cartridge filled with *Gewehrblattpulver*, and it was less accurate as a result. But that changed dramatically when the physical form of the flakes was changed and they were reduced in size and thickness, allowing them to burn faster but also allowing more propellant (3.2g/49.4 grain instead of 2.63g/40.6 grain)) to be loaded into the cartridge. Now the muzzle velocity jumped dramatically, from 620 metres (2035ft) per second to almost 900 metres (2955ft),

■**BELOW: A British soldier, Lee-Enfield at hand, monitors 'no man's land' through a periscope, thus avoiding drawing the unwelcome attention of any German snipers.**

which was little short of sensational. The new cartridge didn't fulfil the ballisticians' dreams, but it came much closer than anything before had done: at 600m (1970ft), the trajectory of an 88 round took it two and a half metres (eight feet) below the line-of-sight, while that of an S round dropped just a metre higher (by way of comparison, the old M/71 round dropped almost five metres/16ft). The new ammunition was adopted as of April 1903. There was an unlooked-for bonus, too: the new light projectile actually had more 'wounding potential' than the old heavy one; the deformation on hitting the target was greater, the jacket often separated from the core on impact, and frequently broke up.

It was necessary to modify the 98 rifles (and the many 88s still in the inventory) in order that they would accept the new ammunition: the cartridge beds had to be reamed out by 0.12mm (an operation which was carried out in four stages, using specially supplied tools, by

Lee-Enfield Number 4, Mark I

See specification above.

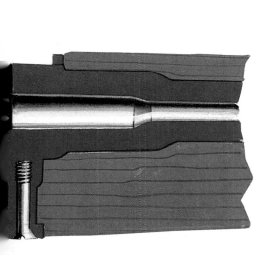

Lee-Enfield Number 4 Mark I

Calibre: .303in (7.7mm)
Weight: 4.2kg (9lb 4oz)
Length: 1130mm (44.5in)
Barrel length: 640mm (25.2in)
Effective range: Over 1000m (3250ft)
Configuration: 10-round
  detachable box magazine,
  bolt-action
Muzzle velocity: 730mps (2400fps)
Country of origin: United Kingdom

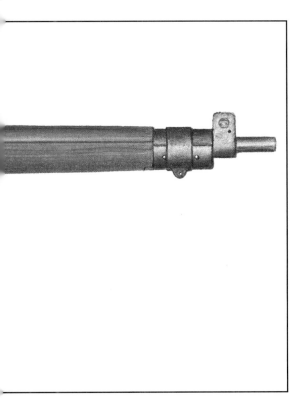

specially trained men who travelled from unit to unit – there was to be no repeat of the fiasco of the ruined M/69 rifles) and the sights had to be altered. It was decided that since the new round's trajectory was so flat, the lowest range setting would be 400m (1310ft), and the new sights were regulated thus; this proved to be a mistake, and during the static, close-range battles of the war which followed, a series of expedients had to be adopted for accurate practice against small targets, the most common of which was to fit a temporary foresight with a longer blade.

THE S AND K ROUNDS

There was to be further research into ammunition in Germany during World War I, most of it carried out by Polte, of Magdeburg, concentrating on projectiles of different types for specialised purposes. Previously, rifle ammunition had been simply 'solid shot': soft lead projectiles which had given way, in turn, to lead hardened by means of an alloy and then to jacketed lead, but with the re-emergence of armour on the battlefield, first in the form of shields, later in vehicles, the power available in the new high-velocity rounds set Polte's researchers thinking about creating a round which could breach it. A 7.92mm (.31in) armour-piercing round for the 98 (and 88) rifles, known as the 'S mitt Kern' (S with Core), 'S.m.K' or 'K-patrone' (K cartridge) was developed, with a hardened tungsten-steel core which was clothed in a lead 'shirt' inside its nickel-plated steel jacket (the lead was necessary to allow the bullet to take the rifling). At 11.5g (177.5 grain) it was 20 per cent heavier than the normal S projectile, and because it was nine millimetres (six-sixteenths of an inch) longer (37mm/one and a half inches instead of 28mm/one and one-eighth of an inch) the propellant charge had to be reduced to 2.9g (44.75 grain). The result was a considerable reduction in muzzle velocity, to 815 metres (2675ft) per second, though the trajectory of the heavy round was flatter than that of the normal bullet at long range.

This came about as the result of a further difference between the two rounds: the new K bullet's body was not cylindrical, as the S bullet's had been, but rather it was tapered towards the tail, the form which has become known as 'boat-tailed'. This shape was introduced after the study of high-speed photographs

taken by means of the new spark-gap technology revealed an interesting phenomenon: at velocities greater than the speed of sound, the 'spitzer' bullet form with a sharply-pointed nose and square-tailed cylindrical body was efficient, for the significant factor was the design of the point and the compression waves it created. But at sub-sonic speed, the form of the tail became increasingly important since the compression waves disappeared, and the dominant factor became the vortices created in the bullet's wake, which both slowed it down and caused it to veer off course. The boat-tailed form went some way towards eliminating the drag by allowing the airflow around the bullet to re-combine more efficiently. (The most efficient shape would be a teardrop, of course, though no-one went that far.) Introducing the new shape into the K round had surprising results – at ranges in excess of 400m (1310ft), the heavier round was actually faster than the lighter. As a direct consequence of this, a heavier version of the normal steel-jacketed round was produced for use in medium machine guns; it was issued to German troops in August 1918, just before the war's end.

Somewhat surprisingly, it was to be the 1920s before boat-tailed ammunition was more widely introduced. The armour-piercing round was most effective – it could perforate four and a half millimetres (three-sixteenths of an inch) of nickel-chrome steel at a range of 1400m (4595ft) and could certainly defeat the eight millimetre-thick (five-sixteenths of an inch) side armour of the early British tanks at short and medium ranges.

Other types of rifle ammunition were developed, too – incendiary rounds, filled with phosphorous; and tracer rounds, intended for machine guns, with a small amount of phosphorous in a hollowed-out tail section. As early as 1916 (and not just in Germany), the material of cartridge cases was changed from relatively precious brass to steel, electro-plated with a copper coating in an attempt to prevent rusting. There was no real difference in performance, and from then on steel cases became more common.

BACK TO SPRINGFIELD

During the Spanish-American War of 1898, it quickly became obvious to men at all levels within the US Army that the

.30in-40 Krag-Jorgensen rifles with which they were armed were deficient, and that a revision was urgently needed. Experiments demonstrated that the problem with the ungainly idiosyncratic magazine could be solved, and that a Mauser-type box magazine, to be loaded from a clip, could be substituted without too much trouble, but there was still the matter of the locking mechanism to be considered. It was clear that the pressures required to propel a bullet at a velocity in excess of 700 metres (2300ft) per second – calculated at something of the order of 2700kg per cm2 /roughly 40,000psi; the existing round achieved just over 600 metres/1968ft per second, and exerted a chamber pressure of 2175kg per sq cm/roughly 32,000psi) – would place an intolerable extra strain on the Krag's single locking lug, and that there was no other course to be followed than replacement.

The first step was to decide on a specification for a new cartridge, and initially the choice fell on a .30in (7.62mm) calibre rimmed round with a 14.25g (220 grain) round-nosed soft lead bullet with a cupro-nickel-plated steel jacket, which was to produce a muzzle velocity of (a fairly modest) 700 metres (2300ft) per second in a rifle with a 762mm (30in) barrel. It was little more than the existing Krag round, marginally longer and with just a pinch more powder. The experimental rifle constructed to go with it was a hybrid of the Krag and the Mauser M93, with the 'two plus one' locking lugs on the bolt (but with the receiver bridge machined through, as the old M/71 Mauser had been) and a charger-loaded single-column non-detachable box magazine (which extended below the stock), and the trigger group of the Norwegian rifle.

THE US M1903

The test rifle was finished at the end of August 1900 and was submitted for testing to begin at the start of October. The trial lasted two months 'as weather and other work permitted', and the recommendations made centred on improvements to the cartridge and magazine: a rimless round (of similar performance) was called for (it having been found that the rimmed rounds were prone to jam when the rim of the upper was behind that of the round below) and the magazine should be of the more recent staggered design, which would allow it to be enclosed within the stock

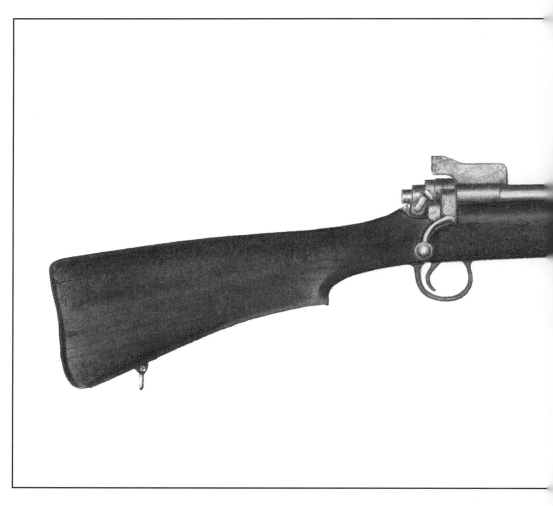

where it was less likely to be damaged. The magazine cut-off – which in the original was modelled on that employed by the Lee-Enfield: a flat plate on a vertical pin, which was swung across to bridge the magazine and depress the cartridges – was criticised too, largely because it prohibited the recharging of the magazine with loose rounds when it was in place, and it was suggested that the cut-off system of the Swiss Schmidt-Rubin, which lowered the entire magazine slightly when the rifle was to be used in single-shot mode, should be substituted.

The first two suggestions were adopted, the last was not, though the cut-off was completely re-designed so that when it was engaged the bolt was prohibited from being withdrawn far enough to strip a fresh round out of the magazine, an altogether more satisfactory – and cheaper – solution; it also performed the function of a disengageable bolt stop. Subsequently, the slot milled in the receiver bridge top was also deleted, and the 'safety' lug's geometry was amended.

Cartridges and test rifles to that specification – 100 of them – were produced, in a variety of different barrel

lengths, from 559mm to 762mm (22in to 30in), all with one turn of the rifling in 203mm (eight inches) instead of the original 254mm (10in), and were issued, in February 1903 to an evaluation board consisting of a cavalry officer and two infantry officers, with an ordnance officer to act as recorder, which was provided with six NCOs to carry out firing tests and demonstrations. All in all, they fired 10,000 rounds through the rifles at the Sandy Hook proving grounds, and demonstrated it at 10 Army posts, and came to the conclusion that the 610mm (24in) barrel should be adopted, along with a cartridge developed at the Frankford Arsenal which gave it the required muzzle velocity. They also recommended a number of slight changes to the rifle's furniture, and the addition of a spring-loaded bolt retainer.

Two rifles in the modified specification were prepared and submitted to the Infantry Board at Fort Leavenworth and the Cavalry Board at Fort Riley, and both accepted them unanimously. The Chief of Ordnance, General William Crozier (who was to achieve lasting fame by rejecting the best light machine gun of World War I, the Lewis gun, because of a personal feud with its inventor, Isaac Newton

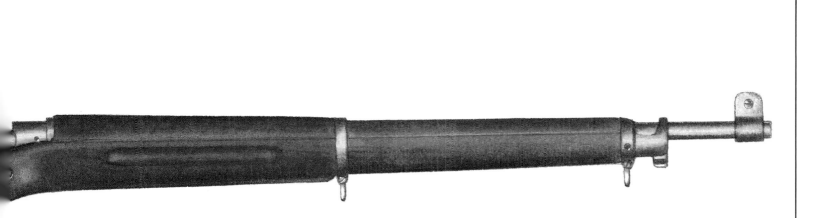

M1917 Enfield (P'14)

Calibre: .30in (7.62mm)
Weight: 4.35kg (9lb 10oz)
Length: 1175mm (46.25in]
Barrel length: 660mm (26in)
Effective range: Over 1000m (3250ft)
Configuration: Five-round internal box magazine, bolt-action
Muzzle velocity: 855mps (2800fps)
Country of origin: United States/United Kingdom

Lewis), recommended its adoption and on 19 June 1903, after what was, for the time, a very brief gestation period indeed, the United States Magazine Rifle, Caliber .30, Model of 1903, together with the Cartridge, Ball, Caliber .30, Model of 1903 was approved by the Secretary of War, and the US Army at last had an up-to-date rifle.

Or at least, it would have, as soon as manufacturing could commence. . . The new rifle was to be made at Springfield, where a single eight-hour shift was supposed to produce 225 each day, and at the new Rock Island Arsenal, which would turn out a further 125. Clearly, it would be some time before deliveries in bulk to the infantry and cavalry regiments would commence, even when, the following month, further new tooling was ordered to up the Springfield production rate to 400 per day. Quantity production began in November, and by 1 July 1904, just over 30,000 rifles had been produced.

A NEW ROUND FOR THE M1903
The firing trials had shown up one potential defect: the hotter-burning, nitro-glycerine-rich propellant required to up the muzzle velocity in the shorter

barrel produced unacceptable erosion with a 203mm (eight inch) rifling twist, and even as the tooling for the rifles was prepared, a series of further test were being carried out. The result was a return to the original rifling specification, one turn in 254mm (10 inches) or 33 calibres. Nonetheless the severe erosion persisted, and in 1904 the propellant load was reduced, which cut the muzzle velocity to 670 metres (2200ft) per second; even so, after little over 1000 rounds had been fired, the rifling in the first 50mm (two inches) of the barrel of a randomly-selected test rifle was completely obliterated (and 40 rounds fired as rapidly as possible actually caused charring in the stock). Clearly, there was a major problem at hand, particularly since it became known that same year that the German Army had adopted a lightweight pointed bullet which gave much better performance.

The result was the development of a new round using 3.04g to 3.24g (47 to 50 grain) of a more powerful but much cooler-burning propellant developed by DuPont, and loaded with a flat-based, 9.7g (150 grain) cupro-nickel spitzer bullet, which produced a muzzle velocity of 823 metres (2700ft) per second and an

extreme range of 3200m (two miles). Thanks to a much flatter trajectory, as well as the reduced windage, as a result of the much slimmer profile, it was consistently more accurate than the old round-nosed 14.2g (220 grain) bullet. On 15 October 1906 the new round was standardised as the Cartridge, Ball, Caliber .30, Model of 1906, which became known universally as the .30in-06, and work began on modifying the tooling which produced the barrels of the Model 1903 rifle, as well as modifications to the existing rifles themselves (though the latter was not to be concluded until stocks of the .30in-03 ammunition had been exhausted, in 1909).

The only major modification to the M1903 rifle was the fitting of a semi-pistol grip stock in place of the straight 'English' stock which had originally been specified, and that did not take place until 1929, but there was a short-lived attempt made to convert it to semi-automatic operation by the addition of the so-called Pedersen Device (more properly – and certainly more confusingly – the US Automatic Pistol, Caliber .30, Model of 1918; see below), and that required a few modifications to the receiver – the magazine cut-off was discarded, and an ejection port for spent cases was cut into the left hand side of the receiver. Almost 102,000 M1903 rifles with these modifications were produced between 1918 and 1920, at which point the programme was abandoned.

THE PEDERSEN DEVICE

The Pedersen Device, the brainchild of John Pedersen, who worked as a designer at Remington's factory in Ilion, came about as the result of a hair-brained, entirely fantastical scheme originally devised to improve the infantryman's chances of survival, as he advanced over no-man's-land during an attack on prepared enemy positions, by the simple expedient of increasing his firepower. If he had a semi-automatic, self-loading rifle, it was argued, he would be able to fire from the hip as he advanced, laying down what was euphemistically and over-optimistically known as covering fire, which would make it impossibly hazardous for the defenders to expose themselves on the parapet. . . The theory had its roots in France where, during the dark days of 1916, casualties were running at over 100,000 per month and something like panic was never too far below the surface, and where almost any new idea received a hearing and often gathered a sizeable group of vocal supporters.

Pedersen, who had no military experience, succeeded in convincing the US military establishment (almost incredibly, but perhaps equally almost understandably, since it actually had very little first-hand experience of 'modern' war itself) of the validity of this tactical scheme. That august body whole-heartedly embraced the notion, and with it the device Pedersen had produced, since it was clearly not feasible to re-equip every infantryman going 'Over There' with a new gun, to transform the M1903 rifle into a semi-automatic weapon in 15 seconds flat. Pedersen's device was blow-back-operated and analogous in action to the vast majority of 'automatic' self-loading pistols (and most sub-machine guns), and was small enough to substitute for the bolt of the M1903 rifle; it was fitted with a barrel which was, in outwards appearance, of the same form as a .30in-06 cartridge, and fired specially designed ammunition (which resembled the .32in ACP pistol round) with a 5.2g (80 grain) jacketed bullet propelled by a 0.23g (3.5grain) charge, which produced a muzzle velocity,

in the M1903 rifle, of 395 metres (1295ft) per second; its energy at the muzzle was only one-eighth of that of the .30in-06 round, but nonetheless, it was – hopelessly optimistically – reckoned to be able to kill at up to 500m (1640ft), if it struck in the right spot. It came equipped with a magazine which held 40 rounds, which was located so that it stuck out to the right of the converted rifle at a 45 degree up-angle.

SENSELESS WASTE

Some 65,000 Mark I Pedersen Devices were produced for M1903 rifles (a version was also produced for the M1917 Enfield rifle which was manufactured in large numbers to make up for the inadequate supply of Springfields available when the USA finally decided to enter the war in 1917 (see below), and also, according to some sources, for the French M07/15 – a modified version of the Berthier rifle as originally issued to colonial infantry regiments, which became the most common variant on the battlefields of the

Western Front – and the Russian M1891, both of which were certainly manufactured in limited numbers by Remington), but were never used in action. They were placed in store along with the rifles modified to take them, and all but a very few were subsequently destroyed in 1931 (to keep them from falling into the hands of gangsters and criminals, it is said. Some reports suggest that destruction took place in 1924-25), the modified rifles being re-fitted with magazine cut-offs (though nothing was done about the ejection port on the left hand side of the receiver) and returned to stock. Ironically, the same insane tactical theory which produced the Pedersen Device was also responsible for the introduction of the Browning Automatic Rifle, one of the best LMGs of the time, which ontinued in front-line service with the US Army until well into the 1950s.

PAYING OFF MAUSER

Clearly, the new US service rifle was a Mauser in all but name, but oddly

(DWM), as Ludwig Loewe & Co. had become in the meantime, submitted a claim for infringement of a patent covering the pointed spitzer bullet. This the US Government rejected because while Mauser had developed it, significant work had been done independently in the USA, too, by a US Army officer named Farley, and on 18 July 1914, DWM brought a legal action demanding a royalty payment of US$1.00 per 1000 on no less than 250 million bullets. Before the case could come to court, however, the war started, and it was set aside. When the USA entered the war against Germany in 1917, the patent was seized by the Custodian of Alien Property, and the Attorney General promptly dismissed the suit. The affair wasn't over yet, however, for after the war a tribunal set up to settle claims against the US Government by Austrian and German nationals found that, even though the patent suit was groundless, the seizure of the patent was illegal, and

on 2 July 1921 made an arbitrary award of US$300,000 in damages to DWM. By the time the award was paid, on 31 December 1928, US$112,520.55 had to be added on in interest!

THE 'AMERICAN' ENFIELD
The Springfield '03 is widely held to be the rifle with which the US Army went to war in 1917, but in fact that is some considerable way from the truth; far more 'doughboys' – fully three-quarters of all those who went 'Over There' – were armed with the British-designed US Rifle, Caliber .30, M1917 than were ever armed with Springfields, and one US Infantry Regiment (the 49th) actually had its M1903s withdrawn and replaced by Enfields.

■BELOW: A Japanese soldier armed with an Arisaka Type 99 rifle, with a large bayonet attachment, stands at attention while officers discuss what to do with Allied prisoners of war.

■ABOVE: Japanese soldiers armed with Arisaka Meiji 38th Year or Type 99 rifles (there was no major external difference between them) crossing a makeshift bridge in China in 1940.

enough, it doesn't appear to have occurred to anyone in the US Government that perhaps Mauser's patents were being infringed until March 1904 when Crozier wrote to Waffenfabrik Mauser, asking that their patent agent call on him to discuss the design of the cartridge loading clip. He got rather more than he bargained for. It was agreed eventually, in July 1909, that the US Army had infringed two patents in the design of the clip, and five more in the design of the rifle, and in May of the following year the US Government agreed to pay Mauser US$0.75 per rifle, and US$0.50 per 1000 clips, up to a maximum of US$200,000.

There was more to come. Hardly had the last payment been made than Deutsche Waffen und Munitionsfabrik

The Enfield in question started life as the Rifle, Magazine, .303in, Pattern 1914 and evolved from an experimental high-velocity rifle in .276in (7mm) calibre, with a Mauser action (that is, with its locking lugs at the front of the bolt), known as the Pattern 1913, which had been approved by the British War Office for issue on a trials basis in 1913, but which had been abandoned on the outbreak of the war due to unsolved problems with its very 'hot' cartridge, including overheating and the risk of premature detonation ('cooking off') and excessive barrel wear.

A RAPID FIRER

This projected replacement for the SMLE had been developed in response to widespread and vituperative criticism of the Lee-Enfield from almost all quarters (the only interest group silent on the subject was the soldiers who were expected to use it, significantly enough). To them it was bad through and through, its bolt-action decidedly inferior to that of the Mauser, even though tests conducted at the School of Musketry against the German service rifle in 1912 showed that the average rate of aimed fire for a 98 rifle was 14 or 15 rounds per minute, whereas for the SMLE it was 28. The all-time rapid-fire record for the SMLE (which admittedly was not established until 1914) was set by a sergeant-instructor there named Snoxall, who got off no less than 38 aimed shots in that time, all of which went into the inner ring of a standard 120cm (four foot) target at a range of 275m (900ft), which by any standard, and any stretch of the imagination, is some shooting! The general standard of musketry in the

■BELOW: The Lee-Enfield Rifle Number 5, universally known as the Jungle Carbine, was simply a cut-down Number 4. Its shortened barrel made for a ferocious and unpopular recoil.

regular battalions of the British Army of the time was very high indeed, in terms both of accuracy and rapidity; German troops who encountered it early on in World War I often assumed that they were meeting machine guns when in fact they were just up against well-trained men with superior rifles.

Nonetheless, the SMLE 'was always bad, its defects always notorious. . .' according to its critics and so the War Office began to look (at least ostensibly) for a possible replacement: the P'13 was the result. It was flawed, but clearly a solid period of development (and perhaps a change of ammunition) would have turned it into an acceptable rifle – though whether it would have been significantly better than the rifle it was supposed to replace is another matter. But it did have one very basic virtue – it had been designed with high-volume production in mind, and the SMLE most decidedly had not. In 1915, by which time it was evident that the war would not 'be over by Christmas' after all, the War Office began to wake up to the fact that it was faced by a short-fall of the most basic of infantry weapons, and turned again to the P'13, hastily ordered it re-chambered for the standard rimmed .303in round and looked around for someone to put it into production. 'Someone' turned out to be the Remington Arms/Union Metallic Cartridge Company's plants at Eddystone, Pennsylvania and Ilion, New York, and the Winchester Repeating Arms Company's factory at New Haven, Connecticut, but in fact it was mid-1916 before enough had been manufactured and shipped to the UK to make it worthwhile issuing them to troops.

THE P'14 RIFLE

On completion of the British contracts, at just around the time that the USA entered the war against Germany, the machinery at the three plants was modified to produce P'14 rifles chambered

for the .30in-06 rimless cartridge (a simple enough matter; all they had to do was revert to the original designs, for the P'14 had been set up for a rimless round to begin with), and the production lines promptly started up again, this time turning out M1917s. Between October 1917 and 9 November 1918, the three plants turned out a total of no less than 2,193,429 M1917 rifles between them, while during the same period, the Springfield and Rock Island arsenals produced a total of just 312,878 M1903s (and production of the M1917 didn't stop then. The total production actually amounted to 2,511,834, and contracts for a further 2,321,566 were cancelled). As late as March 1919 there was still indecision as to which of the two US service rifles should be designated as 'limited standard' and put into storage as war reserve stock, and then a board of infantry officers was convened to decide. It recommended the Springfield, provided that an improved backsight to be located on the receiver (the original sights were mounted in front of the breech case, and the sight radius and accuracy were reduced as a result) could be developed in short order, and pending the development of a self-loading semi-automatic rifle to replace it.

THE THORNEYCROFT ODDITY

By the summer of 1914, the military service rifle had become standardised, firing a small-calibre (seven to eight millimetre/.27 to .32 inches), pointed projectile at a muzzle velocity of up to 800 metres (2625ft) per second, effective out to 1000m (3280ft) and lethal at three times that, its action built around a cylindrical bolt, which was unlocked by rotating a handle through about 90 degrees and was then free to reciprocate, ammunition being presented to it from a box magazine located below the receiver, ahead of the trigger guard, which was charged from a disposable cartridge clip.

We have already dealt with most of the unsuccessful attempts to displace or modify the bolt-action, but there is one variant which deserves our attention since it was the forerunner of the short, lightweight weapon which many of the world's infantrymen would carry into the twenty-first century.

The Thorneycroft carbine first appeared in 1901, its inventor having taken out a patent on his idea in July of that year. Essentially, it was a conventional bolt-action rifle with the trigger group and pistol grip located well in front of the receiver, which was actually enclosed, along with the magazine, within the butt-stock, the bolt running out of the receiver into a channel cut into the woodwork. This was the forerunner of what we now know as the bullpup system, as used in the British SA-80 (L85A1), the French FA-MAS and the Austrian Steyr AUG, as well as several other experimental weapons, the development of which continued in the short-lived SREM (Sniper Rifle,

Experimental Model) of 1944, a peculiar design in which the (straight-pull) bolt was actuated by pulling back on the pistol grip, which came about as a putative solution to a problem snipers frequently encountered – the possibility of giving away their position when actuating the bolt to get off a second shot; the 7mm EM1 and EM2 (which were rejected, as much as anything else, because 'you can't do drill' with a rifle just 890mm/35in long) and the 4.85mm-calibre Individual Weapon.

The real advantages of the Thorneycroft were its size and weight – it weighed 3.4kg (seven pounds eight ounces) against the SMLE's 3.7kg (eight pounds two ounces), and was just 993mm (39in) long overall while the SMLE was almost 1132mm (45in), even though both had the same 635mm (25in) barrel. It was known – erroneously – as a carbine as a result. The School of Musketry tried it in 1902, and complained of excessive recoil (though since its barrel length and the cartridge it fired were exactly the

ABOVE: Lee-Enfield armed Indian troops on jungle patrol in the Southeast Asia theatre during World War II. Many Lee-Enfields remain in service today around the world.

same as those of the SMLE which was also then undergoing evaluation, it is difficult to see why that should have been, except that perhaps its four-groove rifling with a right-hand, instead of a left-hand, twist may have made some difference), awkward handling, and burned fingers from hot cartridge cases. These faults seem to have persisted in an improved model, and testing was suspended in 1903. It would be easy to suggest that conservatism alone would have been enough to have seen it rejected, but the true reason is probably that it simply wasn't that much better – if it was better at all – than the Lee-Enfield. The day of the short bullpup rifle with its trigger group ahead of the action had not yet come – though it would, as we shall see.

CHAPTER 4
SELF-LOADING RIFLES AND ASSAULT RIFLES

Since the eighteenth century, tacticians had sought to ensure that firearms were used concertedly, to create a moving barrier of projectiles which served the dual purpose of denying the enemy's advance and killing or disabling his men.

The brass cartridge made effective repeater firearms feasible, and with that as a starting point it became possible to mechanise the process, and utilise either the recoil or the propellant gas to cycle the action – unlocking the breech and propelling a bolt or breech block backwards against the pressure of a return spring. extracting the spent case, stripping a fresh round out of the magazine and chambering it before re-locking the breech again and re-cocking the action in the process.

The principle was first demonstrated by Hiram Stevens Maxim, inventor of the machine gun, and described in a patent granted on 26 June 1883, in the pre-amble to which he said:

'My invention relates to [a] mechanism chiefly designed to be applied to fire-arms of the class usually called repeating or magazine rifles of which the well-known Winchester may be considered a type. The said invention is designed to utilise the kick or recoil of the rifle or other arm for operating the breech loading mechanism, and is constructed in such a manner that when the arm is discharged, the recoil stores up sufficient energy in a spring or springs to operate the mechanism for extracting the exploded cartridge shells, for cocking the arm, for

■LEFT: Armed with light machine guns and self-loading rifles, a small squad of determined men in an adequate defensive position can seldom be neutralised without support weapons.

transferring the cartridges from the magazine to the rear of the barrel, forcing them into the barrel and closing the breech.'

It has been suggested that Maxim was trying to throw would-be competitors in what would become a race to develop the machine gun off the scent by continual reference to rifles. Nonetheless, the drawings which accompanied his patent application are clearly of a modified Winchester rifle, and when he later came to patent a method of gas operation the following year, again it was a modified lever-action rifle which he used (this time Maxim produced drawings which featured a modified Colt – one of those which never reached production – as well as a Winchester).

TYPES OF ACTION

It is worth considering, though not at great length, the means by which semi-automatic and automatic action (there is no big difference between the two; usually just the design of the sear) can be achieved in a firearm. There are two slightly different locked-breech recoil-actuated systems, generally known as the short and the long, which were used in the first generation of medium- and heavy machine guns, and which are now found in many self-loading pistols, some light- and sub-machine guns and a very few selective-fire assault rifles: the simpler unlocked-breech blow-back system, found in most sub-machine guns and lighter calibre semi-automatic pistols

■**ABOVE: The SLR John Pedersen developed was flawed by his choice of a retarded blow-back action which was overpowered by the ammunition for which the rifle was chambered.**

and in one assault rifle, and the basic gas-actuated system, now used by the majority of general-purpose machine guns and self-loading rifles (SLRs). Clearly, some of these have direct relevance; others are interesting because they were tried out in rifles and more or less failed.

THE SHORT RECOIL ACTION
In the short recoil system the gun's barrel and breech block move back together over a short distance (usually less than one

■**BELOW: Two US Army combat aces – Pfcs Edward Gromowski (left) and Chester Gustafson – with the weapons which made them so effective: the M1 Garand and the vintage BAR.**

centimetre/half an inch), the momentary delay allowing the residual pressure in the chamber to drop to a point where it is safe to open the breech without danger of rupturing the cartridge case. At this point the barrel's rearward passage is arrested, but by one means or another the breech block is unlocked from it and continues on its way, the extractor ensuring that the spent cartridge case goes with it and the ejector seeing that it is expelled. The breech block's motion compresses a spring, which reverses its travel as soon as the point of equilibrium – where its stored or potential energy overcomes the kinetic actuating energy – is reached, cocking the firing mechanism and ramming the next cartridge into the chamber on the way back to re-locking the breech block in battery.

THE LONG RECOIL ACTION
The long recoil system differs only slightly; the barrel and breech block assembly are driven back together rather

further than the entire length of a complete cartridge as contained in a magazine or belt. The two then separate; a return spring drives the barrel forwards into the firing position, while an extractor on the face of the breech block removes the empty case and an ejector throws it clear. The subsequent forward action of the breech block then cocks the action and drives the next round into the chamber before re-locking is established.

THE BLOW-BACK ACTION
The simplest of all the mechanisms is known as the blow-back system; the breech block is held closed to the barrel by the pressure of a spring alone, with no lugs or other mechanical devices locking the two together. On detonation of the cartridge, the breech stays closed until the pressure in the chamber overcomes that of the spring, at which point it flies backwards and cycles the action in exactly the same way as an unlocked locked-breech action. Clearly, this is a simpler solution in mechanical terms, and is thus both cheaper and easier to manufacture and maintain. Blow-back actions are sometimes retarded or delayed by artificially induced friction or by introducing a mechanical

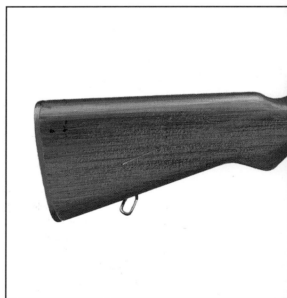

disadvantage which has to be overcome before the cycling can commence.

GAS ACTUATION

In the basic gas-actuation system, propellant gas is tapped off the barrel at a point close to the muzzle (the exact distance between the gas port and the muzzle determines how much gas is used to cycle the action, though that can also be controlled in other ways; it also determines many other factors concerning the design of the primary stage of the gas system), and usually acts on the face of a piston in a cylinder lying above, below, or alongside the barrel, driving it to the rear to propel the bolt and cycling the action in the process (in one major variant introduced more recently the gas acts directly on the face of the bolt carrier). The action can be retarded by either of the means deployed in the recoil-actuated weapon, that is by a locking mechanism, which has to be released before the action can be cycled, or by artificially induced friction or mechanical disadvantage.

THE FIRST SELF-LOADING RIFLES

Considering the relative size constraints of rifle and pistol, it is somewhat surprising that the first self-loading weapon was a handgun, but Borchardt's *Selbstladepistole* of 1893 had been on the market for three years before a semi-automatic rifle appeared, and when it did, it came from a rather unexpected quarter, Denmark, with an even darker horse, Mexico, in hot pursuit.

Soren H. Bang was an inventor, rather than a gunsmith, and drew on the work of another, using a variation on a gas-actuation method Hiram Maxim patented in 1884 as part of his effort to cover all bases (he never produced a gas-actuated gun himself, he just wanted to keep the competition out; Browning designed one 11 years later, and went to extraordinary lengths to hide the fact that it used an action on which Maxim had a patent. The subterfuge worked). Bang utilised a pierced inverted muzzle cone or cap through which the bullet passed and against which a portion of the propellant gas acted, pushing it forward; the cone was connected to an actuating rod, and that in turn, by means of a secondary lever actuated through a rocker arm which reversed the motion, unlocked the breech block and forced it back. The cycle was completed by a recoil spring. Bang's system worked, but not entirely predictably – he had problems in making the operating mechanism light enough to function yet robust enough to last – but he and others persevered with it until after World War I. Its basic principle, considerably modified, was to crop up again in Germany as late 1941, when Mauser and Walther both employed it more or less unsuccessfully in self-loading rifles, as we shall see in due course. Self-loading rifles on the Bang system were issued to Danish marine infantry in 1896, making it the first such arm to be officially adopted.

THE MONDRAGON M1908

Somewhat earlier, an artillery officer in the Mexican Army named Manuel Mondragon had begun experimenting with designs for a self-loading rifle which utilised propellant gas tapped off the barrel by means of a one millimetre-diameter hole situated some 165mm (six and a half inches) abaft the muzzle. In the short period between the projectile passing this port and exiting the barrel, gases at extremely high pressure (typically 3000 atmospheres and more, depending on the size of the propellant charge) passed through the port into a cylinder below the barrel and acted on the face of a piston; the piston was driven back, simultaneously compressing a coiled spring which surrounded its shaft and unlocking and driving back the bolt, the longitudinal movement being converted into rotation by a series of helical grooves in the bolt which acted on oval lugs on the cocking handle, located to the right of the receiver. The rearwards movement of the bolt extracted the spent case and cocked the action, and on its return stroke it gathered a new round and chambered it. In an effort to make the piston work as efficiently as possible, its head was fitted with three copper sealing rings, and in an attempt to make it as secure as possible Mondragon incorporated no less than seven locking lugs, three at the front of the breech block and four at its rear.

Since there were no manufacturers in Mexico capable of producing such a complex article to the required tolerances, Mondragon – with the enthusiastic backing of President Porfirio Diaz, who wished to demonstrate his country's independence in terms of design at least – turned to Switzerland, to Schweizerische Industrie-Gesellschaft of Neuhausen-am-Rheinfalls, better known simply as SIG, ordering 50 rifles in 6.5mm (.25in) calibre in 1893, and 200 more the following year. The second order

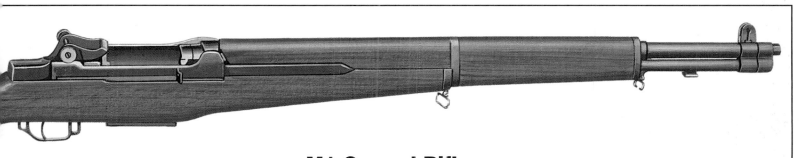

M1 Garand Rifle

Calibre: .30in (7.62mm)
Weight: 4.35kg (9lb 8oz)
Length: 1105mm (43.5in)
Barrel length: 610mm (24in)
Effective range: Over 500m (1650ft)

Configuration: Eight-round
internal box magazine,
gas-actuated self-loading action
Muzzle velocity: 855mps (280fps)
Country of origin: United States

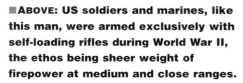

■ABOVE: US soldiers and marines, like this man, were armed exclusively with self-loading rifles during World War II, the ethos being sheer weight of firepower at medium and close ranges.

was for rifles to chamber a pronouncedly idiosyncratic 5.2mm x 68 cartridge Rubin had developed which utilised a collar or sabot around the projectile, an idea which had previously surfaced in the field of artillery, and which was to stay current there, on and off, but which was to be revived for small arms only in the latter years of the twentieth century. Dissatisfied with the experimental Swiss round, Mondragon tried a variety of other chamberings, through .30in-30 WCF and 7mm x 57 to 7.5mm x 54 Swiss, finally settling on the 7mm round (which was of a different form to that Mauser developed for the M/93, and which was not interchangeable with it).

In what was really little more than a show of patriotism, the Mexican Army 'adopted' the rifle (in a very limited sense indeed) as the rather grandiosely-named *Fusil Porfirio Diaz Systema Mondragon, Modelo* 1908, and 4000 were ordered from Neuhausen. Only 400 had been delivered by 1911, at a cost of SFr160 each (approximately three times the cost of a conventional manually-operated repeater rifle at the time), before the

Mexicans realised the error of their ways and reneged; SIG was left with around 1000 completed rifles in its warehouse, and little prospect of ever making its money back on them. The company added a variety of extra refinements, notably the ability to shut off the auto-loading mechanism entirely, whereupon the rifle reverted to being a normal straight-pull bolt-action repeater, and, as we might say, the very reverse – a fully-automatic capability, in which role it could be fitted with a rather spindly bipod and a 20-round magazine (in place of the standard eight-round box). SIG tried to interest various countries' war departments, notably those in Berlin, London, and Washington, in what it was now offering as a light machine gun, but without any success.

Eventually, in 1915, when the German Army had discovered a requirement for a more flexible weapon – than the 98 rifle on the one hand and the heavy MG08 machine gun on the other – to equip its fledgling air force (this, we may recall, was before the days of interrupter mechanisms which permitted fixed machine guns to fire through the arc of the propeller as developed by the Dutchman, Anton Fokker), someone remembered SIG's offer of Mondragons and the entire batch was purchased (much, one may imagine, to the surprise

and pleasure of the Swiss). A version of the over-complicated Tatarek and von Benkö 'snail' helical clockwork magazine, as developed for the long-barrelled 'artillery' version of the P08 Luger pistol (and later adopted for the Bergmann MP18/I sub-machine gun, the first of that genre), was produced for the rifle which upped the ammunition capacity to 30 rounds, and it was re-chambered for the 7mm x 57 Mauser cartridge; thus modified, and known now as the *Fleiger-Selbstladekarabiner Modell* 1915 (though it was actually 1917 by the time it was ready), it was issued to aircrew on the strict understanding that each weapon must be checked by an experienced armourer before and after every mission (and even so, failures were commonplace). The Mondragon self-loading rifle was not a success, but the basic principle was sound, and the system of tapping propellant gas off the barrel near the muzzle and using it to drive a piston which cycled the action was to be widely copied.

THE CEI-RIGOTTI RIFLE
An Italian infantry officer named Cei-Rigotti was one of the first to do so (though there is actually good reason to believe that he was working entirely independently) and also devised a gas-operated, selective-fire, self-loading rifle, chambered for the 6.5mm x 52 M95 cartridge, as used by the Mannlicher-

■RIGHT: One of the drawbacks of a gas-actuated self-loading rifle like the Garand was the need for stringent maintenance, being undertaken here by these men of Merrill's élite Marauders.

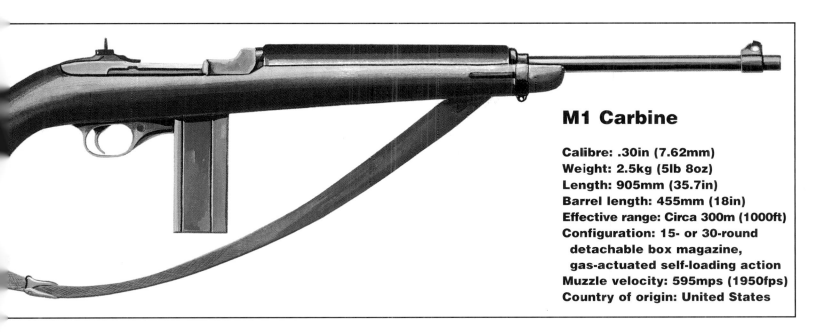

M1 Carbine

Calibre: .30in (7.62mm)
Weight: 2.5kg (5lb 8oz)
Length: 905mm (35.7in)
Barrel length: 455mm (18in)
Effective range: Circa 300m (1000ft)
Configuration: 15- or 30-round
  detachable box magazine,
  gas-actuated self-loading action
Muzzle velocity: 595mps (1950fps)
Country of origin: United States

Carcano service rifle. Gas was led off through a vent located about half-way down the barrel to act on a piston in a short cylinder, which acted as a tappet to operate the bolt via a long rod which lay along the right hand side of the barrel. Its rearwards motion compressed a return spring and unlocked the bolt by means of a lug running in a helical slot, cocked the action and then returned, reloading and re-locking the action in the process. Ammunition was held in 10-, 20-, or 50-round removable box magazines which were conventionally located below the action, in front of the trigger guard. A simple switch selected semi- or fully-automatic fire. For all its failings (and the worst of them was probably caused by unreliable ammunition, while others could have been rectified by further development work), the *Fucile Mitragliatrice* Cei-Rigotti was the first example of the genre which we have come to know as selective-fire assault rifles. Though it was taken up by a major

manufacturer, Officine Glisenti, nothing came of the design, though some elements of it were identifiable later in other weapons.

SELBSTLADEKARABINER

Paul Mauser came up with his first semi-automatic weapon in 1894 (or, to be more precise, a group of his employees headed by the three Feederle brothers developed it for him); it was a pistol, destined to be known as the *Mauser Selbstladepistole, Construction* '96 and to earn itself a reputation as one of the truly great handguns.

The C96 pistol was fired for the first time on 15 March 1896, and Paul Mauser himself demonstrated the new gun to Kaiser Wilhelm II on the Charlottenberg ranges on 20 August. The emperor immediately asked when he could expect to see a rifle with a similar self-loading capacity, and Mauser replied 'Perhaps in five years. . .' In fact, it was to take over three times as long to produce the

Selbstladekarabiner Mauser, and even then the result was far from perfect, largely because Mauser relied on tried-and-tested methods of actuation and failed to innovate. It has to be said that despite his success, Paul Mauser never had any pretensions to genius; even his most fervent supporters agree that his progress was due to doggedness and not sparks of insight, and the history of the development of his self-loading rifle was to be no exception; unfortunately, in this case he was to start from an unworkable premise and never recovered.

MAUSER'S MISTAKES

Mauser's first mistake – and he never rectified it, even though he did eventually make the principle function – was to opt

■**RIGHT: Cal Walther Waffenfabrik developed the *Gewehr* 43, which was commonly used as a sniper's rifle: it was fitted with dovetail mounts for the Zf4 telescopic sight.**

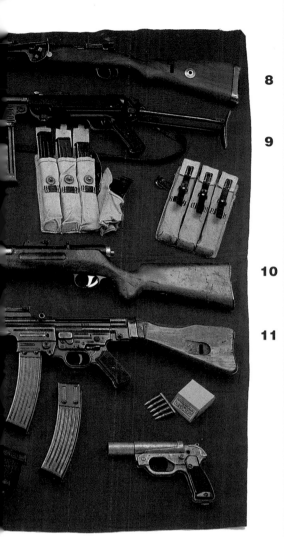

RIFLE 1: The Mauser-designed *Gewehr* 41(W) – only some 20,000 were made.

RIFLE 2: The Walther-designed *Gewehr* 41(W) – more successful but still flawed.

RIFLE 3: The Walther-designed *Gewehr* 43. Half a million were made.

RIFLE 4: The Hungarian-designed 98/40 rifle.

RIFLE 5: The Czech vz/24 rifle – the inspiration for the conversion of the Mauser 98 rifle into the Kar98k.

RIFLE 6: The Czech vz/24 rifle.

RIFLE 7: The Czech-designed 33/40 carbine – issued to mountain troops.

RIFLE 8: The original Kar98k – still the most commonly issued German rifle by the time of the invasion of Poland.

RIFLE 9: The ERMA-designed MP38/40 – erroneously known as the Schmeisser (though his influence can be seen).

RIFLE 10: The Bergmann-designed MP35 – a 'solid and dependable' design.

RIFLE 11: The MP43 – a composite of competing designs. Note the alternative 'Krummlauf' barrel below.

for locked-breech recoil operation; his second – and this one took 10 years to overcome – was to implement it as it was embodied in the C96 pistol, which meant that the barrel of the self-loading rifle had to be free to move in the stock. There can be no doubt that Mauser was aware of the principle of gas actuation (or, indeed, that he knew of the Mondragon and Bang rifles), yet he rejected it out of hand, believing the 'Bang system', as we

RIGHT: This soldier's MP43 is a late model – actually an assault rifle, rather than a machine pistol, despite its designation – with a screw thread at the muzzle for the grenade launcher.

■ABOVE: Wehrmacht assault squads regularly included man-portable flame weapons. The operator was vulnerable and was protected by a team-mate armed with an MP43 assault rifle.

may call it, to be unworkable and mistrusting completely the idea of drilling a hole in the barrel to vent off some of the propellant gas. (He is said to have believed that the vent would burn out in prolonged use, but there is no evidence at all of him even having considered running an extended trial to test that theory; modern practice and experience has proved him wrong, of course. Others believed that the port would reduce the muzzle velocity of the weapon, which shows both a laughable ignorance of the appropriate physical laws and a stupid disregard for the formidable powers of the 'modern' cartridge.) It appears that Mauser's opinion of the potential fallibility of the barrel vent was to influence thinking in Germany for many years – even when development of a self-loading rifle became urgent in 1940, the War Ministry's

■ABOVE: The MP43/44's progress was jerky – senior Wehrmacht figures tried very actively to prevent its adoption since it used ammunition incompatible with other small arms of the period.

Weapons Design Directorate laid down that the barrel of the weapon to be produced was not to be bored to extract gas, and the three failed attempts at a gas-operated design which followed all used a Bang-type muzzle vent. The powers-that-were then relented and the result was some of the outstanding weapon designs of World War II: the FG42 and the MP43/44, the true forerunners of the modern assault rifle, even if the designation of the latter is misleading (it was certainly not a *maschinenpistole* or sub-machine gun).

But to return to Paul Mauser: between

1898 and 1908 he produced dozens of designs for self-loading rifles with moving barrels before realising belatedly that any rifle built to that principle would be unacceptably big and heavy for a man to carry in the field. In 1909, by now aged 71 (it is generally assumed that he had only a supervisory role by this time, and that employees, notably the Feederle

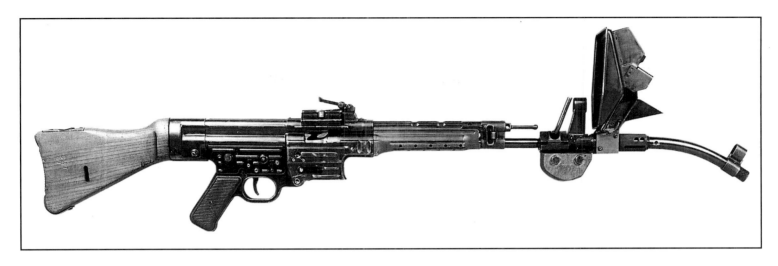

brothers, were actually doing most of the work), he produced a first design with a fixed barrel, utilising a locking system devised by a Swede named Friberg two decades earlier, and subsequently resurrected by Rudolph Kjellman for his unsuccessful machine gun design of 1907. The breech block was locked in battery by two levers or flaps which lay along the rear of the receiver on either side; they were located on vertical pivots and positioned so that when their rear ends were forced outwards into recesses in the receiver walls, their forward ends were brought together behind the breech block to lock it. They were forced out at the front, to lie parallel, by the rearwards movement of the firing pin carrier in recoil, and that allowed the breech block to retire between them, guided by a longitudinal rod which both transfixed it and retained the recoil spring, when the chamber pressure had dropped to a safe level. On the return journey the breech block picked up and chambered a fresh round before being locked in battery again as the flaps were cammed back into position.

It was this mechanism which was to find its way into the self-loading carbine, chambered for the 7.92mm 88S cartridge, which was produced – in very small numbers; records have been lost, but it seems clear that the total did not exceed 2000 – for airship and aircraft crews in 1916 and 1917. (It was also to be utilised in a poorly-regarded pistol Mauser produced and in the only-partially successful Walther Gew41(W), but it came into its own in the Soviet Degtyarev light machine gun which was introduced in 1928 and stayed in front line service with the Red Army until the 1950s; there was certainly nothing basically wrong with it, it just wasn't very well suited to lightweight weapons.) The carbine was

never widely issued to ground troops because it was simply too difficult to keep its action or its cartridges clean enough for it to function predictably – both had to be greased, otherwise extraction of the spent cases of the too-powerful S round, which frequently deformed or split, was often impossible; this problem was to recur in other designs, too, and was eventually addressed by developing a less powerful cartridge, though there was an alternative: to introduce flutes or grooves into the walls of the chamber, a method probably introduced in an otherwise-undistinguished light machine gun manufactured in Italy by Giovanni Agnelli before World War I. Waffenfabrik Mauser was to utilise this latter method in the design of a later self-loading assault rifle, the *Sturmgewehr* 45 – and because its charging procedure was hopelessly complicated. Self-loading rifle development in Germany halted with the end of the war, and only began again a decade later, by which time a variety of effective SLRs had been produced in other parts of the world.

OTHER WORLD WAR I SLRS

Two of the other combatant nations of World War I, France and Russia, produced more-or-less effective self-loading rifles during that period and another, the United States of America, produced one which was to see very long service indeed, but in the light machine gun role rather than as an assault rifle. Historically, the Russian weapon was the first to appear, in 1916. Its designer, Vladimir Fyodora, was responsible for much of the progress made in arms manufacture in Russia during the first decade and a half of the twentieth century, but failed singularly to solve the problem of how to produce a self-loading rifle to accept the over-sized, rimmed

■ **ABOVE: The reasons why the bizarre MP43/44 'Krumlauf', with its curved barrel (this version deflects the bullet through 30 degrees), was developed have never been adequately explained.**

7.62mm cartridge adopted in 1891. Finally he gave up on it, and produced a weapon chambered for the lighter, smaller 6.5mm x 50 cartridge the Japanese had developed for their Arisaka rifles instead (a number of weapons designs which employed this cartridge appeared in Russia at around this time, for no reason which is now clear). It used the short recoil principle, and was rather heavy (at just under four and a half kilograms/nine and a half pounds unloaded) as a result. With its forward pistol grip and 25-round magazine it looked much like the early sub-machine guns, and since it had a selective-fire capability, could indeed be used as one – a dual purpose which was to be continued in later Soviet assault rifles. The *Avtomaticheskaya Vintovka* (automatic rifle) *Sistemy Fyodorova* obr 1916 (AVF) was produced at the state arms factory in Sestroresk until the revolution at the end of the following year, and manufacture started again in 1919; it continued in production until 1924.

MODÈLE 1917 – SAINT ETIENNE

French designers had the same problem with the rimmed M86 8mm x 50R round as devised for the Lebel rifle that Fyodora had encountered with the M91, but the military establishment was not prepared to permit them the same solution. As a result, when the half-baked doctrine of assault by a self-supporting infantry force armed with self-loading weapons took hold in 1916, it found itself with very few appropriate weapons to choose from. Just one, in fact – the *Fusil*

Maschinenpistole MP43/Sturmgewehr StG44

Calibre: 7.92mm x 33 (.31in)
Weight: 5.1kg (11lb 4oz)
Length: 940mm (37in)
Barrel length: 420mm (16.5in)

Effective range: Circa 300m (1000ft)
Configuration: 30-round detachable
box magazine, gas-actuated self-
loading action, automatic option

Cyclical rate of fire: 550rpm
Muzzle velocity: 645mps (2125fps)
Country of origin: Germany

Mitrailleur RSC, the initials being those of the three-man commission which had approved it: Ribeyrolle, Suterre, and Chauchat, the same hapless, inadequate band who, with the addition of a fourth, the ill-named Gladiator, had been responsible a year earlier for the selection for the French Army of the worst light machine gun ever to be adopted: 'Poorly manufactured, of inferior materials, to an abominable design', as one history of the machine gun has described it. (Entirely due to US Ordnance Department boss William Crozier's personal feud with Isaac Newton Lewis, it was with the Chauchat, as the gun was widely known, and not the decidedly superior – and home-grown – Lewis gun that the US Army went to war in 1917, much to the delight of the manufacturer, who off-loaded 35,000 at premium prices at a time when it was next to impossible to even give the suspect guns away elsewhere.)

The *Modèle* 1917 self-loading rifle – normally known as the Saint Etienne after the factory in that city, south of Lyons, where it was produced – was gas operated, and functioned via a barrel vent to actuate a piston attached to a bolt carrier. It was at least an improvement, but not dramatically so – there were

better designs available, but choosing any of them would have created ammunition supply problems since they were not chambered for the 8mm Lebel round and couldn't be easily adapted to it.

The rifle certainly looked wrong, largely because it was still 1330mm (52in) long at a time when most other infantry weapons were 200-250mm (eight-10in) shorter, and it felt wrong because it weighed five and a quarter kilograms (11.5lb) and was imperfectly balanced. It was further condemned by its (fixed) magazine holding only five rounds (which effectively negated the tactical purpose for which it had been devised). It was issued only in small numbers but was neither popular nor successful; a modified version, cut down by 225mm (nine inches) was issued briefly in 1918, but that was not a success either.

BROWNING AUTOMATIC RIFLE
Meanwhile, in the USA, the Mormon gunmaker, John Moses Browning, was entering into the most productive period of his remarkable career. His first commercially-successful design had been for an under-lever-action repeater rifle chambered for the black powder .45in round, which Winchester produced as the

Model 1886. This was the first Winchester to utilise a vertical sliding locking mechanism, and is widely reckoned to have the smoothest action of any such rifle (better even than the under-lever rifle Browning later produced under his own name); it stayed in production – in no less than 10 alternative chamberings – until 1935, by which time very nearly 160,000 had been produced. Browning produced a new version, the first Winchester to be designed specifically for 'smokeless' ammunition, to be known as the Model 1894 (but more frequently as the Klondike Model, since virtually everyone who took part in the gold rush there, four years later, seems to have carried one) and this was even more successful – the millionth one made was presented to US President Calvin Coolidge in 1927, and it was still in production on its 100th anniversary, when, in its most basic form, it sold for just over US$300.

Browning's first weapon of war was a machine gun which Colt put into

■RIGHT: The unsophisticated Simonova SKS, well suited to the Red Army's needs, was the first weapon developed in the Soviet Union to use the 7.62mm x 39 M43 'intermediate' round.

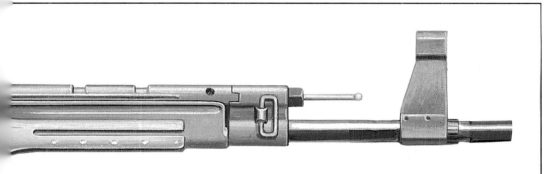

production as the Model 1895 'Gas Hammer', and which was adopted by the US Navy in 6mm (.23in) chambering (the same as the Lee straight-pull bolt-action rifle adopted the same year). Unlike the Maxim guns (if we exclude the design Maxim patented in 1884 but never put into production), it was operated, as its name tries to suggest, by the pressure of the propellant gas in the gun's barrel acting on the breech mechanism. Maxim always insisted that the Browning/Colt design infringed his 1884 patents, which he had renewed, and there is little doubt that he was right despite Browning trying to obscure the issue with a complicated arrangement of levers designed to make it appear, at least, as if his system was based on a different operating principle. It was not.

As a result of this subterfuge, Browning's design appeared somewhat cumbersome; its operating mechanism was partly external, a swinging arm mounted beneath the barrel, the fore-end of which was driven down and back through 170 degrees by gas pressure acting on a short piston, forcing a secondary linking arm to open the breech, extract the spent cartridge case and load a new one, cocking the gun at the same time. Its rather eccentric action led to the gun becoming known as the 'Potato Digger', but while it looked clumsy it was actually very smooth and progressive in action. It was fed by cloth belts similar to those used by the Maxim gun, each one of which had a capacity of 250 rounds.

Browning's second design for a selective-fire weapon was both more conventional and more relevant here, and was to become both popular and successful. Universally known by its initials as the BAR, the gas-actuated

■LEFT: Though the SKS was soon superseded in combat by the AK47, it remained the ceremonial rifle for Soviet forces since its overall length made drilling with it more comfortable.

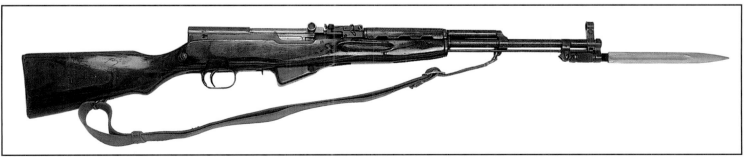

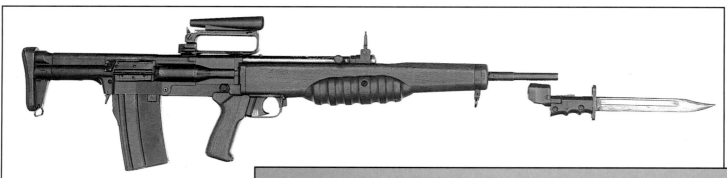

Browning Automatic Rifle did not satisfy its designer, though; he thought it fell between two stools, as it were, and he was right. It was much too heavy at over eight kilograms (18lb), including a full magazine, to be used as a rifle, certainly when fired from the shoulder, and was not capable of any great accuracy, even in single-shot mode, due to its open-bolt action in which the reciprocating parts were held to the rear when the action was cocked and slammed forward when the trigger was pulled. In automatic mode it was too light, and hence inaccurate again, and its 20-round magazine meant it had to be reloaded frequently (but even so, a variant known as the M1918A2, which could not be set

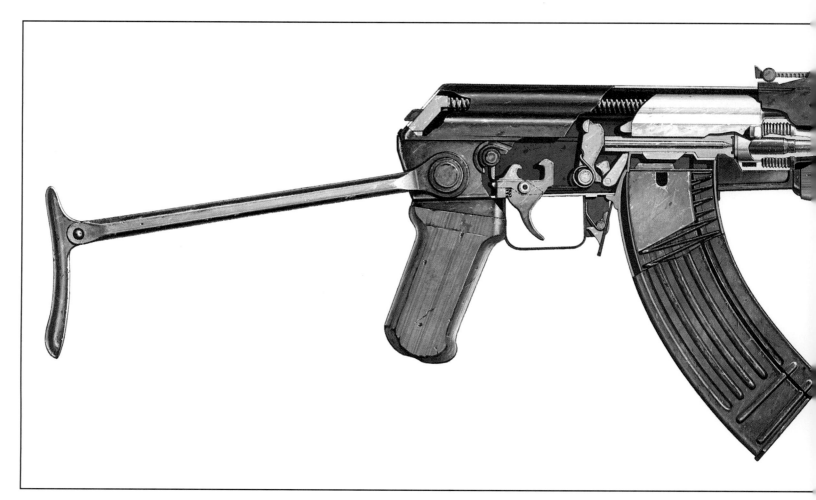

■**LEFT: The Enfield-designed EM2 was one of the first 'bullpup' designs, with its trigger group located well ahead of the action proper, reducing the overall length of the weapon considerably.**

to fire single rounds, but which instead had two pre-set cyclical rates of automatic fire: 300 and 600 rounds per minute, was also produced). For all that it didn't satisfy Browning, it actually lived up to its design requirements very well indeed, because the concept it fulfilled called for a weapon capable of rapid fire from the hip while the infantryman assaulted an enemy position at walking pace. Some versions, the M1918A1 and -A2, were fitted with bipods; all were originally chambered for the .30in M1906 round.

The BAR was adopted by many countries throughout the world, and stayed in continuous front-line service with the US Army and Marine Corps from its adoption in 1917 (it was first

■**LEFT: The Kalashnikov AK was to be adopted by almost all the Warsaw Pact countries, and produced locally in many of them. This is a Romanian AKM with a forward pistol grip.**

employed in combat on 13 September 1918) until the end of the Korean War in 1953, when it (and the then-standard M1 Garand rifle) were both replaced by the M14 self-loading rifle, which itself had a limited capacity for automatic fire. The last BARs in service with the US Army were withdrawn with the coming of the M60 general-purpose machine gun in 1957. It was produced by Colt, Marlin-Rockwell, and Winchester in the United States (and in small numbers by a variety of other companies, including International Business Machines – better known as IBM), and also by FN in Belgium, the state-owned Carl Gustav factory in Sweden, and in Poland, and in a variety of calibres. And while the Thompson may have been 'the gun that made the twenties roar', not a few gangsters and law-enforcement agencies preferred the more predictable BAR – marketed commercially by Colt as the R75 Monitor – to the short-barrelled SMG; among its more celebrated victims were Clyde Barrow and Bonnie Parker.

HOLEK'S ZH29
In a sense, the whole area of self-loading rifle development was polarised at this point – heavy and bulky weapons like the

BAR, which were not well adapted to the battlefield needs of the infantryman, worked; auto-loaders the size and weight (roughly four kilograms/nine pounds or less) of conventional repeater rifles were unreliable, and were understandably unpopular as a result. And it was to be some time before a designer was able to produce something which came close to occupying the middle ground. One of the first to try was the Czech, Emmanuel Holek, who worked at Ceskoslovenska zbrojovka's Brno factory, which was established after the break-up of the Austro-Hungarian Empire at the end of World War I. Holek began work on his rifle in the mid-1920s, but it was the end of the decade before his design was developed enough to be submitted for the sort of rigorous testing necessary to determine if it worked reliably under field conditions. Operation was by means of a barrel vent and piston (despite German resistance, this was fast becoming accepted as the only sensible way to go), and the action used a tilting bolt which was cammed into a recess in one side of the receiver – a sound enough principle, but one which made the manufacturing process expensive (as indeed did the extensive use of aluminium, incorporated for rapid heat dissipation). A similar but more efficient process, in which the bolt (or more accurately, the breech block) tilted on camming surfaces on a carrier which formed an extension to the piston, and was locked in recesses in the receiver wall, was later perfected for light machine guns which the Brno factory was developing concurrently – and which Britain adopted as the Bren gun.

The ZH29, as Holek's SLR was called, was a reliable, competent design, but at four and a half kilograms (10lb) empty it was still reckoned to be too heavy. Nonetheless, it got an enthusiastic reception and was tested widely in a variety of different chamberings (the original had been produced for the 7.92mm x 57 88S round), with and without the capability to fire fully automatically, and with short, medium, and long barrels. In the end, it was its cost which probably mitigated against it.

THE PEDERSEN SLR
That same year, John Pedersen, who in the meantime had entered the US Government's service and had gone to work at the Springfield Armory, produced a new cartridge in .276in (7mm) calibre

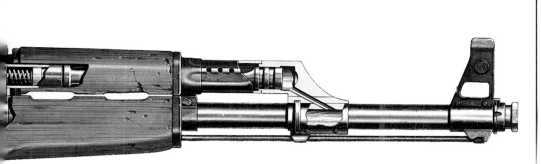

Kalashnikov AK47

Calibre: 7.62mm x 33 (.30in)
Weight: 4.3kg (9lb 7oz)
Length: 880mm (34.65in)
Barrel length: 415mm (16.35in)
Effective range: Circa 300m (1000ft)
Configuration: 30-round detachable box magazine, gas-actuated self-loading action, automatic option
Cyclical rate of fire: 600rpm
Muzzle velocity: 600mps (2350fps)
Country of origin: Soviet Union

(which came close to being selected to replace the .30in-06 round in 1932; it was finally rejected after the personal intervention of General Douglas MacArthur) and a self-loading rifle to go with it, designated the T2E1 but more widely known as the Pedersen Self-Loading Rifle, on which he had been working for seven years, on and off.

Pedersen used a blow-back action, retarded by a variant of the over-centre toggle which Borchardt and Luger had used for their self-loading pistols, but overlooked its one major drawback – like the pivoted flaps Mauser used, it didn't slow the action down adequately and didn't give the gas pressure in the

■ **BELOW: The Czech vz52 was an odd composite, using the actuation of the German Mkb42(W) with the trigger of the M1 Garand; locking of the bolt was achieved by tipping it.**

introduction of fluting into the cylinder, for example, which many modern weapons employ to good effect – but since there were better designs available, the Pedersen stood little chance.

JOHN GARAND'S M1 RIFLE

John Garand was a French Canadian by birth, who worked alongside Pedersen at the Springfield Armory. Garand began work on a design for a semi-automatic, self-loading rifle in 1919, and produced a weapon which worked by a simple method known as primer set-back: the primer was located in the head of the cartridge case in such a way that detonation of the propellant charge pushed it backwards against the firing pin, which was much larger in diameter than usual, initiating a series of actions which led to the bolt being unlocked; simple blow-back did the rest.

Garand had made considerable progress with this design by 1925, when

FN *Fusil Automatique Lèger* (FAL) (Heavy Barrel)

Calibre: 7.62mm x 51 (.30in)
Weight: 5.2kg (11lb 7oz)
Length: 1055mm (41.5in)
Barrel length: 535mm (21in)
Effective range: Over 800m (2600ft)

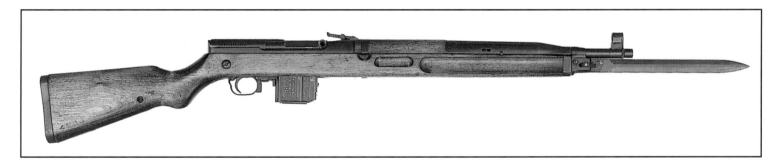

chamber time to fall sufficiently before it opened the breech and commenced extracting the spent case; that meant that the empty case was still pressed hard against the walls of the chamber by the gas pressure, which naturally made the process of removing it all the more difficult. This was less of a factor in a lightly-loaded pistol cartridge, and so the shortcoming hadn't really shown up in the Borchardt or the Luger. Pedersen adopted a similar solution to the one Mauser had, but he waxed his cartridge cases during manufacture instead of greasing them and the rifle's action; there was a difference in the amount of dirt and dust they attracted as a result, but not much!

The Pedersen SLR was tested against a wide range of competing designs by the US Army in July 1929 and rejected, and a similar fated awaited it in the United Kingdom, where it was taken up and championed by Vickers, and later in Japan. Further development might have cured the extraction problem – the

the US Army's Ordnance Department introduced a variation on the old .30in-06 round, with a slightly heavier 11.15g (172 grain) bullet and a different formulation of propellant, called IMR (Improved Military Rifle) powder. The new charge produced a slower, more progressive increase in gas pressure than the old one, which actually made primer set-back ineffective, and Garand began again, this time with a vent close to the muzzle passing propellant gas into a cylinder where it acted on the face of a piston, driving it backwards to work the action.

In Garand's rifle, the piston had eight millimetres (five-sixteenths of an inch) of free movement, which was enough to ensure that the bullet had left the muzzle and the gas pressure in the chamber had dropped to a safe level before a camming surface in a recess in the operating rod came into contact with a lug on the bolt and lifted it up, rotating the bolt in the process and freeing the two locking lugs in the receiver. The rotation of the bolt resulted in primary extraction, thanks to

the profile of the lugs themselves, which freed the spent case, cammed the hammer away from the firing pin, and withdrew the firing pin into the body of the bolt. The bolt was then carried back fully by the operating rod, extracting and ejecting the empty case (this latter by means of a spring-loaded plunger which emerged from the bolt face, another invention of John Browning's), cocking the hammer, and compressing the return spring under the barrel; as it commenced its return stroke under the pressure of that spring, it first actuated a follower in the base of the magazine, which put upwards pressure on the remaining rounds, the topmost of which was picked up by the bolt face and chambered. If no rounds remained, the operating rod was held back and the bolt held open, so that the eight-round clip which had been loaded complete into the magazine, in a system like Mannlicher's but simpler, could be ejected and replaced by a full one. It was also possible to extract a partially loaded clip manually and

Configuration: 20-round detachable box magazine, gas-actuated self-loading action, automatic option
Cyclical rate of fire: 550rpm
Muzzle velocity: 855mps (2800fps)
Country of origin: Belgium

replace it with a full one, though there was little benefit in this since the clips, which were manufactured from spring steel and loaded in the factory, were very difficult both to unload and to reload by hand. As well as developing the action, John Garand also paid considerable attention to the design of a trigger mechanism with an integral safety device, which has since been copied widely.

THE M1 VERSUS THE PEDERSEN

Garand's rifle was tested extensively at his place of work, which was of course the main centre for the development and production of military firearms in the United States, and in 1929 it was put forward for the trial at the Aberdeen Proving Ground alongside the Pedersen SLR, another delayed-action blow-back rifle from John Tagliaferro Thompson (who had started out in this field before being diverted into sub-machine guns, and who was keen to get back into it; Thompson, it transpired, was to be remembered as a one-weapon man, as, of course, was Garand), a modified short-recoil version of the BAR from Colt, the Czech ZH29, and a rifle with a gas-operated toggle-lock action from a German named Heinemann.

The panel of judges had difficulty in deciding between the Garand and the Pedersen, and 20 of each were ordered, in .276in (7mm) calibre. Further testing took until 1932, and the Garand rifle was

then recommended for adoption to replace the M1903 Springfield, largely because at that point MacArthur intervened to block the adoption of the experimental smaller-calibre round, and Garand, who had initially designed his rifle for the .30in-06 round anyway, was able to produce a re-chambered version more quickly than his rival. On 9 January 1936 the Garand rifle was standardised as the US Rifle, Calibre .30in, M1.

Production got under way 18 months later, and by August 1939 some 50,000 had been completed. The early models had screw-on muzzle caps which incorporated the gas vent, but a modification soon appeared with the vent moved back a short distance. A total of eight further modifications took place during the rifle's really quite short service career, some of which never got past prototyping; the most important of them saw an expansion chamber added to the gas system and the separation of the gas piston and actuating rod. Fully half the modifications concerned the fitting of telescopic sights.

By the time the United States of America entered World War II in December 1941 the majority of its regular soldiers had the M1 as their standard arm, and by the end of that war in 1945 huge numbers had been made by the Springfield Armory, Harrington & Richardson, and International Harvesters. Production ceased in the

USA in the early 1950s, by which time a total of some five and a half million had been produced; Garand's rifle was later manufactured by Beretta in Italy, in 7.62mm x 51 NATO chambering, as the BM59, extensively modified with a fully-automatic capability and a larger 20-round capacity magazine, by which time it resembled its successor, the M14, quite closely. It was not superseded there until well into the 1970s.

THE JOHNSON SLR

Garand and Pedersen weren't the only men in the United States designing self-loading rifles at the time, of course. We have noted in passing that Thompson was still active (and still extolling the simple virtues of the blow-back action retarded by the so-called Blish lock – an H-shaped bronze wedge which acted vertically in dovetails cut into the gun's steel receiver body, which relied on the fact that two different metals passing over each other create enhanced friction), but little information on the rifle he submitted to the 1929 trials survives, and he soon returned to the manufacture of the eponymous sub-machine gun which he had been marketing with a lack of success since 1920 but which, with the return of war, was to take off in a big way. A more significant competitor, but one who came too late to be effective, was Melvin M. Johnson, who was connected to the Cranston Arms Co. of Providence, Rhode Island.

Johnson's first effective military rifle was the V9, designed in 1937 (by which time the M1 Garand was already in production, of course) as a recoil-operated weapon with a box magazine, which metamorphosed into the Model 1941. The Dutch adopted the V9 to equip part of their colonial army in Indonesia, and later switched to the Model 1941, which was a more complicated rifle with an idiosyncratic detachable 10-round rotary magazine, the feed lips of which were machined into the receiver, which reduced considerably the chances of misfeeds (or, more often, non-feeds) due to distortion of the magazine as well as permitting the rifle to remain loaded and ready to fire during recharging. The rotating-bolt locking method Johnson devised, with its multiple lugs, was difficult and expensive to produce to the required tolerances, and there were always doubts as to whether all the lugs were actually doing their share of the work; it worked well in principle, though, and was clearly the precursor of the system Eugene Stoner devised for the AR-10/AR-15 series (see below), and which later became very popular indeed. Its 559mm (22in) barrel was easily dismounted, which made the rifle convenient to stow for transportation, though it was also largely unprotected as a result. After initial trials by the US Marine Corps, the US Government adopted it only in limited numbers for use by special forces, notably the clandestine OSS. Like Sir Charles Ross before him, Johnson didn't give in easily, though – he produced modification after modification, but ultimately without real success. By the end of World War II, the Johnson SLR had all but disappeared, and examples are now rare.

LIGHTWEIGHT RIFLES

For all the lip service which had been paid to reducing the weight of an infantryman's kit in the early part of the twentieth century, the rifle hadn't actually been slimmed down much since the introduction of the first repeaters in the 1880s – though shortening them had had some effect, of course. The M1 Garand with which the US Army went to war in 1941 was still four and one-third kilograms (nine and a half pounds) in weight, unloaded, and the simpler British Rifle Number 4 Mark 1 was only slightly lighter. The needs of the soldiery had changed considerably, though, since World War I, which had been largely a

static affair; now they fought on the move, often in arduous conditions, and as a result the search for lighter-weight rifles was resumed.

A LIGHTER, SHORTER WEAPON

Germany had already, as early as 1904, lopped almost 150mm (six inches) off the 98 rifle, producing the Kar98 which weighed nearly four kilograms (eight and a half pounds) unloaded and which was

■ABOVE: Somewhat surprisingly, Britain did not develop its own new rifle after World War II, but instead adopted the Belgian-designed FAL, as seen here in the hands of the crouching soldier.

reworked as the Kar98k (for *kurz* – short) and went back into manufacture in 1935 to become the standard Wehrmacht rifle of World War II. In the United States in 1938 it was suggested that there was a

L1A1 Self-Loading Rifle (FAL)

Calibre: 7.62mm x 51 (.30in)
Weight: 4.3kg (9lb 8oz)
Length: 1055mm (41.5in)
Barrel length: 535mm (21in)
Effective range: Over 800m (2600ft)
Configuration: 20-round detachable box magazine, gas-actuated self-loading action
Muzzle velocity: 855mps (2800fps)
Country of origin: United Kingdom (Belgium)

■**ABOVE: The Belgian FAL was available in a multiplicity of versions: of differing barrel lengths, with wooden or plastic furniture, and with solid or folding stocks.**

requirement for a lighter, shorter weapon than the M1 Rifle, specifically for the use of all but front-line infantrymen, including those fighting with crew-served weapons such as machine guns and mortars, but the request was turned down. However, the idea didn't go away, and it surfaced again two years later.

On 1 October 1940 the US Ordnance Department issued a specification for a self-loading or selective-fire weapon (the latter function was later deleted, and later still reinstated again), no more than 914mm (36in) in length overall and to

weigh under two and a half kilograms (five and a half pounds), to replace pistols and sub-machine guns in all arms except the infantry.

Significantly, this new weapon was not to be chambered for the 'full power' rifle round, but was to employ a lighter, less powerful load in a shorter cartridge, though still in .30in nominal calibre, which was to be developed by Winchester from a .32in-calibre round it had produced for a self-loading sporter rifle of 1905. Its 7.13g (110 grain) round-nosed bullet, similar in profile to a pistol round, was to be propelled by a 0.85g (13 grain) charge to give a muzzle velocity of 570 metres (1870ft) per second, comparable characteristics to that of the 7.63mm round for which the Mauser self-loading pistol of 1906 – a very powerful handgun

indeed at that time, before the introduction of magnum cartridges – was chambered.

THE US M1 CARBINE

The specification was issued to some 25 companies in all. Eleven of them, including Auto-Ordnance (John Thompson's company), Harrington & Richardson, Reising, Savage, and the Springfield Armory eventually submitted designs by the September 1941 deadline, but it was a carbine suggested by Winchester, with a new, simple operating principle designed by David M. Williams, which was selected and standardised the following month as the US Carbine, Caliber .30, M1.

Williams' design tapped gas off the barrel just 115mm (four and a half inches) from the chamber – the chamber pressure was much lower than that in an M1 Rifle, of course, thanks to the reduced-power round – of the 457mm (18in), one-turn-in-24-inches barrel, which acted on a very short piston and drove it back just 2.9mm (two-sixteenths of an inch) to contact the operating slide and transfer its momentum to it.

The slide was then free to move back through eight millimetres (five-sixteenths of an inch), at which point a recess in it engaged the operating lug on the bolt, pushing it up and rotating the bolt to free the locking lugs, which also provided primary extraction, started the cocking action, and retracted the firing pin into the bolt. Free now to move backwards under the pressure from the operating slide and against that of the return spring, the bolt extracted, then ejected the spent case (forwards and to the right), and completed the cocking action before reversing direction, stripping a fresh cartridge out of the 15- or 30-round magazine, chambering it, and rotating to engage the locking lugs once again. The final momentum it imparted to the operating slide was enough to ensure that the gas piston was driven forward into battery.

THE M1A1 AND M2 CARBINES

Like John Garand before him (from whose design he borrowed extensively, of course), David Williams also paid significant attention to the trigger-cum-safety device, and devised a simple yet effective mechanism which proved to be easily convertible to fully-automatic operation when the M2 version of the carbine was produced from November

M14

Calibre: 7.62mm x 51 (.30in)
Weight: 3.9kg (8lb 9oz)
Length: 1120mm (44in)
Barrel length: 560mm (22in)
Effective range: Over 800m (2600ft)
Configuration: 20-round
  detachable box magazine, gas-
  actuated self-loading action,
  automatic option

Cyclical rate of fire: 750rpm
Muzzle velocity: 855mps (2800fps)
Country of origin: United States

1944. Other versions produced included carbines with folding stocks, conceived for paratroops and produced as the M1A1 from May 1942.

In all, something over six million carbines, most of them M1s, were produced by a bewildering array of manufacturers – General Motors' subsidiaries were well represented, but there were oddities like the National Postal Meter Corp., Rock-ola Manufacturing Corp., and International Business Machines (IBM) – and the carbine was later also produced in Italy (by Beretta), in Dominica, and in Morocco.

REISING AND SMITH & WESSON
The M1 Carbine wasn't the only short single-shot weapon produced in the USA at the time; Harrington & Richardson produced the Reising Model 60 in the unorthodox .45in ACP chambering usually reserved for heavy pistols, but which was also employed by most Thompson sub-machine guns and the similar Reising Model 50 and Model 55 SMGs. It was no more successful than the over-complicated machine pistols.

Smith & Wesson tried to get in on the act too, and introduced a decidedly odd carbine, simply constructed but well finished, with a detachable tubular butt-stock which was located in a socket in the pistol grip. Produced in 1939 in 9mm Parabellum chambering, originally as a police weapon, it was apparently adopted

in very small numbers by Britain's Royal Navy in 1941.

GERMAN WORLD WAR II SLRS
For Germany, the provisions of the Treaty of Versailles which formally ended World War I were draconian, thanks largely to the revanchism which was still a strong force in France. Germany's army was limited to 100,000 men, and they were to be armed with only simple, pre-existing weapons. Such clandestine re-armament as did take place concentrated on more significant weapons than the mundane rifle, and, as a result, it was 1940 before the search for an effective self-loading rifle recommenced.

Both Mauser and the relative newcomer Walther (the family firm had actually been making guns in Zella, near Suhl, since the early eighteenth century, but it only became an important force during World War I; its most important contribution to arms manufacture in Germany during the inter-war period, when much of its production was turned over to calculating machines – an exercise it was to repeat after World War II – was certainly the P38 semi-automatic pistol) produced gas-operated designs which, by order of the War Ministry, were not permitted to employ gas vents drilled into the barrel, and which therefore both used variations of the Maxim/Bang system; there were other restrictions, too: no moving part was to be mounted on the surface of the

receiver, and the rifle was to be capable of manual operation should the self-loading mechanism fail. Mauser's proposal was eventually rejected (though some 20,000 rifles were built, and saw action with Waffen-SS troops), but Walther's was taken up and put into production as the *Gewehr* 41 (Walther) or Gew41[W].

THE WALTHER *GEWEHR* 41
Walther's engineers used a somewhat simpler system than Bang to direct propellant gas from the muzzle to act on a piston. A muzzle cap with a truncated conical internal profile was located some way (more than a centimetre, but less than two) from the end of the barrel, an aperture in it precisely aligned with the bore and of the same diameter. Thus, some milliseconds after it left the muzzle proper, the bullet entered the bore in the cap, effectively sealing it (once again, for some milliseconds), and for that brief period the propellant gas behind it was re-directed back around the outside of the barrel, where it acted on an annular piston, which in turn acted on a pushrod atop the barrel, which ran back to the breech and the action in a channel in the (plastic) handguard. The unsuccessful Mauser contender used exactly the same system to this point, save that its pushrod was located below the barrel. The annular piston and pushrod assembly moved backwards only a few centimetres, transferring its energy to a

breech block carrier, and from then on the actuation was conventional.

Locking was by means of the same system of flaps which Mauser had used in the *Selbstladezarabiner* 15, and the load of 10 rounds of ammunition was contained in a fixed box magazine, which was charged from two five-round clips from the 98 rifle.

■ BELOW: The Spanish CETME rifle was developed from a design which Mauser produced close to the end of World War II. The Heckler & Koch G3A4 was then based on the CETME.

The method of diverting the propellant gas via a muzzle cap made the rifle muzzle-heavy, while differential expansion between the barrel and the annular piston led to frequent stoppages, and these were the weapon's main faults, though at almost five kilograms (11lb) unloaded, it was heavy and the combination of short (545mm/21.5in) barrel and full-power ammunition made for heavy recoil and muzzle blast.

When the successor *Gewehr* 43 (Gew 43) and the slightly shorter carbine version were introduced, developed by Walther but also produced elsewhere, the main faults of the Gew41[W] were rectified. The muzzle cone disappeared, to be replaced by a conventional gas vent roughly half-way down the 560mm- (22in) long barrel, which led into a superimposed gas cylinder, where the propellant gas acted on a short piston, momentum being transferred to the breech block carrier by a pushrod. Otherwise the action was largely unchanged, save that the magazine could now be detached. The modified rifle stayed in production until the war's end, though the standard of finish – which wasn't particularly high to begin with – deteriorated drastically; it was seldom issued in large numbers, but was used more frequently as a sniper's weapon: as such, dovetails to take the mounts for a telescopic sight were machined into the receiver as part of the manufacturing process.

REDUCED-POWER AMMUNITION

The process of modifying the Gew41[W] didn't have a high priority, for by 1942 two quite separate programmes to produce assault rifles had come to fruition, one of them, developed by Rheinmetall for the Luftwaffe's parachute troops, using the full-power 7.92mm x 57 88sS ('*schwere Spitzer*' – heavy Spitzer) ammunition; the other, which combined elements of weapons developed independently by Walther and C.G. Haenel (a small company owned by Hugo Schmeisser, the man who designed the first effective sub-machine gun), with a lighter round in the same calibre but just 33mm (one and five-sixteenths of an inch) long, developed to order by Polte, which became known as the 7.92mm *kurz* or *pistolepatrone* (pistol cartridge) M1943. The new round was the forerunner of a new type of rifle ammunition, and thus we need to look at it, and trace its development.

The impetus to produce a new type of ammunition came from two sources. As early as 1892 the talented Czech weapons designer Karel Krnka, who worked closely with Roth, in Vienna, and a Swiss, F.W. Hebler, had begun to collaborate on a 'miniature rifle' project which was aimed at developing a rifle with the same stopping power as those then in use, but one-third shorter and lighter (Krnka also produced a design for a belt-fed machine gun using the long recoil principle which was chambered for a 5mm/.19in cartridge; it is to be assumed that the rifle he and Hebler were working on was to use the same ammunition. Hebler described the cartridge later as being 'three times lighter, the gas pressure and recoil only half as great' as the ammunition in common use. We may recall the miniature round Rubin, another Swiss, produced at around that time, which Mondragon adopted briefly, and speculate on a degree of collaboration – or at least a commonality of purpose – between the two).

The second reason surfaced later, during World War I. It soon became apparent that the sort of cartridges for which the rifles and machine guns of both sides were chambered were actually only useful in the latter. In a rifle, they were just too powerful for all but the most expert shots – men who actually could hit a man-sized target at 550m (1800ft), and sometimes more. To others they were little more than a way of inflicting pain upon one's self, for their use led to badly bruised shoulders (which reduced fighting efficiency all round, for it tended to make men gun-shy). And more importantly, they were entirely unsuitable for the new type of weapons which would be needed to implement new tactical theories.

THE MACHINE PISTOL

We have already touched, with some derision, on the theory of assault tactics which led to the production of the Pedersen Device, the BAR, and the French Saint Etienne rifle in 1917. The concept of advancing in serried ranks across open ground dominated by fixed machine guns was already entirely devalued by then (and orders to do so had already met with large-scale rebellion in the French ranks), but in Germany a different way of breaking the deadlock was mooted: the so-called Von Hutier tactics, first implemented by that gentleman in his 1917 attack on Riga,

■ABOVE: An Italian infantryman from an elite Alpini regiment with his BM59 rifle. The BM59 was a modification of the Garand M1 in 7.62mm NATO calibre.

were actually developed as a staff exercise at German High Command. The mainstay of this method was infiltration by small, self-contained fighting groups using firepower, surprise, concealment, and fieldcraft, and in order to implement it, a new type of weapon, the sub-machine gun or machine pistol, was developed.

THE BERGMANN MP18

The first of these was the Bergmann MP18/I, developed by Hugo Schmeisser, which was chambered for the 9mm Parabellum round which Georg Luger had produced at DWM for his self-loading pistol. Schmeisser chose that round because it allowed him to use a simple unlocked blow-back action in the MP18/I, but of course it had its disadvantages, and first and foremost among them was its lack of real stopping power (its 0.4g/six grain charge gave its 7.45g/115 grain bullet a muzzle velocity of around 380 metres/1245ft per second from the MP18/I's 195mm/seven and three-quarter inch barrel and a maximum effective range of under 200m/656ft). It was adequate for fighting in built-up areas and ideal for close-quarters battle, but just not good enough for the open battlefield, and a variety of men in a variety of different places set out to devise a round which was better suited to the task at hand and which would allow the infantryman to be armed with a lightweight rifle capable of fully automatic fire when required but which would still be effective out to 6-800m (1970-2625ft).

We have seen already how just such a weapon – the M1 and M2 Carbines –

would become the most widely issued of all the small arms adopted by the US Army and US Marine Corps, and how a relatively low-powered commercial round had been adapted for it, but in Germany the realisation that a 'short' rifle-calibre cartridge would be required to fight a war which was already looming came along with wider re-armament and the renewal of universal military service in 1935.

THE VOLLMER/GECO M35

It appears that the first such cartridge was developed as a private initiative by Gustav Genschow & Co. (Geco) in that year, firstly in 7.75mm (.305in) calibre, using a necked case 39.5mm (one and a half inches) long to contain a charge of around 21.6g (5 grain) and a pointed 9g (139 grain) bullet, and later in 7.62mm (.30in) with a correspondingly lighter projectile. The performance was similar in both cases – a muzzle velocity of around 695 metres (2280ft) per second.

This round, which Geco referred to as the M35, was tested by the German Army's Weapons Office in conjunction with a carbine designed around it by Heinrich Vollmer, a talented designer who was doomed never to make a big impact because he lacked really influential friends at a time and in a place where they were more essential than ever. Vollmer's *Maschinekarabine 35* had an idiosyncratic form of gas actuation, constrained by the boring of a

simple barrel vent being forbidden, but it also had a further peculiarity – a locked-breech action which fired from an open bolt (which we have already noted was less than ideal in one sense, due to the mechanical shock caused by the closing – and in this case, locking – of the bolt after the trigger was pressed). And as if that wasn't enough, its cyclical rate of fire was close to 1000 rounds per minute – Vollmer had to devise a pneumatic brake to slow it down.

We need spend no more time on the MKb35; it was by no stretch of the imagination a great rifle, and only 25 were ever made (by hand, of course, at a cost of 4000 Reichsmarks each – at a time, in the summer of 1938, when the Mark III and IV tanks which were just going into production were only costing around 100,000 Reichsmarks apiece), and were it not for a simple happenstance, it would probably have long disappeared from the literature. The MKb35's only real claim to fame is that one example, along with a small supply of M35 ammunition for it, fell into Soviet hands in 1945; the Red Army's technical branch

was not impressed with the carbine, but the Geco round was a different story: it was suspiciously similar in every way to the 7.62mm x 39 round which was adopted in 1947 for the Simonov and later for the Kalashnikov self-loading rifles as the M43 (there is no satisfactory explanation for the designation; many commentators have taken it to be the year of its introduction, and that would seem logical, but there is no evidence to support that), and which was to be the official rifle ammunition for the entire Communist bloc for a further 30 years, and for which millions of rifles still in everyday use are chambered. It is safe to say that the Soviets were impressed by the 7.92mm x 33 *kurz* round (see below) for which the MP43/StG44 was chambered, but it is significant that it wasn't the one they chose to copy – though perhaps their preference for the 7.62mm calibre which they had adopted so long before was the real influence.

The short cartridge which the Germans did adopt was developed – although, that is probably too strong a term – by Polte Werke of Magdeburg by

ABOVE: An Israeli infantryman in training with a Galil assault rifle. Based on the AK47 action, it is lighter than the FAL and the German G3 thanks to its being chambered for the 5.56mm round.

the simple expedient of reducing the 7.92mm x 57 cartridge case to 33mm (one and five-sixteenths of an inch) in length (and reducing the rim diameter marginally, to remove the possibility of anyone trying to chamber a short round in a weapon designed to accept the original), filling it with 2g (31 grain) of propellant and trimming the projectile to 7.95g (123 grain). This specification gave a muzzle velocity, in the assault rifles which were designed around it, of about 650 metres (2135ft) per second, which was shown to be enough power to penetrate a steel helmet at 700m (2300ft).

The Vollmer/Geco development programme was halted by the War Ministry in Berlin in 1938, with the excuse that war was imminent and this was no time to be attempting to develop new weapons. Even if Vollmer lacked

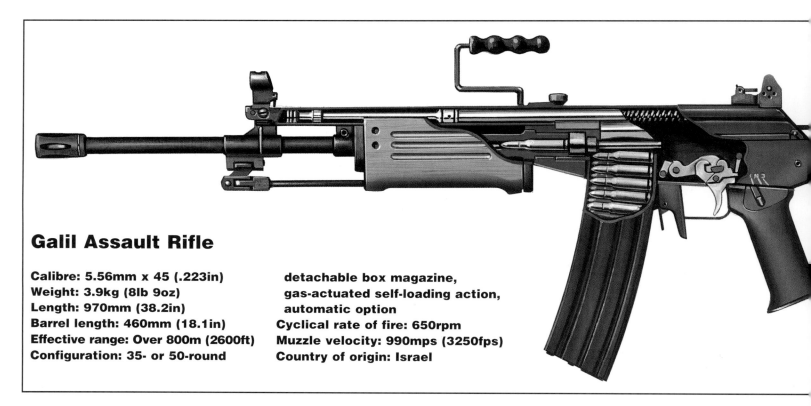

Galil Assault Rifle

Calibre: 5.56mm x 45 (.223in)
Weight: 3.9kg (8lb 9oz)
Length: 970mm (38.2in)
Barrel length: 460mm (18.1in)
Effective range: Over 800m (2600ft)
Configuration: 35- or 50-round

detachable box magazine,
 gas-actuated self-loading action,
 automatic option
Cyclical rate of fire: 650rpm
Muzzle velocity: 990mps (3250fps)
Country of origin: Israel

friends in high places, he must have realised soon enough that this was no more than a brush-off, for two rather better-known gunmakers were later instructed to begin work on machine carbines with a similar specification to his own: C.G. Haenel Waffen- und Fahrradfabrik (Weapon and Bicycle Works) and Carl Walther. The truth was that Vollmer's MKb35 was simply not suited to mass-production techniques and required too much complicated – and therefore expensive – machining. The Waffenamt didn't make the same mistake with the specification handed down to Haenel and Walther in late 1939 or early 1940, and it was made clear from the start that the emphasis was to be on simplicity of construction.

THE WALTHER MKb42[W]

The Walther design, which emerged as the MKb42[W], was ultimately unsuccessful, but it had some interesting features. Despite the problems they had had with the annular piston in the Gew41[W], the development engineers at Zella stuck with this arrangement for the new weapon, though the port from which it derived its propellant gas was now a conventional vent instead of a muzzle cap. This piston worked within a cylindrical housing, and a sleeve attached to it first freed the front-locked tipping block then propelled it backwards to cycle the action. As a result of the form of its gas cylinder, the Walther gun was

instantly recognisable by its distinctive cylindrical combined fore-stock and handguard and its lack of a gas tube parallel with the barrel, but apart from that it was generally very similar in appearance to the Haenel MKb42[H] – both had pistol grips and curved, 30-round capacity magazines and were almost identical in overall length, though the Walther's barrel was 40mm (one and a half inches) longer than the Haenel's at 405mm (16in). Some 8000 (other reports say around half that number) MKb42[W]s were produced, and they were extensively tested in Russia over the winter of 1942.

HUGO SCHMEISSER'S DESIGNS

The successful Haenel design from Hugo Schmeisser was also centred around a tipping block (which had the advantage of requiring no rotation, and so could be square in section rather than round, with camming surfaces and lugs which operated in a plane in the walls, floor, or roof of the receiver; that meant that considerable economies could be achieved in the machining process), but it had a more conventional gas tube and piston, the latter acting on a bolt carrier, shifting it back and down to unlock the action, when it carried the bolt backwards to cycle the action. Like the Walther, the Haenel fired from an open bolt (that is to say that when the action was cocked and ready to fire the bolt was held to the rear, with the breech open and the chamber

empty. As we have noted, this made for a marked loss of accuracy in single-shot operation, but allowed better cooling when bursts were fired) but the most important feature it shared with the gun from Zella was its pressed-steel construction. Haenel had no experience with this method and had to go outside to Merz Werke, an office machine manufacturer in Frankfurt; Walther's earlier foray into that same branch of business now paid off. Schmeisser was involved with the development of the MP40 sub-machine gun at the same time, and used a similar technique for the formation of its receiver; it was very much an idea whose time had come. Merz Werke refined Schmeisser's original designs considerably in converting them to pressed-steel construction; the receiver was stamped out of sheet steel, strengthening ribs were pressed into it, and camming channels and recesses for other components were machined into it before it was folded into shape and welded into a box.

Even to those without a knowledge of machine shop technique, it is clear that the 'new' method offered huge time and cost advantages over the traditional. Fifty examples of Schmeisser's design were delivered for evaluation in mid-1942, and over the following autumn and winter around 8000 MKb42[H]s were produced and tested on the Eastern Front alongside the Walther. The result was acceptance of the former, which went into

factory in Oberndorf as the *Maschinenpistole* 43 with an overall length of 940mm (37in) and a weight of five kilograms (11.25lb) unloaded.

THE *STURMGEWEHR* 44

Over the following year the MP43 was further modified slightly – it got mountings for a telescopic sight, and a different grenade launcher mount – and became firstly the MP44 and then the *Sturmgewehr* (assault rifle) 44 – a designation which was certainly a good deal closer to its actual role.

An MP44 took some 14 hours to make and cost about 70 Reichsmarks (by way of comparison the Kar98k was cheaper, at 56 Reichsmarks, but took longer to produce and required more and more complicated machining). Because of the cost, and because it did not use the standard 7.92mm x 57 ammunition, the MP44 was not immediately adopted for general service (though nonetheless, by February 1944 production was running at 5000 per month) and it was not until July or August, 1944, after the Allied invasion of France, that it was actually adopted officially as the StG44.

It is said that Adolf Hitler himself was responsible for both suppressing it and then adopting it, and that is more than feasible; Der Führer was an inveterate meddler where new weapons were concerned, believing that as an old soldier himself, he knew what was really needed on the battlefield, even though

production, after its trigger lock assembly had been changed over to that devised for the Walther (Schmeisser had adopted the rather rudimentary safety device which he employed on the MP40 sub-machine gun – engaging the cocking handle in a recess in the left hand side of the receiver – which failed very easily, whereupon the weapon was rendered active without the bearer realising it) in July 1943 at Haenel's own factory in Suhl, at Erma Werke in Erfurt, and at the Mauser

conditions had changed out of all recognition since he had served.

By far the strangest modification to the StG44 (or any other comparable weapon, come to that) was that produced in 1944 to allow the weapon to shoot around corners. Quite what was expected of the *Maschinenpistole mit Vorsatz* or *Maschinenpistole mit Krummlauf* as it was known is not clear, though the usual suggestions include a means of clearing combat pioneers off tanks as well as the obvious ('Vorsatz' means 'design'; the letter J, P, or V was added, distinguishing between the three sub-variants. 'Krummlauf' means 'in a curved path'). One variant, the MP44K/30, had a 30 degree bend in the barrel, another, the /40 (which seems to have been no more than a paper exercise), a 40 degree bend and the third, the /90, turned the projectile through a full right-angle. It wasn't enough simply to bend the barrel and fit mirror sights, of course; gas vents were also drilled into it to allow propellant gas to be expelled progressively, reducing the muzzle velocity from 650 metres (2135ft) per second to little over 300 metres (985ft) per second in the process, which certainly ensured that the weapon would never

■**BELOW: Since the eighteenth century, Switzerland has maintained a large and active arms industry. This is the mid-1990s SIG SG-550 – a conventional SLR but built to the highest standards.**

have been of any use at anything but short ranges. It is said that as many as 10,000 MP44K/30s were ordered (and certainly, there are many in museums and perhaps even in private collections), but little evidence of it seeing any action.

PARATROOPER REQUIREMENT

At roughly the same time as the Haenel and Walther assault rifles were being tested in Russia, an alternative design, this time using the full-power 7.92mm x 57 88sS round was also undergoing trials. The *Fallschirmjaegergewehr* ('Paratrooper Rifle') 42, as the selective-fire weapon was eventually to be designated, has been described in glowing terms by many experts, and we must conclude that its lack of success was due more than anything else to the diminished importance of the arm-of-service for which it had been developed by the time it became available. It is said that the FG42 project came about as a result of a request from senior paratroop officers preparing for (or perhaps fresh from) Operation Merkur – the hard-fought battle to take the Mediterranean island of Crete in the third week of May 1941, who complained that the combination of Kar98k rifles and sub-machine guns with which they were armed didn't give them enough firepower. They wanted a full-power rifle, less than one metre (39in) in overall length, accurate enough, when equipped with a

telescopic sight, to be used by a sniper at long range yet able to produce sustained fire, capable of firing grenades, strong enough to be used as a club in close-quarters fighting and weighing less than four kilograms/nine pounds (the weight of the existing rifle). Their request was made initially to the Luftwaffe's weapons section (German paratroopers were enlisted in the air force, not the army) and was re-directed to the equivalent office in the army, which was responsible for the development of infantry weapons. Not entirely surprisingly, it was dismissed as 'utopian' and the officers in question were told that they would have to wait for the operational version of the Gew41, which was then undergoing initial testing. Undeterred, they returned to the Air Ministry, which resolved to approach its suppliers of aircraft machine guns and cannon, notably Gustloff-Werke, Krieghoff, Mauser, and Rheinmetall-Borsig, with a view to developing such a weapon. Mauser offered a revamped MG81, a design originally conceived as an aircraft-mounted machine gun, which was much more an LMG than a rifle, and Gustloff-Werke made no submission; the other two proposed new designs and that from Rheinmetall-Borsig was selected.

FALLSCHIRMJAEGERGEWEHR 42

The successful contender was devised by Louis Stange, who had started work in

1904 as an apprentice to Hugo Schmeisser's father, Louis, not long after Rheinische Metallwaren und Maschinenfabrik had acquired the family firm of Dreyse. By 1934, when he produced much of the mechanism of what was to become the MG34 – far and away the best infantry machine gun of its day – Stange had risen to the post of chief designer. Though only 7000 FG42s were ever produced, it was to prove seminal, the spiritual forerunner both of the selective-fire assault rifles which came to dominate in military circles from the 1950s onwards and of the 'bullpup' designs which began to appear 20 years later.

We noted that the American rifle of the eighteenth century acquired a considerable downward angle to its butt-stock, so that the recoil would tend to throw the gun's barrel even further up, rather than driving the whole weapon straight back into the shoulder, and that same feature was found to some degree at least in all the rifles which succeeded it – until the FG42 came along. It was a fairly conventional auto-loading rifle, with a piston propelled by gas tapped off the 510mm- (20in) long barrel at just about the centre point, acting over a long stroke to release and cycle a rotating bolt locked by two forward lugs, but it had a cunning – though by no means complex – variation which allowed it to fire from a closed bolt when the selector was set to

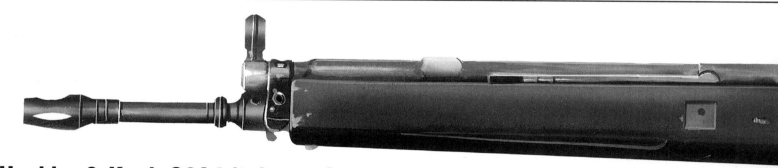

Heckler & Koch G3A4 (telescopic stock)

Calibre: 7.62mm x 51 (.30in)
Weight: 3.85kg (8lb 8oz)
Length (stock extended): 980mm (38.6in)
Barrel length: 450mm (17.7in)
Effective range: Over 500m (1650ft)
Configuration: 20-round detachable box magazine, delayed blow-back self-loading action, automatic option
Cyclical rate of fire: 550rpm
Muzzle velocity: 810mps (2650fps)
Country of origin: Germany

■LEFT: A German infantryman with an extending-stock Heckler & Koch G3A4 rifle. The rifle was based on the Spanish CETME, which was itself developed from a Mauser design.

four and a half kilograms (10lb), was actually the first effective general-purpose assault weapon. Stange foresaw that, and produced prototypes of a belt-fed version (though there is no evidence that he also experimented with interchangeable light- and heavy barrels, another pre-requisite for the transformation of a rifle into a sustained-fire weapon).

At first sight, the FG42 looks unbalanced, for the magazine protrudes horizontally from the receiver on the left hand side; indeed, the rifle *was* unbalanced as a result, particularly when the 20-round box was fitted (the early models came with either 10- or 20-round magazines, the later with only 20-round boxes; the two were not interchangeable) but this was unavoidable, for Stange had taken a bold conceptual step, the import of which has been missed even by some of the most perceptive analysts: he had to use a horizontal magazine because he moved the entire breech back to a position directly above the trigger assembly, and saved the equivalent of the magazine's depth in the rifle's overall length, which was just 940mm (37in) – the same as that of the Haenel-designed MKb42[H] – but with a 510mm- (20in) long barrel in place of the latter's 365mm (14in) tube as a result. It would be interesting to know if Stange ever made the whole leap and considered placing the action far enough behind the trigger assembly so that the magazine could have gone back to its conventional place, vertically below the receiver.

single-shot and from an open bolt when set to automatic, thus solving the stability-versus-cooling problem neatly and satisfactorily. Instead of being carried within the bolt, the firing pin was actually integral with the piston, on its upper surface; the bolt was a complex hollow cylinder which fitted over it. There was a forward bent or recess on the underside of the piston for repetitive fire and a rear bent for single shots; they were offset to left and right respectively, and the type-of-fire selector simply pushed the trigger sear which located in

the bent to left or right. To compensate for the heavy recoil of the 88sS round, Stange devised a buffer system and utilised a semi-floating butt-stock upon which it acted. He also fitted a muzzle brake which diverted some of the propellant gases to the sides. A folding bipod and a folding bayonet were also fitted.

The early version of the FG42 was made entirely of metal; later versions of the rifle had a wooden butt-stock and a pistol grip which was much closer to the vertical. The FG42, which weighed only

THE FG42 IN ACTION

The FG42 rifle first saw action on 12 September 1943, when a paratroop unit led by the legendary Otto Skorzeny landed in cargo gliders on a plateau on the Grand Sasso in the Abruzzi region of Italy and successfully rescued the deposed Italian dictator, Benito Mussolini, from the hotel where he was being held prisoner by the pro-Allied government of Marshal Badoglio, though somewhat surprisingly it is reported that not a single shot was fired in the whole of that operation. The weapons issued to Skorzeny's men were production prototypes; series production, which was

undertaken by Kreighoff (which produced 5000 rifles) and I.C. Wagner (which produced around 2000 more) didn't start until the winter of 1943-44.

MAUSER'S ASSAULT RIFLE

And what, one might ask with a certain justified curiosity, was going on at Oberndorf while the FG42 and the MP43/44 were being developed? After all, Mauser had been in the forefront of German rifle development since the very beginning of the modern era. . . In fact, there, too, the reduced-power *Pistolepatrone* 43 round was being used as the basis for a selective-fire assault rifle (after a similar round in 7mm/.27in calibre which DWM developed itself, as well as the same company's own 9mm Parabellum round, had been rejected) which first saw the light of day in incomplete form in mid-1942 as the deceptively named Gerät 06H ('Gerät' simply means device). Even though it was not perfectly developed, the rifle had one vital new feature – a breech block locked by rollers instead of cams, which allowed it simply to reciprocate without any up-and-down or side-to-side motion and with no rotation. This same principle had first been applied to the MG42 machine gun, developed from the MG34

for which Mauser had provided the (rather different) locking mechanism, and is held to have been the invention of Dr Ing. Gruner of the Grossfuss Metall- und Lackierwarenfabrik, a company with no previous involvement in firearms design and manufacture at all, whose main product was sheet-metal lanterns (though one authority believes the original design to have been patented in Poland by Edward Stecke in 1937 – the same year that Gruner first showed his demonstration model – and others suggest that it was more properly attributed to Rheinmetall-Borsig's Louis Stange). As a tribute to its effectiveness, we may note in passing that the MG42 was known to be able to operate at a cyclic rate in excess of 1200 rounds per minute; its basic design was still in production 50 years after it first appeared.

Ernst Altenberger was Mauser's chief designer at the time (and had been responsible for the MG34 locking mechanism), but much of the actual work on the new assault rifle design was consigned to Wilhelm Stühle. He modified the locking mechanism of the 06H so that the bolt head, with its two locking rollers, was linked flexibly to the bolt carrier by means of what he called a 'steering piece'

in the form of a flat arrow-head, which forced the rollers outwards to lock into recesses in the receiver walls.

The action of the prototype Mauser assault rifle in its original form was almost identical with the Tokarev, and Stühle was able to modify it to roller locking quite easily; he must have realised early on, however, that he could dispense with the complicated and expensive gas cylinder and piston arrangement, and return to the method of actuation Paul Mauser himself had preferred – retarded blow-back, with the rollers supplying both the locking and a good part of the retardation. In the prototype of the MKb43, as the project came to be known, the resistance of the jamming effect of the steering piece acting on the locking rollers was sufficient to hold the breech closed until the projectile had left the barrel. The rollers then retracted into the bolt head, which was then free to begin its rearwards motion. After the bolt and carrier had completed their cycle of extraction/ejection/cocking and inserting a fresh round, locking was accomplished by the steering piece forcing the rollers out into their recesses once more, whereupon the trigger/hammer assembly was unlocked and a fresh round could be

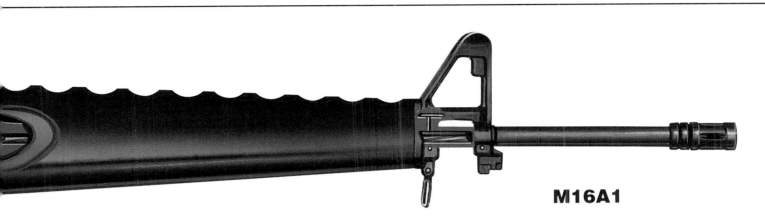

M16A1

Calibre: 5.56mm x 45 (.223in)
Weight: 2.85kg (6lb 5oz)
Length: 990mm (39in)
Barrel length: 510mm (20in)
**Effective range: Over 500m
 (1640ft)**
**Configuration: 20- or 30-round
 detachable box magazine,
 gas-actuated self-loading action,
 automatic option**
Cyclical rate of fire: 800rpm
Muzzle velocity: 990mps (3250fps)
Country of origin: United States

■LEFT: Since its introduction in the early 1960s the M16 rifle has become the standard by which other 5.56mm self-loading assault rifles are judged. It will almost certainly survive years yet.

fired. Stühle solved the problem of expanded cartridges sticking in the chamber by machining grooves or flutes into the chamber wall, so that some part of the propellant gases was forced down the outside of the spent cartridge case, equalising the pressure inside and out and preventing it from expanding.

Four examples of the new rifle were completed by hand in late 1943 and were dispatched to the Army Weapons Office for trials at the Kummersdorf test range, while independent experts were asked to produce estimated production schedules. It soon became clear that not only did the new machine carbine perform as well as it had been expected to, but that it would take barely half as long to manufacture (and cost half as much) as the Haenel-designed MP44 which was even then going into production. Production tooling, including dies for the pressing out of the sheet metal components, and a sample run of a 'zero series' of 30 rifles, designated as the *Sturmgewehr* 45[M] was ordered, and manufacture, but not

assembly, was completed just as the war ended; no Stg45 ever saw action.

THE SECOND 'SPANISH' MAUSER

Its story was far from over, however, for a group of ex-Mauser employees including Ludwig Vorgrimler, who had worked closely with Altenburger and Stühle, later re-created it at the Centro de Estudios Technicos de Materiales Especiales in Madrid as the re-styled *Fusil d'Assalto Modelo* 58, employing a trigger group like that of the FG42, which permitted automatic fire from an open bolt and single shots to be fired from a closed bolt. The M58 was originally chambered for the 7.92mm *kurz* round, then modified to accept a different short cartridge (with an aluminium projectile) in the same calibre before it was standardised for the CSP003, a low-powered version of the 7.62mm x 51 NATO round which produces a muzzle velocity reduced by around 20 per cent, to about 785metres (2575ft), though somewhat surprisingly it could also handle the standard version; the two are dimensionally identical. The CETME design was taken up by another group of ex-Mauser employees (though this time they had stayed in Oberndorf-am-Neckar) who set themselves up as Heckler & Koch and produced it as the G3. It was adopted as the official rifle of the Bundeswehr in 1959 and was subsequently taken up by virtually every army outside the Communist bloc which did not adopt the FN FAL. H&K later relied on the roller locking action as the basis for a wide range of other assault rifles (qv) as well as light machine guns and machine pistols.

THE SWISS SLR
SIG in Switzerland also adopted the same locking method for the SG510, which was available to military customers in 7.62mm NATO and Soviet chamberings as well as in a single-shot 'sporting' version as the AMT, and in a modified form, using the same locking system but with gas/piston actuation, for the SG530 rifle (see below) in 5.56mm x 45 calibre.

In common with most arms manufacturers trying to sell into the very competitive export market, SIG produced its 510 and 530 series rifles (and the later, gas-operated, rotating-bolt 540 series) in a multitude of forms, with varying barrel lengths and weights and different types of furniture.

These were by no means the first Swiss self-loading rifles, for the design department at SIG's Neuhausen factory had been at work on the genre on its own behalf ever since it had come up with the marginal 'improvements' to the Mondragon, back in 1915. Throughout the 1920s, Kiraly and End, its two most prolific members, developed the KE series of recoil-operated SLRs, none of which got past the prototype stage (though one was produced as an LMG, and was sold in small quantities to China). Joined by Gaetzi in 1930, they produced a number of basically similar but no more successful gas-operated designs which relied on long gas tubes running the length of the barrel, and then one with a short gas tube leading to a cylinder which ran alongside the bolt.

Then, in 1953, by means of an aberration of magnificent proportions, SIG produced a unique machine carbine utilising the 'blow-forward' system which some machine gun designers had briefly entertained (but never put into production; as far as one can determine, the idea came into consideration only as a way of avoiding the more practical methods already in use, which were protected by patent) around the turn of the century. In the AK53, as the ill-fated rifle was known (only 50 were made), the entire barrel was propelled forward by firing the cartridge (and the assistance of a large coiled spring), leaving the case, gripped by the extractor claw located in the cannelure, to be ejected. The barrel was then returned to battery by means of a second spring, stripping a fresh round out of the magazine, cocking the action and re-setting the first spring in the process. The system permitted a cyclic rate of fire of some 300 rounds per minute to be achieved, and no provision for single-shot operation was made since the rifleman could achieve the same result by rapidly releasing the trigger.

Finally, in 1955 a practical self-loading carbine, utilising the Mauser roller-block locking action, was produced as the AM55, and was adopted by the Swiss Army in somewhat modified form as the StGw57, to replace the by-now rather venerable straight-pull bolt action Schmidt-Rubin in its final form, the Kar31. This was the last Swiss service rifle to use the 7.5mm (.29in) round. It was from this rifle that the SG510 SLR was developed, independently of CETME and Heckler & Koch.

SIMONOV AND THE AVS
The need to equip German soldiers with self-loading rifles became pressing in 1941 because after Operation Barbarossa,

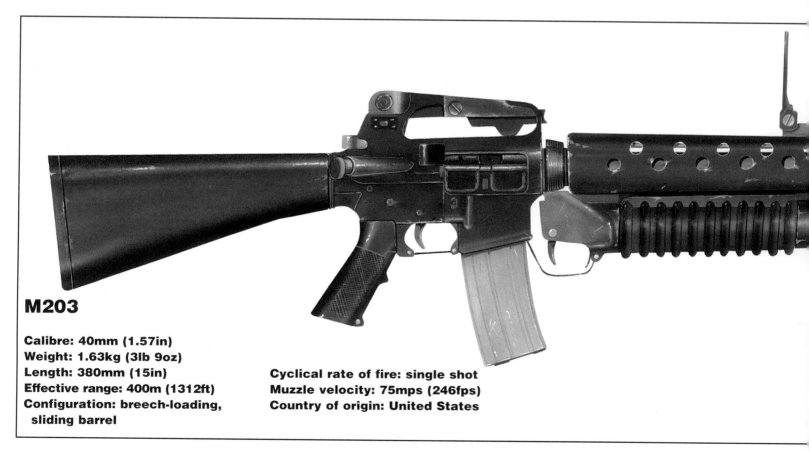

M203

Calibre: 40mm (1.57in)
Weight: 1.63kg (3lb 9oz)
Length: 380mm (15in)
Effective range: 400m (1312ft)
Configuration: breech-loading, sliding barrel

Cyclical rate of fire: single shot
Muzzle velocity: 75mps (246fps)
Country of origin: United States

the invasion of the Soviet Union, they were frequently confronted by 'human waves' of fanatical infantrymen who were often armed with semi-automatic weapons themselves and against whom only superior firepower succeeded.

In 1936 the Red Army adopted a rifle designed by Sergei Gavrilovich Simonov, who is sometimes described as the last of the 'old guard' Russian designers, having begun work as a trainee technician, probably at Sestroresk, before the revolution. By 1927 he was working in the design and development department at the Tula Arsenal under Vladimir Fyodora, and the *Avtomaticheskaya Vintovka Simonova obr* 1936, usually known as the AVS or AVS36, was his first adopted design. It used a piston operating in a gas tube above the barrel to operate a rather unusual locking system which relied on a vertically-sliding block to lock the bolt and carrier into the receiver. The cocking handle reciprocated with the bolt, which was an unpopular feature, particularly when the selective-fire weapon was used in automatic mode (and also meant that the interior of the receiver was open to mud and dirt). It suffered from excessive recoil, which Simonov tried to correct by fitting a two-port muzzle brake.

The AVS was not a success, though the simple tactical principle for which it was

evolved continued to be employed, and it was superseded in 1938 by a self-loading rifle designed by another eminent Tula-based Soviet designer, Feydor Vassilivich Tokarev, who also produced light machine guns and a very popular semi-automatic pistol, the TT-33.

TOKAREV AND THE SVT

The *Samozaryadnaya Vintovka* (self-loading rifle) *Tokareva obr* 1938 (SVT38) and its (very similar) successor, the SVT40, also used a superimposed gas tube fed from a vent just abaft the muzzle, but the locking mechanism was somewhat simpler – a block cammed downwards at the rear into a recess in the receiver floor, which was lifted and released by the rearwards movement of the bolt carrier, guided by slots in the receiver walls. It too suffered from the effects of muzzle blast, and a six-port brake was fitted.

In 1940, after the Soviet Union had shown its capacity for war by invading Poland, a more robust version with a revised muzzle brake was produced; a few of these latter rifles were modified for selective fire, and others were cut down to carbine length for use by the cavalry units the Red Army still employed. Both the Simonov and the Tokarev rifles were light enough in weight, at under four kilograms (nine pounds), unloaded, and all were of similar overall length (1220mm/48in) with barrels from 615mm

■ **ABOVE: Like all its kind, the M16 demands regular maintenance and cleaning – a fact which eluded the US Army when it was first introduced, leading to a reputation for failure.**

to 635mm (24-25in) in length, which gave them a muzzle velocity of 770 metres (2525ft) with 7.62mm x 54R M1891 ammunition.

SIMONOV AND THE SKS

During the Great Patriotic War (World War II), Simonov had produced a self-loading anti-tank rifle designed around the existing 14.5mm x 114 round – a massive cartridge with a 65g (1003 grain) projectile and a 31g (478 grain) charge which gave it a muzzle velocity of around 1000 metres (3280ft) per second.

It was a conventional design which performed adequately enough as a mechanism (the concept of the anti-tank rifle as an effective weapon against 'modern' armour on the open battlefield was probably invalidated even before it appeared, though it was still effective occasionally during fighting in built-up areas) and it was this action which he employed in a new infantry rifle, Simonov's most important design, the *Samozaryadny Karabin Simonova* or SKS, the first Soviet rifle to use the 'new' intermediate, reduced-power 7.62mm x 39 round which was copied from the original devised in Germany by Geco.

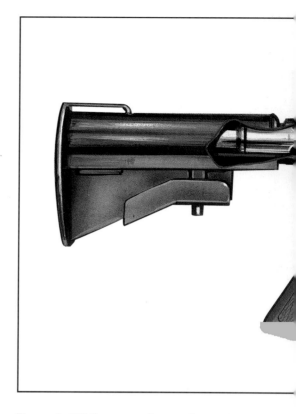

■LEFT: The current M16 – the -A2 version – is normally equipped with a lightweight M203 launcher for 40mm grenades, making it ideal for house-to-house combat situations.

This cartridge was known in the Soviet Union as the M1943, though there is no real reason to think that it was developed in that year. In any event, World War II was over before the SKS appeared, and it was to have a relatively short life as a front-line weapon with the Red Army despite being simple, sturdy, and reliable for the reason that a much better rifle, the Kalashnikov (see below), the most popular weapon ever seen, was to be produced hard on its heels.

The action of the SKA was similar to that of the Tokarev. The propellant gases behind the projectile escaped through the port in the barrel to impinge upon the piston in its superimposed cylinder. The piston acted upon a tappet which lay above the chamber, which transferred the momentum to the bolt carrier and compressed a spring which immediately returned tappet and piston to the ready position. The bolt carrier had eight millimetres (five-sixteenths of an inch) of free travel, during which the gas pressure in the chamber dropped to a safe level, before it lifted the rear end of the bolt out of locking slots in the floor of the receiver, whereupon bolt and carrier continued on together, cocking the hammer and compressing the return spring while extracting the spent case, which was thrown clear to the right on encountering the ejector in the receiver floor. As soon as the pressure in the spring overcame the momentum of the bolt assembly it reversed direction. If there was a cartridge remaining in the magazine it stripped it out, the extractor located itself in the cannelure and it was chambered, ready to fire, otherwise the bolt was held back so that the receiver was open, the guides in the bolt face positioned to accept a fresh charger loaded with 10 rounds, which were stripped out and down into the magazine. A light backwards pressure on the cocking handle was sufficient to release the bolt to chamber the first round after the empty charger was removed. The magazine could be topped up with single rounds, but in order to accomplish that, the cocking handle had to be held back manually. The safety catch was located behind the trigger guard, and when engaged, by pressing it forwards and upwards, it both blocked the trigger and obstructed the trigger finger. The floor plate of the magazine could be swung open for cleaning and to unload.

The SKS was manufactured all over the Communist bloc, in the People's Republic of China and in North Korea as well as in the Warsaw Pact countries, in its millions. It has been said that it was perhaps a little overweight for the reduced-power round it fired, though in fact it weighed just just under four kilograms (eight and a half pounds) unloaded, half a kilogram less than the shorter AK rifle which replaced it, in its original form; it looks heavier, perhaps, thanks to its 'old-fashioned' wooden furniture. Despite being chambered for the reduced-power round, which enabled a hand-held rifle to deliver automatic fire reasonably accurately, the SKS was never given a selective-fire capability.

THE KALASHNIKOV

The successor to the SKS was destined to become the most widely distributed rifle ever, the *Avtomat Kalashnikova*, more commonly known by its initials, AK, or simply by its designer's name. Mikhail Kalashnikov, born in Siberia in 1920, left school at 17 and became a railway clerk. Two years later, called up for military service, he was posted to a driving and vehicle maintenance school. By 1941, when Germany invaded, he was a senior sergeant in command of a tank himself, and was badly wounded that autumn at Byransk. While a convalescent he designed a sub-machine gun and a machine carbine, neither of which were accepted, but then, in 1947, he came up with the assault rifle which bears his name, which was adopted in 1950 or 1951. In 1959 he revised the design to make manufacture easier, and the result became known as the AKM (for *Modernizirovanni* – 'Modernised') and later produced the folding-stock version, the AKM-*Skladyvayushchimsya*.

The AK series rifles are above all robust and virtually soldier-proof – a very important attribute since many of the men who were to carry it were technically illiterate, to say the least. The action is simple: gas is drawn off the barrel near the muzzle into the superimposed cylinder and propels the piston and bolt carrier – the two are integral – through a short stroke, eight and a half millimetres (five-sixteenths of an inch), during which time the gas pressure in the chamber drops to a safe level (excess gas passing into the cylinder is vented off at this point through a series of small holes drilled in the wall; there is no gas regulator). A slot in the bolt carrier engages a stud on the bolt, and the rearwards motion is translated into a rotation through 35 degrees, releasing the locking lugs. There is no primary extraction during rotation and unlocking, but instead an over-size extractor claw is fitted in the bolt head (and the interior of the chamber is fluted). The bolt, carrier,

Colt XM177E2 Commando

Calibre: 5.56mm x 45 (.223in)
Weight: 2.4kg (5lb 5oz)
Length (stock extended): 760mm
(30in)
Barrel length: 365mm (14.4in)
Effective range: 400m (1350ft)
Configuration: 20- or 30-round

detachable box magazine,
gas-actuated self-loading action,
automatic option
Cyclical rate of fire: 800rpm
Muzzle velocity: 830mps (2720fps)
Country of origin: United States

and piston are now free to continue on their way, extracting the spent case (which is thrown out of the port on the right hand side of the receiver when it passes over the ejector built into the guide rail), cocking the hammer, and compressing the return spring. The bolt is brought to a halt by its impact with the rear of the receiver. Re-locking is accomplished in the last eight and a half millimetres (five-sixteenths of an inch) of the bolt carrier's travel by a simple reversal of the unlocking process, and the bolt carrier and piston then continue for some five millimetres (three-sixteenths of an inch) to eliminate any chance of partially releasing the bolt should the carrier rebound on hitting the stop. The cocking handle forms part of the bolt carrier, and reciprocates with it. There is no hold-open device to indicate that the magazine is empty (which is held to be the AK's most serious shortcoming). The 30-round curved magazine cannot be re-charged on the weapon, but must be removed. The AK is a selective-fire weapon, single-shot or automatic fire being selected by a long change lever mounted on the right hand side of the receiver, behind the ejector port and directly above the trigger guard, which also acts as the safety catch, blocking the trigger and physically preventing the bolt face from coming back past the head of the top cartridge in the magazine (the design of the change lever has also been heavily criticised). The trigger

mechanism is based on that which Garand designed for the M1 Rifle, but the hammer has two working surfaces on the bent and there are two hook-shaped opposed sears on the trigger itself; the change lever disengages the rearmost sear when set to automatic, but otherwise it engages the hammer after a round has been fired, and will not release it until the trigger has been released. The AKM is fitted with a cyclic rate of fire reducer, though it is complicated in design and only very marginally effective, relying on inertia during the cycle.

Due to its having a barrel only 415mm (16in) long and a short sight base, there are good theoretical reasons why the AK shouldn't be a particularly accurate rifle, but in practice adequate single-shot groups can be obtained by average marksmen out to about 300 metres (985ft); over that, performance starts to fall off drastically, but on the modern battlefield that seldom matters. Thanks to the characteristics of the M43 round, effective automatic fire is possible out to that same distance, and a slight tendency for the muzzle to climb and veer off to the right was largely corrected on the 'modernised' version, which has a small compensator – hardly more than an angled cut-off – on the muzzle. Some versions of the AK and AKM are permanently fitted with grenade launchers; some have fixed, folding bayonets; some (particularly AKM-Ss) have still shorter barrels and forward

pistol grips; some have wooden furniture and some have plastic – others both.

The differences between the AK and the AKM are substantial but not immediately obvious. The forged and machined receiver of the former was replaced by a one millimetre-thick steel pressing, formed into a U-shape and rivetted to inserts which comprise the locking recess, the barrel bearing and the front and rear blocks. This meant a considerable saving in weight – from just over four kilogrammes (nine and a half pounds) to slightly over three kilograms (just under seven pounds) – could be achieved, and the folding-stock version is somewhat lighter again. The rotating-bolt action which Kalashnikov designed also found its way into a light machine gun, the *Ruchnoy Pulemyot Kalashnikova* or RPK, which conveniently uses the same magazine as the rifle, and into the rather different belt-fed PK, which was chambered for the old, long 7.62mm x 54R M1891 round.

THE CZECH ALTERNATIVE

The only Warsaw Pact nation not to adopt the AK as its standard service rifle was Czechoslovakia, where a Brno-developed selective-fire SLR known as the Samopal vz58 was adopted instead. Though outwardly very similar to the Soviet design in its 'modernised' form, the vz58 is actually quite different, utilising a tilting bolt and a trigger mechanism which is both simpler and smoother. The

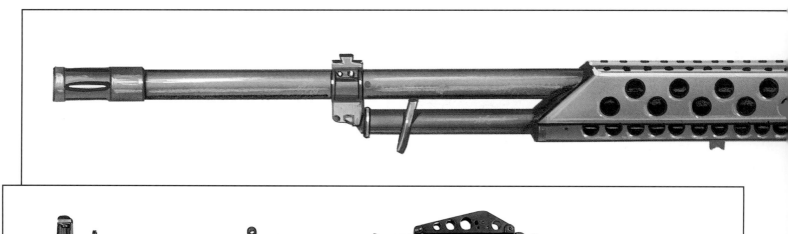

Beretta AR-70/90

Calibre: 5.56mm x 45 (.223in)
Weight: 4.2kg (9lb 4oz)
Length: 1000mm (39.35in)
Barrel length: 450mm (17.8in)
Effective range: 500m (1650ft)
Configuration: 20- or 30-round
  detachable box magazine,
  gas-actuated self-loading action,
  automatic option
Cyclical rate of fire: 650rpm
Muzzle velocity: 950mps (3116fps)
Country of origin: Italy

vz58 was used by the Czech Army in 7.62mm x 45 calibre, but was also manufactured in 7.62mm x 39 calibre for export. It was produced with a folding metal butt-stock and with wooden (later, compressed woodchip impregnated with plastic) furniture, but that latter feature

was introduced in the interests of saving weight, not money; the vz58 was well made and well finished.

IMPROVED IN FINLAND

Finland, which was never quite sure whether it was a Soviet client-state or

not, adopted the AK in the 1950s, and later began producing an improved version as the *Ryannakkokivaari Malli* ('Assault Rifle') 62, usually known outside its country of origin as the Valmet, after the company which manufactured it, which looked rather

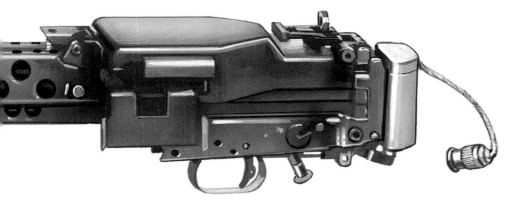

Stoner 63

Calibre: 5.56mm x 45 (.223in)
Weight: 5.4kg (11lb 14oz)
Length: 1022mm (40.23in)
Barrel length: 508mm (20in)
Effective range: 800m (2624ft)
Configuration: magazine or belt
Muzzle velocity: 1000mps
  (3280fps)
Country of origin: United States

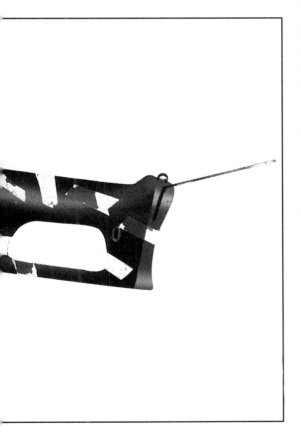

■**LEFT: The Stoner M63 weapons system – it encompasses everything from an SMG to a general-purpose machine gun; this is the basic rifle version – was a brave attempt to introduce a standardised, modular approach to the arming of infantry and support troops.**

different thanks to an extensive re-design of the furniture and the introduction of a tubular steel butt-stock with a simple crossbar rivetted on, but which was almost identical to the original under the skin. More recently the lightweight Valmet M76 and M90 have been introduced, in both 7.62mm Soviet and 5.56mm NATO chamberings.

REPLACING THE M1

As early as 1944, when US troops were preparing to land in France, doubts as to the effectiveness of the M1 Garand were already being expressed. They were centred on the rifle's weight, its limited ammunition capacity, and its lack of a selective-fire capability; it resulted, after the war was over, in a number of design studies for a replacement, the first of which, designated the T20, was a Garand with a 20-round magazine and capable of automatic fire. The next essay was a tilting-block design designated the T25, which was chambered for a new round, the T65 (which was really nothing more than an M2 .30in-06 with its case shortened by 12.2mm (half an inch); it was to be adopted, after considerable pressure was applied by Washington, as the standard NATO round, its calibre now expressed in metric units as 7.62mm x 51), developed at Springfield.

It was tested against the British EM2 and the Belgian FN FAL, both of which were chambered for a 7mm (.27in) cartridge, and both of which will be considered in due course, and all three were rejected. The next stage was the T47 (an improved T25), and the T44 (an improved T20 which was also chambered for the T65 round). Meanwhile, FN produced some FALs for testing which were also chambered for the T65 round, and this was designated the T48. Harrington & Richardson formed a partnership with FN to manufacture the T48, and were responsible for further developments locally. During winter firing trials in 1953-54 the T48 developed

problems, and though they were cured before the re-run the following winter, they were enough to sway the opinion of the US Army's Ordnance Department. A rifle in 7.62mm NATO chambering developed by Eugene Stoner of Armalite, the AR-10, was rejected too, in 1956 (though there was much more to come from that quarter, as we shall see in due course).

THE M14

On 1 May 1957 the US Secretary of the Army announced that the T44 rifle would be adopted for the US military in two versions, as the Rifle, Calibre .30in M14 and M15, the former with a lightweight barrel and no selective-fire capability, the latter with both. The M15 project was dropped the following year, and the light-barrelled rifle was instead given a selective-fire capability.

In essence, the M14 rifle is little more than an updated, slimmed-down M1, around half a kilogram (one pound) lighter but with the same rotating bolt design which John Garand had perfected 30 years earlier. The men armed with it were trained to use it in single-shot mode in all but the most pressing circumstances, since it was too light to produce accurate sustained fire with its full-power ammunition, even with a muzzle compensator, and its barrel tended to overheat dramatically, though a light bipod was supplied to turn it into a squad support weapon, and a variant, the M14A1, was produced (in small numbers) with pistol grips front and rear. A folding-stock version also appeared, in even smaller numbers. A version for snipers was produced by the sensible but simple expedient of matching particularly

131

ABOVE: Soviet naval infantry parade proudly through the streets of Moscow before the collapse of the Soviet Union, bearing their Kalashnikov AKM rifles across their chests.

accurate barrels to the best actions and fitting them with Redwood telescopic sights. After the M14 was discontinued, this very accurate specialist weapon was re-designated the M21 and stayed in use well into the 1980s. Production of the M14 ceased in 1964, by which time around 1,200,000 had been made.

REPLACING THE LEE-ENFIELD

The British Army soldiered on with its bolt-action Lee-Enfields until the 1950s, the only major development during the course of World War II being the introduction of a lightened (by almost 900 grammes/two pounds) version of the Rifle, Number 4 with its barrel drastically shortened (by 162mm/six inches to 478mm/18.7in) and its fore-stock and handguards cut away so that it resembled a sporting rifle more than a military type. It was fitted with a heavy rubber butt-pad in an (unsuccessful) attempt to compensate for the increased recoil from the shortened barrel, though the same modification also caused a serious loss of accuracy, for which there was no solution. The Rifle, Number 5 was

developed in 1944 for operations in Southeast Asia and the Pacific, and became known (though never officially) as the Jungle Carbine. It was not widely issued (slightly more than 250,000 were produced, in all), and it was not sorely missed when it was withdrawn from service. Many found their way onto the civilian market in the United States after they had been declared surplus to requirements in the 1950s, and sold for US$29.95 or less, though the price later rose dramatically as the rifle became scarcer and a collectors' market developed; the asking price in France, for example, at the time of writing was FFr4000 – over £400 Sterling/US$650. By way of contrast, the asking price for the much more common but mechanically identical Rifle, Number 4 was FFr1500.

THE FN FAL

The Lee-Enfield was finally replaced in British and Commonwealth service by a version of Fabrique National's *Fusil Automatique Lèger* or FAL, as rejected by the US Army. This was developed from a pre-war design which appeared eventually as the *Fusil Automatique Modèle* 1949, often known as the SAFN (*Saive Automatique*, FN) or ABL (*Arme Belge Lègère*). It used a tilting block, locked into a recess in the receiver floor and released by camming lugs in the

receiver sides, which was very similar to the system developed for the zv26 LMG, which metamorphosed into the British Bren gun, and which Tokarev then used for his SVT40. Designed by Dieudonnè Saive, it was first manufactured at Enfield (Saive fled to the UK at the time of the German invasion of his homeland, in May 1940) as the SLEM (Self-Loading Experimental Model) in 1946. It was eventually produced in a variety of different chamberings, and sold widely to export customers in the early 1950s even though it was fairly expensive thanks to the high standard to which it was manufactured.

The first prototypes of the SAFN's successor were demonstrated in February 1948, chambered for the German 7.92mm *kurz* round, and appeared in a modified form in 1950, chambered for the lightweight, lower-powered 7mm (.27in) round which the British were trying to introduce, for which the experimental EM1 and EM2 rifles were also chambered. (These rifles, which were among the first modern bullpups, and as such were to be very influential, we shall examine in due course, for they sit rather more comfortably with the next generation of military rifles. A bullpup version of the FN FAL was produced, too, but didn't get past prototype form.) The rifle used the simple Saive action with a removable 20-round box magazine and had a full pistol grip and a straight-through butt-stock (either in wood, or a folding version in tubular metal) reminiscent of the German FG42. It had one novel feature – a carrying handle located at the point of balance, which folded down to lie alongside the right hand side of the magazine just below the receiver when not in use. More important perhaps was its adjustable gas regulator, by means of which it was possible to compensate for a build-up of deposits in the gas cylinder by increasing the amount of gas fed to it.

The FN FAL's operation was straightforward. Gas was fed from the barrel via the regulator to the gas cylinder, where it drove the light, spring-loaded piston back to strike the top of the front face of the bolt carrier. The carrier, which almost surrounded the bolt in an extended, inverted U, travelled freely for around eight millimetres (five-sixteenths of an inch) – during which time the pressure in the chamber dropped – before its unlocking cam lifted the rear of the bolt out of the locking recess in the receiver floor. The bolt and carrier were then free to travel back together against the resistance of the recoil spring which ran the length of the butt-stock, and the action cycled in the normal way, re-locking occurring when the locking cam surface on the bolt carrier forced the rear of the bolt back down into the recess and held it there. Manual cocking was by means of a handle on the left hand side.

In its original form, the FAL was a selective-fire weapon, the change lever-cum-safety catch located on the left hand side, just to the rear of the trigger. When adopted by the British Army as the L1A1 Self-Loading Rifle, the capability for automatic fire was deleted; it was of limited value with full-power ammunition, the rifle being too light to hold on target, even when a bipod and an extended heavy barrel were fitted. Some other users in NATO and elsewhere followed that example, but most retained the selective-fire capability. At just under four and a half kilograms (nine and a half pounds) empty (and five kilograms/over 11lb with a full magazine) it was no lightweight (though the introduction of plastic furniture went some way towards correcting that shortcoming), and the 7.62mm NATO round for which it was chambered was already reckoned to be over-powerful for normal use in a rifle of this type.

Nonetheless, the FN FAL was to be very widely adopted; it was manufactured in eight countries as well as in Belgium, and chosen as their standard service rifle by around 30, though it has since been superseded in virtually all but the very poorest of them.

In 1966, Ernest Vivier, who had worked alongside Saive on the original design, was responsible for transforming the FAL into the *Carabine Automatique Léger*, using a rotating bolt system with interrupted thread locking, making more extensive use of plastic and with a 470mm (18.5in) barrel in place of the 533mm- (21in) long tube fitted to the heavier weapon. Most significantly, the CAL was chambered for the 5.56mm (.223in) round which FN developed from an original design by Remington, and which was to become the new de facto standard. We shall look more closely at that round, and the other rifles chambered for it, in due course. As originally introduced, the CAL had a novel and interesting addition to its selective-fire capability: the change lever had a fourth position, 'burst', in which three rounds would be fired every time the trigger was pressed. This same, quite desirable, feature was also incorporated in other assault rifles, of course, and has since become more common.

THE MAS 44/49

While the FN FAL, the Heckler & Koch G3 and the M14 were the most common full-power self-loading rifles, they were not the only ones developed and issued in the decade following the end of World War II. The first, in fact, came from France, and was developed at Saint Etienne, work on it having started as soon as the country was liberated from German control in 1944. A small number of prototype self-loading rifles were

actually manufactured before the war (as the MAS38-39) but were never produced in any quantity, but a revised version, the MAS44, was put into production before the end of the war and some were issued to the French troops who took part in the last battles in Germany and to those who were rushed to Indo-China in 1945-46 in what was eventually to prove a futile attempt to regain control there.

The most significant feature of the MAS44 and its more widely distributed successor, the MAS49, was its lack of a gas piston. Instead, the propellant gas which was vented into a narrow, tubular chamber set above the barrel (from about mid-way down it in the early rifle; from rather closer to the breech in the later) and impinged directly onto the bolt carrier of an action which was otherwise very similar to that of the Tokarev and the Anglo-Belgian SLEM, with a tilting block. This method was greeted with considerable scepticism by critics who believed that the inevitable build-up of solid deposits within the action itself would rapidly lead to frequent stoppages, and it is true that weapons with such an action do require frequent inspection, but when the same method was adopted for other self-loaders (most notably the AR-15/M16) the level of criticism died down.

Somewhat surprisingly, given the French disposition for things home-grown, the 7.5mm x 54 M1929 round for which the MAS36 had been developed was almost set aside for the MAS49 in favour of the American M2 .30in-06 round, many millions of which were available for free at the time of its

■BELOW: **The Russian AK103 rifle uses the action of the AK74M, but is chambered for the 'old' 7.62mm x 39 M1943 round. A shorter barrelled version (the AK104) is also available.**

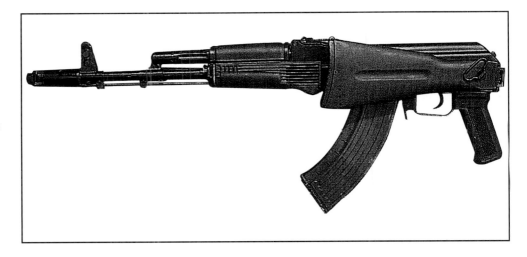

introduction, and after 1953, when the 7.62mm x 51 NATO round became the standard, some were modified to accept that. In the end tradition prevailed, however, and France remained out of step with her allies. The MAS44/49 (there was really very little difference between the two) were distinctly old-fashioned in appearance, with integral 10-round box magazines and full wooden furniture. The most important additions to the later model were dovetails to fit a telescopic sight and an integral grenade launcher. Unusually, there was no provision for a bayonet to be fitted, though some few were modified, probably locally, to accept the short spike bayonet from the MAS36. Despite some use of aluminium, the MAS49 was a heavy weapon at over 450g (10lb) unloaded, though examples with folding aluminium stocks were also produced. It was with the MAS49 that the majority of French troops fought the two disastrous wars which brought down the curtain on their nation's empire, in Indo-China and Algeria, and with some modification (notably a shortening of the fore-stock, the addition of a bayonet fitting, and the incorporation of a muzzle brake into a launcher re-configured to accept American grenades) it stayed in front-line service as the MAS49/56 until the late 1970s/early 1980s, when it was progressively replaced by the bullpup FA MAS.

SWEDEN'S AG42

Another World War II-vintage self-loading rifle to dispense with a gas piston was developed by Eklund and Ljungmann at the Swedish Government's firearms factory as the *Halvautomatiskt Gevär* 42 or AG42, in 6.5mm x 55 calibre, though this time the bolt rotated, guided by camming tracks in the carrier. The main point of interest in the Swedish rifle was perhaps that it was issued to troops less than a year after the first drawings were laid down – a remarkable feat, but one which produced a variety of deficiencies in the finished weapon, most of which were cleared up when it was re-launched as the AG42B in 1953. It was also manufactured in Egypt for its army – in the days before it became a client-state of the Soviet Union – in 7.92mm 'Mauser' calibre, as the Hakkim, and in Denmark by Madsen, who modified the gas tube so that it was coiled around the barrel – this prevented fouling deposits from forming so quickly within the receiver, but was next to impossible to

clean itself; the Danish Army declined to adopt it and took Heckler & Koch's G3 instead.

TOWARDS A SMALLER BULLET

Hardly had NATO established the 7.62mm x 51 cartridge as its standard for infantry assault and light support weapons in 1953 than the Americans, who had bullied their allies into accepting it despite its various shortcomings, simply because they were emotionally attached to the .30in-06 which it resembled so closely, issued a specification for an altogether lighter assault rifle which, in the natural way of things, would have to be chambered for a much smaller, lighter round.

Thanks largely to one man, Eugene Stoner, the round in question turned out to be the 5.56mm x 45. Remington had previously sold it commercially as the .222in, and it combined a projectile weighing just 3.56g (55 grain) with a 1.55g (24 grain) charge in a

Kalashnikov AKS74

Calibre: 5.45mm x 39 (.214in)
Weight: 3.0kg (6lb 10oz)
Length (stock extended): 940mm (37in)
Barrel length: 415mm (16.35in)
Effective range: 300m (1000ft)
Configuration: 30-round detachable box magazine,
  gas-actuated self-loading action, automatic option
Cyclical rate of fire: 600rpm
Muzzle velocity: 900mps (2950fps)
Country of origin: Soviet Union

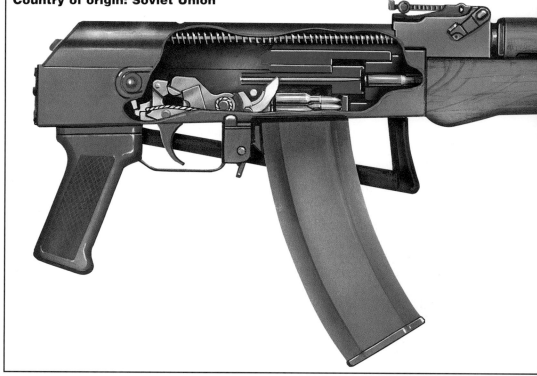

■RIGHT: The 5.45mm-calibre Kalashnikov was also produced with a much-shortened barrel as the AKS74U. Note the rather old-fashioned conical flash hider on the muzzle.

proportionally smaller cartridge case than that of the 9.7g (150 grain) and 3.0g (47 grain) M59 ball round (the US NATO 7.62mm/.30in standard; other NATO countries' ammunition varied slightly – the British L2A2 ball round, for example, was marginally lighter, with a lighter charge), and was thus well under half its weight. In the form in which it was adopted it had what one expert has called 'a fortuitous combination of bullet mass and stability, which resulted in a projectile which tumbled rapidly when it struck its target and delivered up its energy in massive fashion rather than. . . passing through the target with minimal energy transfer'.

Stoner was not alone in thinking that 5.56mm (.223in) was an adequate calibre

■LEFT: Very similar in overall appearance and design to the original AK47, the AK74M is really little more than an updated version re-chambered and re-barrelled for the new round.

when it was the Belgian version which was adopted.

The decision to adopt the new miniature round was to have far-reaching consequences, and force a programme of re-equipment which was every bit as comprehensive as that of the 1880s following the invention of smokeless powder. Within 10 years, all the world's major armies (and not a few of the minor ones, too) which had not already adopted new weapons in the new calibre were to do so, expending hundreds of millions of dollars in the process. Not surprisingly, the Soviet Union, as it still was then, was also quick to adopt a sub-6mm short round – in this case a 5.45mm x 39 cartridge – but did so without a major re-design of the weapon which was to fire it.

STONER AND ARMALITE

The Armalite Corporation was formed in the late 1940s, and was taken over by aircraft manufacturer Fairchild in 1954, at which point a retired US Marine named Eugene Stoner was appointed chief engineer. That same year, the group was asked to design a 'survival' rifle (a light weapon, intended chiefly to kill small game for the pot rather than for combat purposes) for the US Air Force to replace the existing Harrington & Richardson-designed M6, an all-steel folding combination gun with a rifled .22in (5.56mm) barrel above a smoothbore .410in (10.5mm) barrel. They came up with a bolt-action design chambered for the .22in Hornet cartridge, known as the AR-5 or MA1; just 762mm (30in) long and weighing one and a quarter kilograms (two and three-quarter pounds), it was a 'take-down' rifle which was easily separated, without tools, into butt, receiver, magazine, and barrel, the latter three (which were largely made of aluminium) fitting inside the former, which was a hollow moulding made of glassfibre-reinforced plastic. The rifle floated in either configuration. Though the MA1 was entirely effective, the USAF declined to adopt it, deciding that it had too many of the existing model in its inventory (though it was to be adopted for clandestine operations, firing sub-sonic ammunition and equipped with a

for an assault rifle; designers Ernest Vervier and Maurice Bourlet at Herstal-lez-Liège went to work on a miniature-calibre rifle, a version of the FN FAL known as the CAL (see above), which was never a startling commercial success but which did provide considerable data on the behaviour of a new 5.56mm round which the Belgians were promoting as an alternative to the American round which Stoner had adopted.

Externally, the SS 109, as the Belgian variant of the new round came to be known, was identical with the American, but its ballistic characteristics were quite different; the American M193 was optimised for performance at up to 400m (1320ft) – though even by that point, the

drop in the bullet's trajectory was right at the edge of the acceptable envelope, at around 76cm (30in) – while the SS 109 was considerably better at longer ranges. At that time (the mid-1970s), NATO had yet to make up its mind about an ammunition standard to supersede the 7.62mm round: Britain was pushing for a 4.85mm (.19in) round; Germany for one of 4.6mm (.18in) calibre (or a revolutionary caseless 4.75mm/.187in round), while France (which was no longer a full member of NATO, but which still had a very loud voice within its councils) and Belgium, as well as the USA, urged a 5.56mm (.223in) round of some description. The affair was finally settled in a protracted trial in 1978-79

silencer, by a variety of special forces). An essentially similar design, but this time in .22in Long Rifle (rim-fire) calibre and with a blow-back action, known as the AR-7 'Explorer', was produced for the civilian market, but, with a US$49.95 price tag, enjoyed little success.

Prior to joining Armalite, Stoner had designed a self-loading rifle with a conventional cylinder and piston, utilising a Mauser-type revolving bolt. Like the diminutive survival rifles, it had a glassfibre butt-stock and was made largely of aluminium; it never went beyond the prototype stage, being essentially a design exercise, but it exemplified Stoner's thinking; it became known as the AR-3, and metamorphosed into the AR-11, which was designed as a testbed for the high-velocity .222in Remington cartridge which itself turned into the 5.56mm M109.

THE STONER SYSTEM

At roughly the same time as the AR-3 prototypes were being produced, in 1952, Stoner had also started work on a new military self-loader which eventually became known as the AR-10. It dispensed with the gas cylinder and piston and instead, like Saive's SLEM, the AG42, and the MAS44/49, allowed the propellant gas to act directly on the bolt carrier. Its most important component was the multi-lug front-locking rotating bolt which was subsequently used in the AR-15 rifle as well as in semi-automatic shotguns and in the Model 63 multi-purpose weapon which Eugene Stoner was to develop after he parted company with Armalite (and in Armalite's later AR-18 and a variety of later derivative designs, including the British and Austrian bullpups, see below); it was certainly his most important contribution to the design of modern firearms, though it was not entirely original – its design owes much to the work, two decades earlier, of Melvin Johnson.

The Stoner system in its original form worked by channelling gas from the barrel vent two-thirds of the way between breech and muzzle through a stainless steel tube above the barrel into a space within the cylindrical shell of the bolt carrier, forcing it back. After some three millimetres of free travel, during which the gas pressure in the chamber fell to a safe level, a camming slot in the internal wall of the carrier located with a pin on the bolt, causing it to rotate clockwise through 22.5 degrees around its axis, so

that the seven locking lugs on the bolt head were aligned with the seven grooves cut in the barrel extension (there was a slot which housed the extractor where the eighth lug would have been). The carrier then drew the bolt to the rear to start the operating cycle. There was no primary extraction, and re-locking was a mirror-image of the unlocking process, assisted by a coiled spring housed in the butt. The trigger and hammer and the safety/selector mechanism Stoner used were virtually identical to that employed in the M14.

Stoner originally chambered the rifle which became the AR-10 for the M2 .30in-06 round, and only in 1955 was it modified to accept the 7.62mm NATO round. In the course of the development programme he tried several innovations which failed, one of them being a revolutionary barrel which combined an aluminium outer tube with a titanium liner. After the AR-10 was rejected as a replacement for the M1, in 1956, Armalite cast around for other customers, and the following year reached an agreement with the Dutch state arsenal, Artillerie-Inrichtingen, to produce it. Tooling up took far too long, largely because like the US Army the Dutch declined to adopt the rifle (they chose the FN FAL instead), and by the time it was possible to manufacture the AR-10, most potential customers had gone elsewhere; a few were sold to Burma, Nicaragua, Portugal, and the Sudan – none of them first-line military powers – and in 1958, after only 5000 AR-10s had been made, the agreement with the Dutch company was allowed to lapse. By this time the 5.56mm-calibre AR-15 was also ready to go into production, and in January 1959 Colt's Patent Firearms Company obtained a licence to manufacture both rifles, which turned out to be possibly the soundest decision the company had made since it secured the rights to produce John Moses Browning's self-loading pistols in the USA, in the early years of the century. It soon became obvious that the AR-10 had missed its market, and it was never put into production, Colt's choosing to concentrate on the lighter weapon instead.

THE AR-15/M16 RIFLE

Much of the physical form of the new rifle – its straight-through profile, which carried the axis of the barrel directly to the butt, and its combined rear sight/carrying handle in particular – was

copied directly across from the AR-10, as of course were the direct gas action, the multi-lug rotating bolt and the trigger and safety mechanisms. The AR-15 was simply scaled down from the earlier weapon to meet the requirements issued by the US Army's Infantry Board for a rifle which was not to exceed two and three-quarter kilograms (six pounds; in fact the AR-15 never achieved this, and an early M16 with a loaded 20-round magazine and a sling actually weighed over three and a half kilograms/eight pounds) when loaded, with a selective fire capability and similar ballistic characteristics to the M1 rifle out to 450m (1500ft). On the face of it, this seemed a tall order, but in fact the only serious problem facing Stoner and his team was the non-availability of suitable ammunition.

A NEW PROJECTILE

As we have seen, the choice finally fell on the .222in Remington round with a 3.56g (55 grain) bullet, which achieved a muzzle velocity of 920 metres (3020ft) per second but which dropped 840mm (33in) in 400m (1310ft) and only developed half the kinetic energy of the M2 .30in-06 round, which dropped 595mm (23.5in) over the same distance. Armalite turned to the Sierra Bullet Co. to develop a new projectile, and the result was a boat-tailed design which not only had more efficient aerodynamics but also displayed the tendency to tumble on impact described above, negating the criticism of its poor hitting power. The cartridge case was lengthened slightly to allow a greater propellant charge, which upped the muzzle velocity to 990 metres (3250ft) per second, and the redefined round became the .222in Special (and in military circles the M193) until Remington launched a similar round as the .222in Magnum, whereupon it became the .223in Remington. It is suggested that it would have been more sensible for Armalite to have set out to develop a new round entirely, in something like .26in (6.6mm) calibre, with a projectile of between 5.2-5.8g (80-90 grain) instead of adopting the .222in round that Stoner had previously experimented with. A glance at the characteristics of a cartridge which falls within those parameters is instructive – the .257in Winchester Magnum, for example, with a 5.64g (87 grain) bullet produced a muzzle velocity of 1166 metres (3826ft) per second, almost

■RIGHT: Men of the French Foreign Legion's 2e *Regiment Étranger Parachutist* on ceremonial parade with their 5.56mm FA MAS bullpup rifles at their home base near Calvi in Corsica.

identical kinetic energy to the .30in-06 round, and dropped less than 200mm (eight inches) at 400m (1312ft). The British, who had been 'dissuaded' (see below) from adopting a 7mm (.27in) calibre, later described the 6.25mm (.246in) round developed at Enfield as being an ideal compromise, with the hitting power of a 7.62mm NATO round and the recoil of a 5.56mm M193 round.

SUCCESS AND MODIFICATIONS

After comprehensive testing in a variety of different locations and some subsequent modification, the AR-15 was adopted by the US Air Force in 1961, and the US Army and US Marine Corps, after a great deal of grumbling and disagreement, followed suit two years later, by which time Colt's had already achieved some success in selling into export markets, particularly in Southeast Asia (it was later to go into production under licence in both the Philippines and Singapore; its low weight and small size made it popular with infantrymen in the region, who tend to be somewhat smaller in stature than those in the West). By 1966, the US Government had bought a total of 413,500, and then acquired a sub-licence to manufacture it from Colt's for US$4,500,000, contracting further production to Harrington & Richardson and General Motors. By the time 10 years had passed, total production had reached perhaps four million.

When it was first issued to troops in Vietnam they were told that the M16 was self-cleaning – a desirable state of affairs which has yet to be achieved – and, accordingly, most soldiers left it severely alone, which led in short order to jams and stoppages and at length to a full-blown Congressional Enquiry, where it was determined that it was necessary, after all, to clean the weapon, particularly since the propellant in the cartridges had been changed, apparently without any announcement having been made, from tubular IMR to a new compound formed into small balls. This increased the production of gas and in turn both stepped up the rate of fire and the rate of carbon deposition in and around the bolt carrier. When it cooled, solidified, and hardened, this carbon

formed a bond strong enough to prevent the bolt unlocking, and since it could not be freed manually, by pulling back on the cocking lever, this rendered the rifle useless. The remedy was three-fold: a cleaning kit was issued, along with instructions on how to use it; the chamber was chromium-plated; and the recoil buffer was modified to reduce the rate of fire.

The only other modifications made to the rifle in the early period were to tighten the rifling from the original one turn in 356mm (14in) to one turn in 305mm (12in) after it was shown that in sub-zero temperatures (when the air is much thicker, of course) the light bullet was not attaining enough rotational velocity to keep it stable (it was its marginal stability which gave it its tendency to tumble on impact, so any modification made in this area had to be very subtle, if that feature were not to be lost), and to fit a bolt closing device,

which allowed a dirty (or imperfect) round to be driven fully home into the chamber manually – a most unsatisfactory arrangement, in technical terms, but one which was greeted enthusiastically by the soldiery. The 30-round magazine was also standardised, and the rifles thus modified were known as M16A1s. In 1982, when the US military bowed to pressure from its NATO allies and adopted the Belgian SS109 round, with its longer, heavier projectile (23.45mm against 18.8mm, and four grammes against three and a half), it became necessary to re-configure the M16's barrel, and Colt's took that opportunity to improve the rifle in other ways, too. The new barrel, which was heavier and therefore stiffer and more accurate, was rifled with one twist in 178mm (seven inches), and was fitted with a new type of muzzle compensator/flash suppressor; in addition, the fore-grip was re-profiled, the

■ABOVE: A very different situation, but the men – and the rifles – remain the same. Legion parachutists disembark from a Puma helicopter, FA MAS rifles very much to the fore.

rear sight was improved, a deflector was fitted to the ejector slot (which was much appreciated by left-handers, who had previously been troubled by hot cases hitting them in the face) and the provision for fully-automatic fire was removed and replaced by a three-round burst capability. The improved rifle was first issued, as the M16A2, in small numbers in 1983, and large-scale replacement of the earlier version began in 1986.

THE M203

Like most designers of self-loading rifles, Stoner believed that weapon could supplant – or at least supplement – the light machine gun in the role of support weapon at the squad level, and he developed a heavy-barrelled version of the AR-10, fitted with a bipod, and then went on to produce a more basic conversion to belt-fed ammunition, at which point he developed a quick-change

barrel and a traversing tripod, too. He had no takers for his expedient LMG, nor for the 'carbine' version, with its shortened barrel, but that didn't stop him producing prototypes of the AR-15 in the two configurations, and here he had rather more success. Colt's put the short barrelled version into production – with a further refinement, a telescoping butt-stock – as the Commando, and saw it used extensively in Vietnam and after by US Special Forces, and the magazine- and belt-fed LMG was manufactured as the Colt Automatic Rifle (an obvious though unacknowledged homage to John Browning), but with poor results.

A rather simpler and more traditional approach to the problem of providing local fire support was to equip rifles to launch anti-personnel grenades, and many M16s were to be fitted with under-barrel launchers for 40mm (one and a half inch) grenades, as standardised for the M79 hand-held launcher, which resemble a much-enlarged pistol round. After many different units were tested, the M203 version was adopted – a simple tube which slid forward on a fixed rail to allow a round to be loaded and which had its own trigger located just ahead of the

M16's magazine housing. This wasn't the first time this type of rifle grenade had been deployed – the Italian Army used a similar system during World War II – but it did a lot to popularise it; the alternative – grenades which resembled spigot mortar rounds, which had no propellant charge, but which fitted over the muzzle of a rifle and were launched by means of a specially powerful blank round (or, more recently, in a development pioneered by FN, by a conventional bulleted round) – continued to be popular.

SYSTEM 63

Stoner was actually more committed to the multi-purpose/multi-role weapon than most designers, as his next offering was to show. System 63, as the family of weapons was originally known, was designed after Stoner left Armalite, and was produced by Cadillac Gage, which was better known for its light armoured vehicles. It comprised 15 assemblies in all, and could be made up in five forms: as a sub-machine gun, a carbine, an assault rifle, a light machine gun, and a sustained-fire general-purpose machine gun. They all shared a common receiver, and the variations were in the different barrels, the butt-stocks, the ammunition feed mechanisms, and the choice of box magazines or belts. Both the US Navy and the US Marine Corps put the M63 through comprehensive battle testing in Vietnam, and liked it, but no order was forthcoming.

THE LOW-COST OPTION

Armalite went through major changes in 1961; it was hived off from Fairchild to become a separate, independent company as Armalite Inc., and it lost its chief engineer, but it continued to develop self-loading rifles, and in 1964 launched the AR-18, intended for low-cost production and chambered for the commercial (and readily available) .223in Remington cartridge. The AR-18 took elements from practically all the earlier Armalite designs but was very different from the AR-10/AR-15 since it employed a gas cylinder-and-piston system – though by no means a conventional one (neither did it resemble the earlier Armalite SLRs physically; in fact, it looked at first glance very much more like the FN FAL). In the AR-18 the gas was vented from a port some two-thirds of the way down the 465mm (18.25in) barrel into a superimposed stainless steel cylinder in the form of a hollow spigot, over which fitted a slightly longer female piston. The spigot had three sealing rings at its rear end; when the piston had been driven back just 12.5mm (half an inch), four vents in it passed over the rings, and all the remaining gas passing that way escaped under the top of the fore-stock. The piston impacted with a two-part spring-loaded operating rod, which in turn imparted momentum to the bolt carrier, turning the Stoner-type bolt and initiating the cycle. The bolt carrier was located on two longitudinal rods which passed through its length; these guide rods also located the twin recoil springs.

The firing pin was fitted with a heavy retaining spring where that of the original AR-15 had been free-floating, to prevent accidental discharge should the rifle be dropped vertically on its butt while loaded. The mechanism has been compared with that of the World War II-vintage Gew43.

The outstanding feature, if one can call such a basic principle that, of the AR-18 was the way it was designed to be manufactured: from 28 simple parts manufactured on the sort of machine tools – lathes, milling machines, and the like – found in any decent workshop: 14 stampings, three machined castings, six mouldings and four more complex machined parts – the barrel, the barrel extension, the bolt carrier, and the extractor. The body/receiver was formed from a single stamping, wrapped into a box, and welded on the underside, the guide ribs for the bolt rotating pin being spot-welded along the left hand side; the two-part fore-stock was moulded in high-impact plastic (and had a stamped metal heatshield inside), as were the pistol grip halves and the (folding) butt-stock. Armalite estimated that a production run of only 50,000 units was enough to justify setting up a manufacturing plant, which is a very small number indeed of any manufactured item.

It was produced in Japan by the Howa Machinery Corp. from 1967, after the US military had tested it, liked it, and turned it down (on the grounds that while it was better than the M16, it wasn't so much better that the US Government should forego a large part of the US$4,500,000 it had invested in purchasing the right to produce the latter), and from the following year by Armalite itself in California; it was available in the standard military version, with a selective fire capability, as the AR-18S with a severely shortened barrel, designed to be used as a sub-

machine gun, and as the AR-180, with the trigger mechanism heavily modified to give single-shot fire only (it was so heavily modified simply so that it would be incapable of being converted to automatic), for use by police forces and as a 'sporting' arm. The AR-18 and its variants were also to be manufactured in the United Kingdom by Sterling Arms, one of a new breed of independent gunmakers set up, like Armalite, to carve out a share of what was to become, by the 1980s, a multi-billion dollar market for military small arms.

OTHER 5.56MM SLRS

As we noted earlier, most of the factories outside the Communist bloc producing self-loading rifles during the 1960s and 1970s adopted the new soon-to-be-standard 5.56mm (.223in) calibre. Some employed the action they had used in their first-generation weapons: Heckler & Koch produced the HK33, and used the roller-locking delayed-blow-back action from the G3; and in Spain CETME also continued to use the same action in its Model L and shortened Model LC. Others took elements from an earlier design and modified one or other of the components: FN devised a new bolt locking system for the CAL; while SIG went further, and produced the 530 with its composite action, which had a large-diameter gas cylinder and piston, the latter acting on a bar which retained the locking rollers in the recesses in the receiver. As soon as this bar was released, the residual pressure in the chamber forced the breech block back, whereupon the two pressures – from chamber and piston – carried the breech block to the rear and

■ **BELOW: The Heckler & Koch HK33 was the successor to the very successful G3. In 5.56mm x 45 calibre, and making extensive use of plastics, it was also considerably lighter.**

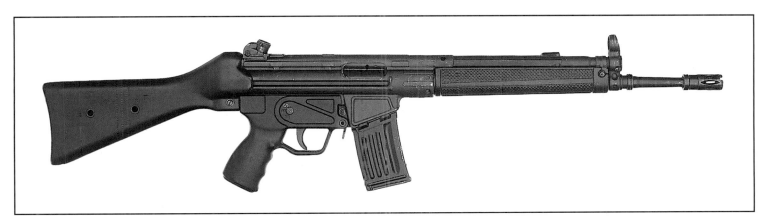

convinced of the merits of the roller-locking system. Beretta – which had been producing an updated version of the M1 Garand, which closely resembled the M14, as the 7.62mm BM59 – then developed a weapon of its own, the AR-70. The new rifle retained the simple two-lug rotating bolt locking system used in the M1 and the AK series, Beretta having rejected the Stoner multi-lug system on the grounds that to machine a bolt head and barrel extension with seven lugs and recesses sufficiently accurately so that each took an equal share of the load was practically impossible (and, equally, entirely unnecessary – an opinion shared by many; they perhaps missed the point that a multi-lug system cuts down the degree of rotation required to release it: compare the Mauser system – two lugs at 180 degrees and thus a 90 degree throw – with the Stoner system – lugs at 45 degrees and a 22.5 degree throw), and the tilting block, as used by the FN and others, as not guaranteeing symmetrical locking (the same fault which plagued the Mauser M/71, as we may recall).

The resulting rifle appeared in the early 1970s, and somewhat to Beretta's surprise was not immediately adopted by the Italian Army (though special forces units did take it up). The design was updated somewhat over the next decade, and its faults – for example, the bolt guides of the original had been pressed into the sheet-metal box which formed the receiver, and tended to distort; they were replaced by welded–on guides – were progressively eradicated.

One very worthwhile innovation was introduced, too: the barrel, which was retained by a hexagonal nut, instead of being screwed into the receiver, had a collar upon which that nut bore; this ensured that the chamber was located exactly, in relation to the bolt face, and removed the necessity to adjust the headspace (the distance between the bolt face and the head of the cartridge) when the barrel was changed. The AR-70/90, as the improved version was known, was adopted in 1990 in three versions: the standard rifle, with a fixed butt-stock and a 450mm (18in) barrel; a carbine, the SC-70/90, with a folding metal skeleton butt-

cycled the action in the normal way. The return spring was unusually placed – inside the piston – and acted against a backplate attached to the receiver; this arrangement meant that a variety of butt-stocks – or none at all – could be fitted.

The later SIG 540 – which was available in both 5.56mm and 7.62mm NATO chamberings – was a less unusual design, being piston-operated with a rotating bolt, while the Model 550, which was eventually to be adopted as the StG90 to be the Swiss Federal Army's standard service rifle, was an updated version making more extensive use of plastics to keep the weight down. It was manufactured only in 5.56mm calibre; a short-barrelled version, however, the SIG 551, was also available.

The new rifle offered all the refinements expected of a state-of-the-art combat weapon in the last years of the

twentieth century, including three-round burst capability and the ability to launch grenades using conventional ammunition instead of over-powered 'ballistite' rounds, which had to be loaded singly. The standard-model SIG 550 was equipped to hold three magazines, side by side, the changeover from one to the next being accomplished by a simple sideways push (this method was pioneered in a World War II-vintage sub-machine gun, the German MP40, and also featured in an independently-produced variant of the M16A1 designed for use as a light machine gun).

BERETTA'S ASSAULT RIFLES

While preparing the design which became the 530 in the mid-1960s, SIG had begun negotiating with Beretta with a view to producing a second-generation SLR jointly, but the project foundered when the Italian company would not be

■RIGHT: Like any combat arm, the FNC must be capable of working reliably in all sorts of conditions and in any sort of climate. Mud is a particularly tenacious enemy, of course.

stock; and the SCS-70/90, with the folding butt and a 320mm (12.5in) barrel.

THE FNC AND THE SAR 80

After failing to obtain significant orders for its first-generation miniature-calibre rifle, the CAL, FN later adopted a simplified system much like that Beretta used in the AR-70, with twin locking lugs in place of the interrupted thread system. which had proved costly to manufacture and none too reliable, and a system of regulating the gas supply which vented excess gas to the atmosphere in the same way that the AR-18 did, but rather more simply with a conventional piston which was driven past exhaust ports in the cylinder wall. The construction of the new rifle, known as the FNC, was simplified, too, and made more use of pressed steel, light alloys, and plastic. It was available with 450mm (18in) or 365mm (14in) barrels rifled to suit either the M193 or the SS109 round, and with either a fixed, plastic or a folding, tubular metal butt-stock; it was adopted by the Belgian and Swedish armies, and also by Indonesia, where it was manufactured under licence.

In neighbouring Singapore, Chartered Industries – one of the Asian companies which acquired a licence to manufacture the M16 – later collaborated with Sterling, which produced the AR-18 in the United Kingdom, but which had some design experience too, to devise another assault rifle to the same low-cost specification, and came up with the SAR 80, which utilised the AR-18's action virtually unchanged, as did the bullpup Enfield XE series, the last evolution of which the British Army was to adopt as the L85A1/SA80, and which is described in more detail below. Like the Beretta AR-70, the SAR 80 had an innovation which permitted the barrel to be replaced rapidly, without any need to check the headspacing; in this case it consisted of a key, rather than a collar, but was also retained by a locknut. A fore-stock dimensionally identical with that of the M16 was fitted, to allow the M203 grenade launcher to be added, and like virtually all 5.56mm-calibre assault rifles, the magazine housing was also compatible with that of the American

rifle. A modified version, the SR 88, was produced some years later, with all the gas fittings – cylinder, regulator, and piston – chromium plated, to reduce the build-up of fouling deposits. and with its lower receiver manufactured as an aluminium forging to save weight. The manufacturers wisely offered customers a choice of fixed or folding butts, both of them adjustable for length by means of spacer pieces, barrel lengths, selective-fire options (fully-automatic or three-round bursts), and a variety of sighting systems, the upper receiver cover being fitted with standard dovetails.

GUNS BEFORE FALAFELS

From the time of its creation in 1947, the modern state of Israel experienced considerable difficulties in obtaining reliable supplies of up-to-date weaponry, and this led inevitably to the creation of an indigenous arms industry. In terms of small arms, perhaps its best known product was the almost-ubiquitous Uzi sub-machine gun, the invention of Lieutenant-Colonel Uziel Gal, but equally effective, if not quite so popular outside its homeland, was the assault rifle designed later by Israel Galil. From the early 1950s, the Israel Defense Forces had been armed (at least in part) with the FN FAL (and, indeed, had employed the heavy-barrelled version as its squad support weapon) but the events of 1967, when they launched the pre-emptive Six Day War, convinced them that a lighter rifle was required. and they issued a

specification for a weapon chambered for the M193 5.56mm round. The M16A1, together with the Stoner M63, was considered along with the HK33 and two home-produced prototypes, one from Gal and one from newcomer Galil.

Galil, who was of Russian origin himself, had a considerable regard for Kalashnikov's rifle, but knew its weaknesses, too. When he set out to design a rifle to meet the Israelis' special needs, he copied its strengths and designed out its shortcomings as best he could, though in fact its primary fault – its ultimate inaccuracy – was an attribute of the reduced-power 'intermediate' 7.62mm x 39 round, and that was cured by substituting the 5.56mm round (Galil resisted the temptation to slim the weapon down; the result was a heavy rifle for its type, at four kilograms/over eight and a half pounds, unloaded, which was very stable as a result). Galil also tackled the defective design of the selector/safety lever, which the original manufacturers should probably have taken in hand themselves years before, substituting a small thumb-operated lever (on both sides of the receiver, so that it was accessible to both left- and right-handers) above the pistol grip in place of the long, awkward (and decidedly noisy) lever of the original, and added a carrying handle similar to that fitted to the FAL. The exterior styling was not at all like the Soviet assault rifle, but inside the Galil ARM was almost pure Kalashnikov. It

■RIGHT: Designers at the Royal Small Arms Factory at Enfield first produced a bullpup rifle in 1948, but it was nearly 40 years before such a weapon was adopted by the British Army.

was issued with a removable bipod (which also functioned as a wire cutter and a bottle opener!) and with 35- and 50-round magazines. It was adopted in 1973, and soon after the South African Defence Force, which had strong links to its Israeli counterpart at that time, began issuing an identical weapon as the R-4.

UPDATED KALASHNIKOVS

Meanwhile, the rifle which had been the basis for the Galil was also the subject of some modification to bring it more in line with contemporary tactical reality – which meant the adoption of a high-velocity, miniature calibre round.

The round in question was in 5.45mm (.214in) calibre in a cartridge case the same length – 39mm (one and a half inches) – as the old intermediate round, and comparable in performance with the M193, but apart from the necessary re-chambering and re-barrelling, the rifle which was to fire it was virtually unchanged from the AKM, save for the addition of a muzzle brake which reduced the recoil to almost nil (at the expense of deflecting the blast sideways, which was disconcerting, to say the least, to the firer's neighbours) and the adoption of plastic for the magazine body.

The AK74M can be distinguished immediately from the original AK by the presence of a deep groove in the butt-stock. It was also produced as the AKS74U with a folding skeleton butt, which saved a further kilogram and reduced the unloaded weight to under three kilograms (six pounds).

Like its predecessor, the AK74 was widely distributed around the Soviet bloc and was still in production at the time the Warsaw Pact finally became moribund, distributed then by the Russian State Corporation for Export and Import of Armament and Military Equipment, Rosvoorrouzhenie. The rifle and carbine were also offered in 5.56mm NATO chambering, as the AK101 and AK102, and in the old 7.62mm x 39 chambering as the AK103 and AK104, black plastic being the standard furniture.

BULLPUP RIFLES

There is an area of wasted space in the conventional rifle – the portion which

separates action and butt-plate, and which serves, quite literally, only to keep them apart, allowing the weapon to be anchored at the shoulder while keeping the trigger at arm's length and the sightline accessible to the eye. From the eighteenth century the area in the butt-stock was sometimes used as storage, for small tools, patches and the like, and Christian Sharps even put a small coffee mill there. By the time of World War II we occasionally see it being reduced to tubular metal, and either hinged or collapsible, thus saving weight and also space when the weapon was not in use. That practice was to become more common with the wider adoption of the assault rifle which doubled as a light

automatic weapon, and was more often employed from the hip (or just in two hands) as a result, but that did nothing to address the question of how to reduce the overall length of a rifle to be fired from the shoulder. As early as 1901 a gun designer came up with the simple, novel idea of locating the receiver and action in the butt, which allowed a full-length barrel to be incorporated into a weapon shorter than the average cavalry carbine, but as we have seen, the bolt-action Thorneycroft Rifle was rejected, and probably not just because it was innovative, but also thanks to the awkwardness of its action at a time when much was made of the average ability to get off 20 aimed shots per minute.

It took the perfection of the self-loading rifle during World War II, which removed the need to cycle the action manually, to validate what we now call the bullpup concept, though it was not until some time after the war that 'short' rifles were to be developed in any number – and even then, there was resistance to them. As we have seen, Louis Stange took the first step when he moved the breech of his FG42 back to a point above the trigger assembly, but of course that meant the magazine being located horizontally, which did nothing to improve the weapon's balance. The Swiss Federal Arms Factory, Waffenfabrik Berne, produced a short rifle, the Model 47/49, which was little more than a copy of the FG42, in an unsuccessful attempt to replace the bolt-action Kar31. Its action was moved back further still, to a point above the pistol grip, but it still had to have the problematic horizontal magazine and it was rejected.

Even as the Swiss Federal Army was rejecting the Model 47/49, a team in the design department at Britain's Royal Small Arms Factory at Enfield, led by Colonel Noel Kent-Lemon, was roughing out a design for a new SLR, while Saive in Herstal-lez-Liège was producing the prototypes of what was to become the FN FAL. In one of those (the third) Saive went all the way down the road Stange had pointed out, and located the trigger group well forward of the breech, allowing the magazine to migrate back to its 'proper' position, below the receiver but now in back of the pistol grip, but he was set back on a more conventional course in no uncertain terms by Renè Laloux, FN's dictatorial and hyper-conservative director, who went on to criticise the 'buttless' concept (as it was quite erroneously known in Belgium) in the fiercest possible manner at every opportunity. But Saive was not Laloux's real target – it was at his designer's former colleagues in Enfield that he was aiming, for they had embraced the notion too, and showed some signs of actually being able to popularise it.

A NEW ENFIELD

The EM1/EM2 (Enfield Model 1 and 2) rifles (the former was abandoned part-way through the development programme; it was too complex and expensive ever to have stood a chance of being adopted) came about originally as a result of a 'decision in principle' taken in 1945 that the bolt-action Rifle Number 4

(and the expedient Number 5) should be replaced by a self-loading weapon, in .276in (7mm x 43) calibre, firing a 8.1g (125 grain) bullet at a muzzle velocity of 765 metres (2510ft) per second, which was to supplant every other small arm in the British Army, from pistols to LMGs. (The specification of the round came about as a decision of the 'Ideal Calibre Committee', though it was certainly not a new notion – we may recall that a similar had been selected for the P'13/P'14 rifles, three decades and two world wars earlier, and the equivalent which Pedersen developed in the USA almost ousted the .30in-06. It eventually appeared as the 7mm, Mark 1Z, and was generally known as the .280in in the UK, and in Belgium, where it was adopted as the cartridge for the new FN rifles, including the ill-fated bullpup, as the British Intermediate Round.) Of course, there were inevitably conflicts of interest in a weapon which was to be short enough to be useful to vehicles' crews but accurate enough for infantrymen, and, rather than compromise, the decision was taken to utilise a bullpup design which allowed a short weapon to have a full-length barrel, with the breech and action in the butt-stock, well behind the trigger group.

The EM2, which was ready for full-scale trials at the end of 1948, was unconventional both inside and out. Just 890mm (35in) long, yet with a 625mm (24.5in) barrel, its magazine was half-way down the (tubular pressed-steel) butt and its superimposed carrying handle doubled as the base for a simple, non-magnifying optical sight. It weighed three and a half kilograms (under eight pounds) unloaded and just four kilograms 300g (nine and a half pounds) with a full 20-round magazine. Its action was locked by a pair of front-pivoted flaps, like those employed in the Mauser *Selbstladekarabiner* 15 and elsewhere, but reversed, and was actuated by a piston operating inside a superimposed cylinder, the rear of which carried a suspended firing pin (which was housed within the breech block/bolt and which controlled the locking flaps) as well as an extension which cocked the hammer. It was tested throughout the following year in the UK, and in 1950 its demonstration team took it to the Aberdeen Proving Ground in the USA. There and at Fort Benning, between May and November, it underwent comparative trials against the FN FAL prototype and the indigenous T25, with the M1 Garand acting as a

control comparator. It was the least prone to stoppages in both single-shot and full automatic modes (with an overall average of 4.54/1000 rounds fired), and was the most accurate, but as we have seen, it was rejected anyway (although so were the others, of course) because the 7mm round, even when increased to 9g (140 grain) was deemed to be too light to guarantee a disabling wound (at least, that was the official reason; the truth was actually much more mundane – it was foreign). The British decided to adopt the EM2 and the 7mm round anyway, in 1951 but were dissuaded by their senior partner in the newly-formed NATO; the EM2 was shelved (though there was a last-gasp attempt at redefining it, re-chambered for the 7.62mm x 51 round and with the selective-fire capability deleted, by British commercial gunmakers BSA), and the FN FAL was selected as the new British service rifle in its place – but the concept was far from forgotten.

A NEW STANDARD FOR NATO

It re-emerged, much modified, to the public at large in June, 1976, with the announcement that RSAF had developed a new 'Individual Weapon' (and a very similar 'Light Support Weapon', with around 80 per cent commonality of parts) in a new calibre – 4.85mm x 49 – which fired a 3.63g (56 grain) bullet at a muzzle velocity of 900 metres (2953ft) per second (the 7.62mm NATO round had been discredited in the meantime, of course, thanks to the belated realisation in the USA that it was far too powerful, and hence entirely useless in a selective-fire assault rifle). This new rifle – and more particularly for the moment, the ammunition it fired – was entered along with the M16A1 and a slightly-modified version of the Galil, produced under licence in Holland and known as the MN1, with the M193 round; the FN CAL, with the SS109 round, and the Heckler & Koch G11, which employed an entirely new 4.75mm caseless round (of which more below) for the NATO ammunition trials of 1978-79; we may note that though this was nominally an ammunition trial, had either of the sub-5mm rounds come out the winner, there would have been very far-reaching consequences for the arms industries of the other competitor nations. The French, by now no longer a full member of NATO, cheered the 5.56mm round on from the sidelines, having just adopted the FA

MAS (see below). In the event, the Belgian 5.56mm round, the SS109, was chosen as the new NATO standard for individual weapons, while the 30-round M16A1 magazine was chosen as the magazine to contain it – a surprising choice, since that particular unit was in fact a bodged adaptation, combining a curved lower portion with the straight upper part of the original 15-round Armalite design for the AR-15, and was not at all easy to manufacture; perhaps it was a politically-motivated decision.

THE UK'S INDIVIDUAL WEAPON

The British team returned home, and immediately set about re-engineering the XL series, as their new rifle and light support weapon were known, to accept the chosen round. Since the outcome of the trials had been widely predicted, and the possibility that the new weapons might have to be produced in 5.56mm calibre had been taken into account during their design, this was no particularly difficult matter, and in due course revised versions were adopted by the British Army as the L85A1 Individual Weapon and the L86A1 Light Support Weapon in 1985. In their action, the rifle (which was widely known as the SA80) and sub-LMG were essentially similar to

the Armalite AR-18, described above. Relocating the trigger well forward of the action caused no problems; a simple transfer bar connected the trigger and the sear and the remainder of the trigger group proper, which was conventionally located behind the magazine. The fire selector switch and safety catch were located above the pistol grip, where they could be operated by the thumb of the right hand, and those functions were carried by a transfer bar, too.

Since the sight base of the rifle was unacceptably short for standard open sights to be effective, it was decided very early on in the development process to fit a magnifying, light-gathering optical sight as standard, the first time 'ordinary' riflemen's weapons had been so equipped. The sighting system went through a number of evolutions itself, and the final version, known as the SUSAT (Sight Unit, Small Arm, Trilux), gave 4x magnification and enhanced vision at night. In case of failure or breakage, the optical sight, which was mounted on a long longitudinal dovetail and locked by an over-centre lever, could be removed and an emergency iron rear sight, kept inside the hollow, moulded-plastic pistol grip, substituted. Non-infantrymen – vehicle crews, engineers,

support troops, and the like – were to receive a simplified version, with the optical sight removed and a carrying handle-cum-rear sight, similar to that fitted to the M16 series, in its place. An emergency iron foresight was permanently fitted at the front extremity of the hand guard; it was folded down out of the way when not required.

Even with the SUSAT sight in place, the rifle weighed fractionally under four kilograms empty (eight and a half pounds), thanks to the pressed-steel construction and plastic furniture (such as it was). In terms of overall dimensions versus barrel length, the concept worked splendidly, enabling a weapon just 785mm (31in) long to have a 518mm-(20.4in) long barrel, and to be remarkably accurate as a result. The Light Support Weapon variant was fitted with a (non-removable) barrel some 125mm (five inches) longer than that of the rifle. The other significant difference lay in the trigger group – the LSW fired from an open bolt on both single-shot and automatic settings, while the IW fired from a closed bolt in both cases. Thanks to a combination of an unenviable reputation for unreliability in the very first production examples – a problem soon solved – and a high price tag, the SA80 never sold in anything other than token quantities outside the UK.

THE FRENCH SOLUTION

Despite having produced a working, practical bullpup design before anyone else, the British were not the first to adopt such a rifle for their armed services; that distinction went to the Austrians with the Steyr AUG (see below). They were also beaten by the French, even though it took a considerable time for the Ministry of Defence in Paris to actually adopt the new rifle, the FA MAS (*Fusil Automatique, Manufacture d'Armes de Saint Etienne*), the Heckler & Koch HK33 having been a strong contender. It was among the first European standard service arms to be produced in 5.56mm calibre (though it was optimised for the American M193 round, not the later NATO-standard SS109, having been completed long before the NATO

■LEFT: This Royal Marine has used masking tape to break up the outline of his telescopically-sighted L85A1. The optional sight uses the same mount as the normal SUSAT unit.

■ RIGHT: The L85A1/SA80, like most of its modern counterparts, is a relatively simple design, constructed along modular lines so that a damaged part can be quickly and easily replaced.

ammunition trials were concluded in 1979), and like the AUG it was equally at home in the hands of a left-handed or a right-handed shooter. The change-over was remarkably easy to accomplish in the FA MAS – a steel pressing, rubber covered, which was a clip-fit over the upper edge of the butt-stock and retained by the pin which held butt-stock to receiver, was supplied to act as a cheek-piece; it was symmetrical, fore and aft, and could be mounted on either side of the stock, over one or other of the twin ejection ports. Simply swapping the extractor from one side of the bolt face to the other – a blocking piece occupied the corresponding slot on the other side; it was a simple operation which the soldier himself could perform – completed the conversion. The weapon would be less than ambidextrous if the cocking lever were located on one side or the other, of course, so it was set in the centre of the upper plate of the receiver, below the carrying handle, in the same position in which it was located in the original Armalite AR-10.

A RADICAL APPEARANCE

The FA MAS was even more idiosyncratic in appearance than the SA80 (though an unusual outward form compared to that of the 'traditional' self-loading rifle was to become a common feature of the new genre of course, just as the SLR had differed so much from the bolt-action rifle which had preceded it), with a carrying handle which doubled as a sight protector, like that of the AR-15/M16, except that in this case it protected both fore- and rear sights, for it ran to almost half the entire length of the weapon, along the full length of the receiver, giving rise to the rifle's soubriquet, *le Clarion* (the Bugle). Inside, it was more unusual still, with a form of unlocked, delayed blow-back action originally developed some 30 years earlier for the French general-purpose machine gun, the AAT 52, (*Arme Automatique Transformable*) at the same design studio, where it was, if anything, even more out of place, since the automatic weapon was chambered for the 7.5mm x 54 M1929 full-power round, and was later modified to accept equally powerful 7.62mm x 51 NATO ammunition. As one respected commentator, Thomas Dugleby, put it: 'A weapon firing a cartridge with pressures in the 50,000 pounds per square inch [22 tons per square inch; 3500 atmospheres] region from an unlocked breech needs very little to go wrong [with it] before becoming a distinct liability to its user.'

It is widely held that even miniature-calibre rifle cartridges are simply too powerful to be used in a weapon with an unlocked blow-back action, since the extraction inevitably begins before the projectile has left the muzzle and gas pressure in the chamber has fallen to a safe level, which leads to the empty case bulging as it leaves the protection of the chamber, which in turn means an ever-present danger of the action jamming (like the other modern blow-back designs we have already looked at, the FA MAS's chamber had to be fluted, otherwise reliable extraction would have been doubtful anyway).

A CRUCIAL LEVER

At the very start of this chapter we looked at ways of delaying the rearwards movement of the bolt or breech block, and considered such methods as artificially-augmented friction and the application of mechanical disadvantage; it was the latter of these which the FA MAS and the AAT 52 employed, by the simple expedient of linking the bolt and its superimposed 'carrier' by a lever, pivoted at its lower end against a hardened steel pin across the floor of the receiver so that during the rearwards 'stroke' it acts as a Class Three lever (one in which the effort falls between the fulcrum and the load; the effort in this case is the force provided by the propellant gas, working to move the bolt backwards; the load is the bolt carrier) and switches over to being a Class Two lever (one in which the load falls between the fulcrum and the effort) as it returns to battery. The lever is actually in the form of an H with an offset crossbar, the linkage being accomplished on the exterior of both bolt and carrier and the cross-bar serving to withdraw the firing pin into the bolt as part of the rearwards movement.

The delay/accelerator lever works in two ways. Firstly, it diminishes the force with which the bolt acts on the bolt carrier, and thus slows it down, during the first part of the cycle when the pressure in the chamber is pushing it back, and it augments the speed with which the recoil spring, transmitted by the bolt carrier, acts on the bolt when it returns to chamber a fresh round by the same means. The ratio of amplification and reduction is around two to one. The profile of the lever is such that as it is turned through 45 degrees, it disengages from the pin which retains it, allowing the entire assembly of bolt and carrier to shoot to the rear and cycle the action, and is re-engaged when the bolt is brought to a halt by the breech case and the carrier continues forward – a simple scheme, but both ingenious and effective.

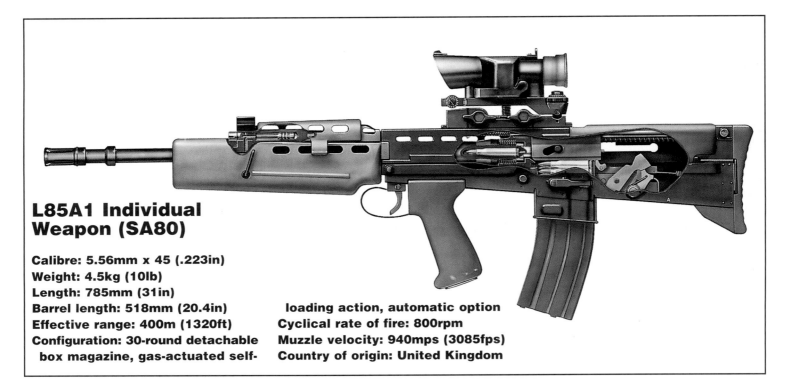

L85A1 Individual Weapon (SA80)

Calibre: 5.56mm x 45 (.223in)
Weight: 4.5kg (10lb)
Length: 785mm (31in)
Barrel length: 518mm (20.4in)
Effective range: 400m (1320ft)
Configuration: 30-round detachable box magazine, gas-actuated self- **loading action, automatic option**
Cyclical rate of fire: 800rpm
Muzzle velocity: 940mps (3085fps)
Country of origin: United Kingdom

Whether it is ultimately strong enough is another matter. Firing a grenade by means of the over-powered 'ballistite' projectile-less cartridge (the recoil from which is so great that the rifle is not shouldered in the conventional way; instead the butt is placed under the arm, where it can travel back freely, and the thumb is not wrapped around the pistol grip, but lies alongside it, above the trigger finger. In fairness, one should perhaps point out that the same safeguards apply to all rifles which fire grenades by this means) must be something akin to hair-raising – and probably not just metaphorically, for the handbook issued with the rifle discusses the possibility of the delay/accelerator lever breaking under the extra strain . . .

The 757mm- (30in) long FA MAS, with its 488mm (19.2in) barrel, was rather more compact than the SA80, and at three kilograms 600g (eight pounds) unloaded was also slightly lighter; thanks to its shorter barrel (and sight base) it was noticeably less accurate than its British counterpart or the more popular, more widely distributed Austrian Steyr which was the only other first-generation bullpup rifle to go into series production (see below). By virtue of its blow-back action, it also had a very much higher cyclical rate of fire, and for that reason, a three-round burst setting was provided along with fully-automatic and single-shot. The hammer group wherein that selection was made, by means of two levers, was a self-contained unit in a plastic casing which was pinned to the receiver wall and could be replaced quickly and simply – another worthwhile innovation. It operated on the escaping cam principle, like the very simplest of clockworks, 're-cocking' the hammer actually being re-setting the driving spring, and was connected to the trigger by a long rod.

AUSTRIA'S 'UNIVERSAL RIFLE'

By the late 1960s, Josef Werndl's Österreicher Waffenfabrik Gesellschaft had long been a division of a conglomerate named Steyr-Daimler-Puch AG, the biggest industrial group in Austria, trading as Steyr-Mannlicher AG, but it still made excellent rifles, among them the version of the FN FAL which the nation's armed forces carried. The nation's Office of Military Technology was quicker than most to read the writing on the wall which foretold the demise of the 7.62mm round, and a senior officer who was also a professional engineer, Colonel Walter Stoll, was instructed to start work in conjunction with Steyr-Mannlicher on a replacement in 5.56mm calibre. The result was the world's first plastic-bodied, modular firearm, the futuristic AUG (*Armee Universal Gewehr*).

Stoll took as his inspiration the bullpup concept embodied in the British EM2, he related in an article he later wrote for the Austrian Army's magazine, but from the outset held to Stoner's view, that the new weapon should be flexible enough to perform not just as a rifle, but as a short machine carbine and a light machine gun too, and the gun which he produced for technical tests was equipped with 400mm (15.7in), 500mm(19.7in), and 600mm (23.6in) tubes. It was compared with the FN FAL in 7.62mm NATO, the Czech M/58 in 7.62mm Soviet, and the FN CAL and the Colt Automatic Rifle in 5.56mm M193, and proved to be in no way inferior and, in fact, superior to all of them in terms of ease of handling,

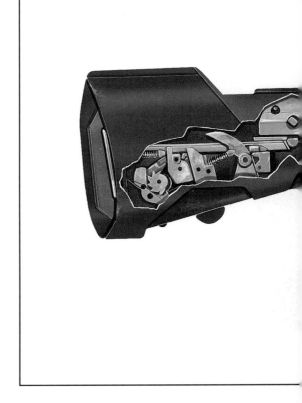

accuracy, and controllability. Further testing and troop trials showed up no hidden faults, and in 1977 the new rifle was accepted as the standard Austrian service arm under the designation *Sturmgewehr 77*.

PLASTIC AND MODULAR

The new rifle was called revolutionary in that it had a 'body' made entirely of plastic, with a receiver, barrel, and trigger/hammer group inserted in it, but in fact that was more in the way of a return to the traditional method, substituting a man-made material for wood, and moulding for carving or machining. The object was not to save weight – at three kilograms 600g (eight pounds), the AUG was comparable with its metal-bodied competitors – but in the interests of economy and durability. Like the EM2 concept rifle, it had a low-magnification (x1.4) optical sight fitted as standard; the mount and tube for this was formed as an integral part of the receiver, and thus doubled as a carrying handle. The barrel was provided with a handle, too, which doubled as a forward pistol grip, there being no real fore-stock to speak of, which made removing it, even when it was hot, a simple process of retracting the cocking slide (located on the top of the receiver, to the left of the forward sight pillar) and turning it up into its retaining notch, pressing the

barrel locking button, and rotating the barrel through one-third of a turn. Once the barrel had been removed, the entire receiver, along with the bolt and guide rods (which are actually tubes, with the recoil springs inside) could be separated from the stock and further stripped down as necessary. Removing the hammer group was equally straightforward – a locking catch retained the rear sling swivel, which in turn locked the butt-plate to the stock. With that removed, the hammer group could be taken out whole.

All the individual groups were treated as modular units, and would be replaced in the field and returned to the armoury for repair; the replacements could be identical units to those removed, or they might be variants – any one of the three lengths of barrel, for example; a receiver with a carrying handle which contains standard dovetails for mounting a telescopic sight or a night-vision sight, in place of the simple optical sight, or a hammer group which gave single-shot and three-round bursts in place of one which was set up for single-shot and fully automatic fire. The bolt itself was issued with either a left-hand or a right-hand extractor, and switching ejection from one side to the other was a matter of swapping one for the other and changing the port over. The rear sling swivel could be located on either side of the butt-stock. There was no change lever; rather, the

trigger pull itself determined the type of fire, with a light pull giving single shots and a more determined effort, overcoming the resistance of a second spring, giving either a three-round burst or sustained fire, depending on which hammer group is fitted. The trigger itself was a plunger unit, like those found in electric drills, and its guard was formed to include the entire hand, making operation wearing cold-weather clothing much simpler. The cocking handle served as the safety catch, since the entire action was locked when it was turned into its retaining notch. The 30-round magazine was also plastic, of course, though in this case it was impact-resistant transparent polycarbonate, so that the rifleman could check the contents visually – an innovation which other manufacturers were quick to adopt. A 42-round magazine was also available, for use in the LMG role.

Internally, the Steyr AUG was essentially similar to the AR-15/M16, with the propellant gas acting directly on the bolt carrier (the gas tube formed an integral part of the receiver) to release the multi-lug bolt head locked into the barrel extension before driving the carrier and bolt backwards to cycle the action. The single most important refinement was the so-called 'suspended bolt' design – the carrier was not in contact with the plastic of the body, but was supported on the guide rod/tubes

FA MAS (*Fusil Automatique, Manufacture d'Armes de St. Etienne*)

Calibre: 5.56mm x 45 (.223in)
Weight: 3.6kg (8lbs)
Length: 757mm (30in)
Barrel length: 488mm (19.2in)
Effective range: 400m (1320ft)
Configuration: 25-round detachable
box magazine, gas- actuated
self-loading action,
automatic option
Cyclical rate of fire: 900rpm
Muzzle velocity: 920mps (2990fps)
Country of origin: France

which extended all the way to the butt plate, with an air space all round it.

The AUG was later adopted by the armed forces of half a dozen other nations, including Australia and Saudi Arabia, and a single-shot variant known as the AUG-P, became a popular police weapon despite a hefty price tag of almost US$1500 in the USA (an M16A2 in law enforcement specification cost around US$1000). An outwardly similar weapon, but with blow-back operation, is also available in 9mm Parabellum chambering to provide markedly lower penetrating power – important for law enforcement agencies to consider.

BACK TO OBERNDORF

Heckler & Koch was one of the first arms makers in Europe to adopt the 5.56mm round, for the HK33 which was introduced in the 1960s, but by the middle of the following decade the company was already looking towards the future and considering not just alternative, still smaller calibres, as the British were, but also an entirely new type of ammunition, developed by Rottweil, now Dynamit Nobel's German subsidiary. The small conventional round under development, in 4.6mm (.18in) calibre, was optimised for an effective range of just 300m (1000ft); the rifle built around it, the HK36, was an adaptation of the HK33 except in its magazine arrangement, which was both complicated and idiosyncratic. The magazine was integral with the receiver, and was charged with 30 rounds of ammunition from an open-ended aluminium container, the ends of which were covered by a flimsy membrane. To charge it, one pulled a spring-loaded chain from the bottom of the magazine, which caused the magazine platform to descend and then to latch in the open position, when the 30-round package could be inserted through an aperture in the rear of the housing. A second pull on the chain released the platform, which rose under the pressure of the magazine spring and bore on the cartridges through the open end of the container, which sealed the loading port. Since the ammunition packs were prepared at the manufacturers, the rounds within them

were protected from dirt and moisture. It was claimed that this system was cheaper than a detachable box magazine system and saved weight, not so much in the weapon as by removing the need to carry loaded magazines around.

The other weapon Heckler & Koch was developing alongside the HK36 was very different indeed, and represented a true attempt to carry small-arms technology forward by the twin means of proposing a new type of ammunition and an entirely new type of action to go with it. It was produced as a private-initiative extension of the US Government's SALVO research programme, which looked at the feasibility of improving an infantryman's battlefield performance by providing him with a weapon which fired more than a single projectile, from multiple barrels, by the use of multiple projectiles in a single round (by no means a new idea; the British tested it before World War I), or by firing a burst at a very high cyclical speed. This last approach was the one adopted in another US Government initiative, the SPIW (Special Purpose Individual Weapon) development programme, and also by Heckler & Koch, whose new rifle fired not individual single shots, but three-round bursts, at a cyclical rate of 2000 rounds per minute, so that the burst lasted for just one

millisecond and the third round was on its way to the target before the shooter was affected by any recoil.

CASELESS AMMUNITION

In a sense, Dynamit Nobel turned back the clock about 120 years with the new type of ammunition it developed, for it dispensed with the conventional metallic cartridge case altogether, and instead was composed of pure compressed nitro-cellulose propellant with no binder or adhesive added (but with a waterproof, flame-resistant coating), with a partially-encapsulated projectile. It was almost rectangular in cross-section (the shorter sides were very shallow trapezoids, so the round was actually octagonal), to optimise space in the magazine, some 12mm (half an inch) wide and 32.5mm (one and a quarter inches) long overall from its head to the tip of the projectile which was of a nominal 4.75mm (.187in) calibre. At the heart of the compressed propellant, immediately behind the projectile, was a small 'booster charge', which was rather more volatile than the propellant proper, and which quite literally blew it apart in the chamber before detonating it, providing the ideal surface area for controlled combustion. The all-important gas pressure curve was exactly the same as that produced in a

■RIGHT: The 5.56mm Austrian Steyr-Mannlicher AUG bullpup, in its three basic forms, with optional short- and ultra-short barrels, taking the concept of modularity to a logical conclusion.

metallic cartridge with a more-or-less granular filling. One hundred rounds of the new ammunition occupied less space than two 20-round magazines of 7.62mm NATO ammunition, and was lighter.

The primary innovation in the rifle which was designed around the new round, the H&K G11, lay in the breech block, which was cylindrical in cross-section, a little under 50mm (two inches) in diameter, and lay across the axis of the barrel at right-angles. This cylinder was pierced at right-angles to its axis by a chamber suited to the round, which finished in a rifled barrel extension into which the protruding portion of the projectile (around 12mm/half an inch of it) was seated. Loading took place with the chamber vertical, and the breech block was rotated through a quarter turn to align the round with the barrel and with the firing pin (it is unclear why H&K's designers did not dispense with the mechanical trigger and firing pin/percussion primer arrangement and substitute electrical firing, though one may imagine that there was a very good reason, perhaps connected with timing). There was an ejection port bored through the barrel extension in which the breech block was housed, through which the chamber could be cleared manually should the need arise. Motive force for the rotation of the breech block was provided conventionally, by a piston acting in a cylinder into which propellant gas was introduced through a vent in the barrel, but the way in which it worked was most unconventional.

The barrel, gas cylinder, breech, and magazine (the latter lay atop the barrel, and reached down its entire length; the rounds were held in it vertically in a single row) were held firmly together, but were free to reciprocate within the framework of the receiver. Upon a round being fired, the gas piston was propelled to the rear, ultimately striking a buffer and reversing its direction, whereupon the barrel assembly also moved towards the rear, chambering a fresh round in the process. When the piston arrived at its battery position in relation to the barrel assembly, the next round was fired, and the process began afresh, though this time the initial location of barrel assembly was some way to the rear of where it had been originally. The process continued through the firing of the third round, by which time the 'free' barrel assembly reached the buffer. The hammer was then disconnected from the sear, and the cycle was over; the barrel assembly returned to battery, taking the piston with it, and on its arrival the hammer was re-connected to the sear, so that a new cycle could be initiated by pressing the trigger again. From the shooter's point of view, the entire operation felt like firing a single round, for he was unaffected by recoil until all three projectiles were on their way.

LOOKING FURTHER AHEAD

There was a problem, however, and it is one which has resisted solution: the build-up of heat in the weapon soon causes rounds to 'cook off', or discharge spontaneously, a phenomenon sometimes, but far less frequently, found in weapons firing conventional cased ammunition, since the cartridge case acts as a heat sink, and carries much of the heat away from the breech as it is ejected. Thanks to this and problems with obturation, the H&K G11 was actually withdrawn from the NATO ammunition trial of 1978-79 before its conclusion, and no rifle firing caseless ammunition has surfaced since.

Though the direction Heckler & Koch went in with the G11 proved to be a false trail, the basic principle of serial ultra-rapid fire using either conventional projectiles or flechettes (very light arrow-like projectiles which are fin- rather than spin-stabilised and contained within a sabot while they are in the barrel) has been widely accepted, and it appears that the way to achieve the necessary 2000-plus rounds-per-minute cyclical rate is to separate the processes of firing and feeding ammunition to the breech. One way to achieve this in a single-barrel weapon is by means of a three-chambered revolving cylinder which is recharged from a large capacity box magazine in a single operation (the rounds in the magazine being in three columns) after the burst has been fired.

The three bullpup rifles which entered service in the 1970s and 1980s validated the short rifle concept sufficiently well to put an end to any attempt to develop the breech-before-trigger format any further – not that it actually had that much further to go in any event – and future rifles are only likely to get smaller, and lighter, still. New types of ammunition such as the flechette round and conventional projectiles in calibres in the two to four millimetre range will ensure this. Looking rather further ahead, it is not inconceivable to imagine new types of ammunition including a guidance package of some sort in the projectile, linked directly to a target acquisition system, for it is quite certain that the military rifle of the future will be the central component in an integrated fighting system which will include passive and active sensors and detectors, collecting data which will be routinely transmitted to a tactical control centre for instantaneous analysis as well as presenting the individual soldier with a clear picture of the battlefield around him, no matter what the physical conditions, and including such much-needed features as automatic identification of friend and foe.

■ LEFT: The Steyr AUG proved to be just as popular outside its country of origin. The Australian Army adopted it in place of its FAL/SLRs, and so have other armed forces, including police forces.

CHAPTER 5
SPORTING GUNS AND SNIPER RIFLES

Until well into the twentieth century, the majority of guns produced for the commercial market were everyday utility items: tools, just like farming implements, the prime function of which was to keep meat on the table and to dispose of dangerous pests and predators.

There were exceptions, certainly – rich men hunted for sport long before the rifle arrived on the scene, and adopted it wholeheartedly as soon as it did, and there were marksmanship contests with very serious prizes between riflemen just as there had been for archers – but the basic requirement for the majority of gun-owners was for a plain, reliable, sturdy weapon at an affordable price.

MATCH RIFLES

We have seen how obsolete military rifles were sold off to soldiers and ex-soldiers (and by extension to the public at large; there were no restrictions anywhere in the world on the private ownership of firearms at that time) at well under original cost price during the latter part of the nineteenth century, and soon organisations to promote target shooting as a sport (and, originally at least, to maintain a certain standard of skill-at-arms within what would be the core of a 'citizen army'), like the National Rifle Associations (NRA) of both the UK and the USA, came into being, and most of the important shooting matches held today date from that time.

By just after the turn of the century manufacturers had begun making specially selected current rifles, of the standard which went to equip the best marksmen, available to members of the public at reasonable prices, usually through the NRAs, for the purpose of encouraging rifle practice; the Springfield Armory, for example, began selling M1903s in 1910, having previously sold match-quality Krags for five years.

National Match competitions were inaugurated in 1903 in the United States, and international matches, many under the auspices of the International Shooting Union, were well established by then (the Palma Match, which was inaugurated in 1876, was revived in 1901; it was shot over 800, 900, and 1000 yards – 730m, 820m, and 910m respectively) by eight-man teams competing with selected but unmodified service rifles, and rifle shooting was an Olympic sport. Since the type of rifle to be used was standardized, a great deal of energy and money was expended on producing super-accurate ammunition with very high velocity and a flat trajectory; for example, the .30in-06 ammunition the USA's Frankford Arsenal produced for the 1925 Palma Match had a computed mean radius – a theoretical accuracy – of just under four and a half inches, which translated into 13.5in 10-shot groups, 20 times out of 20, at 1000yds (910m); in order to compete, commercial ammunition makers such as Remington and Winchester had to do better still. Much of what we now know about the behaviour of bullets in flight was learned as a result of the between-

■ LEFT: Competitive shooting is a mix of physical control and technology; the control takes years to acquire, but the technology, such as this expensive SIG-Sauer SSG 3000, one simply buys.

■ABOVE: The Barrett Model 82 A-1 Light Fifty is one of the most powerful firearms on sale to the general public. It is chambered for the same .50in round as the Browning M2 machine gun.

the-wars international and inter-service shooting matches.

Particularly since World War II, rifle manufacturers have gone through a similar process to the makers of cars, motorcycles, and the like, and come to rely to some degree on competition results to demonstrate the quality of their products. The result has been the emergence of rifles with selected actions and barrels and purpose-designed aperture sights, mated to stocks which are adjustable in every conceivable way – for length and height of the butt and the position on it of the cheek-piece, and for the size, position, and inclination of the grips, fore and rear. There are distinct differences between the rifles to be used in different positions, too.

BOLT-ACTION DOMINANT

Most modern match rifles are bolt-action; as late as the 1950s and 1960s, the Martini falling block action was still popular for small-bore rifles (for example, those chambered for .22in Long Rifle

rounds), which are used both indoors and out, but slowly the bolt took over, and by the 1980s it had come to dominate the field entirely. Heavier calibre manually-loaded rifles, for outdoor use over longer ranges, are almost exclusively bolt-action weapons. The best were very expensive, with price tags of US$5000 and more (the Heckler & Koch PSG-1 Marksman rifle in 7.92mm/.308in calibre is almost twice that). Most were available with left-hand action and stock. There were also self-loading target rifles on the market, based on a variety of military actions – the M1/M14 action was popular, as was Stoner's, as developed for the AR-15.

HUNTING RIFLES

Hunting for sport with a rifle is a relatively new popular pastime, with its seat firmly in North America, and is largely unknown in many other parts of the world. It's not surprising, then, that many of the rifles which fall into this category come from American gunmakers, although European manufacturers, particularly Germans, and Far Eastern manufacturers are represented, too.

Sports or trophy hunting in the nineteenth century was an elitist activity, the pursuit of rich men who could afford

to lavish very considerable sums of money on hand-built guns from the likes of Boss, Rigby, Holland & Holland, and Westley Richards in London, which was still recognised as the centre of gunmaking excellence.

In truth, there was often very little sportsmanship involved – a tiger hunt in nineteenth century India, for example, either involved hundreds of beaters driving the beasts towards a party of hunters installed in howdahs – box-like structures set atop an elephant's back – or bait, usually a goat or a calf, which was staked out and surrounded by hunters in secure hides.

The object of the exercise was to kill the tiger with the least possible danger to one's self, and as a result, large-calibre rifles firing very heavy projectiles (up to 14.6mm/.577in Nitro Express, which fired a 48.5g/750 grain bullet with a muzzle velocity of 625 metres/2050ft per second were – and still are – available) were much in demand.

The 'hunters' also often carried large-calibre double-barrelled, or even quadruple-barrelled, break-open pistols as an additional means of self-defence, too – these combination pistols became known as 'howdah' pistols as a result. The best of them were said to come from

■RIGHT: The Calico M-900 carbine is primarily a self-defence weapon chambered for the low-powered 9mm Parabellum round. This version is equipped with a laser target indicator.

Charles Lancaster, who also made excellent rifles).

DOUBLE-BARRELLED RIFLES

Most of the rifles so employed were combination guns, too – almost always double-barrelled side-by-sides – for there was virtually no chance of them failing entirely; even if one barrel misfired, there was always the second, and there was no danger of the action jamming, while by its nature such a gun gave a very fast two-shot sequence, particularly if fitted with a single sequential trigger.

Such rifles are still available today, from a number of small, specialist manufacturers but also from larger concerns such as Beretta, Brno, and Krieghoff, and some are configured as over-and-unders. All such double-barrelled guns are break-open designs with simple box- or side-locks; some have double triggers but most are fitted with just one.

The 'old' makers of custom guns still produce double-barrelled rifles to order, but at an astronomical price, and even the best quality factory-made doubles can be very expensive – Beretta's Model 455, hand-made to order and extensively hand-engraved, goes for around US$50,000.

A more mundane off-shoot of the double-barrelled 'big game' rifle is the combination of a rifled barrel and a smooth-bore barrel, usually set one above the other. The combination of .22inLR and .410in shotgun is a popular one (and we may recall that the Springfield M6 survival rifle which Stoner tried to supplant with his AR-5 and AR-7 rifles was configured in just this way) but a number of manufacturers offer combinations of heavier calibre – 12-bore and .30in-06, for example.

MODERN REPLICAS

There is also a large and ever-growing market, in the United States in particular, for replicas of rifles of a by-gone age, not just for display but also to use as hunting weapons. Far and away the most sought-after single-shot weapons are the excellent replicas of Christian Sharps' rifles and carbines in a variety of forms, particularly a number of re-creations of the Model 1874 and Model 1875 in .40in (10.15mm), .45in (11.4mm), and .50in (12.7mm) calibres, chambered for rounds loaded with anything from 3.2g to 9g (50 to 140 grain) of black powder and with barrels from 558mm to 863mm (22in to 34in) long (Sharps' replicas are also available in 'modern' chamberings, from .22inLR up to .40in-65 WCF). Good examples sell for between US$700 and US$1500 – a great deal less than one would have to pay for an original.

Replicas of Rolling Block Remington rifles and 'trapdoor' Springfields are also popular. There is also a ready market for replicas of muzzle-loading rifles, with either flintlock or (more commonly) percussion cap ignition. Modern-style black powder muzzle-loaders are available, too, usually with telescopic sights, from a number of small, specialist manufacturers.

Many of the classic American under-lever-action repeater rifles of the nineteenth century are also available in replica, many of them manufactured in Italy, which has acquired an enviable reputation for such weapons thanks to companies such as Uberti. By far the most popular among them are the Henry and Winchester copies, particularly those of the Model 1873. The enduring

■BELOW: The Calico M-951 with its full butt-stock; more recently, a forward pistol grip and a muzzle compensator have been added. It comes with 50- and 100-round capacity magazines.

popularity of this genre of rifle in the United States is amply demonstrated by the fact that two rifles from the very end of the nineteenth century were still available over 100 years later from the companies which first produced them: Marlin's Model 1893, which is now produced as the Model 336, and the hammerless Savage 99 with its idiosyncratic rotary magazine. The Winchester Model 94 was still in production past its centenary, and was joined by the more recent (and rather different) Browning lever-action rifle, the BLR, manufactured in a variety of forms in Japan.

MARLIN'S RIFLES

John Marlin began making handguns in the period just after the American Civil War; in 1875 he acquired the rights to manufacture a successful black powder rifle, the Ballard. He abandoned that design with the coming of smokeless powder, and devised an under-lever-action, tubular-magazine rifle very similar in character to the Winchester, which emerged in its final form in 1893.

Marlin used a cylindrical bolt which was locked at the rear by a vertical rod attached to the actuating lever-cum-trigger guard, close to its pivot point, at the front, and arranged so that when the latter was lowered and pushed forward the bolt was unlocked and then pushed back out of the receiver to the rear, extracting and ejecting the case in the chamber (to the right, rather than upwards as in the Winchester) and pressing the hammer back past the full-cock position. Simultaneously, the cartridge carrier or lifter dropped to allow the next round to pass into it from the under-barrel magazine. As the actuating

lever was pulled back up into the battery, the cartridge carrier was elevated and the bolt pushed forward, allowing the hammer to come to the full-cock position, where it was retained by the trigger sear, and chambering the fresh round (the Winchester action differed in that the return of the cartridge lifter was

Galil Sniper

Calibre: 7.62mm x 51 (.30in)
Weight: 6.4kg (2lb 14oz)
Length: 1115mm (43.89in) extended
Barrel length: 508mm (20in)
Effective range: Over 800m (2624ft)
Configuration: 20-round box magazine
Muzzle velocity: 815mps (2674fps)
Country of origin: Israel

■BELOW: The Federal XC-800 and XC-450 carbines (the sub-designator refers to the calibre – 9mm Parabellum or .45 ACP) are examples of the modern 'no frills' approach to self-defence arms, with all-steel construction. The butt-stock is telescopic, and the gun can be stripped in a matter of seconds.

■BELOW: Israeli Military Industries set
BELOW: Israeli Military Industries set up a subsidiary to market its products for general use. One such was the Galil rifle, repackaged for civilians with a very attractive straight-through wooden stock. It was available in the civilian equivalent of the two NATO calibres – .223in Remington and .308in Winchester.

accomplished at the end of the forward stroke of the actuating lever, and ejection was vertical, from the receiver top, which prevented a telescopic sight from being easily mounted; this failing was later modified when such sights became more popular– and cheaper – later in the twentieth century). Both rifles had two-

piece firing pins, and positive safety was achieved by moving one section out of line with the other.

It is estimated that around eight million Marlin 1893s and near-contemporary Winchester 1894s were sold in the 100 years following their introduction – a figure probably equal to

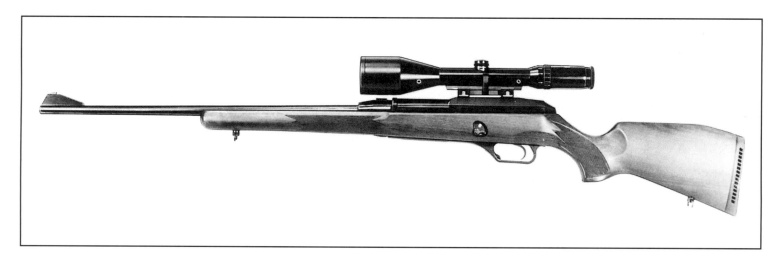

■**ABOVE: The Heckler & Koch HK-940 is an oddity – a conventional self-loading hunting rifle using the same action as the company's military weapons but chambered for the .308in Winchester.**

the total of all the rest of the 'sporting' rifles sold in that period put together – and this despite the fact that neither could handle a 'modern', high-powered cartridge as introduced from about 1910 (the throw of the action is too short for these longer rounds, and they have no primary extraction, without which it is next to impossible to remove spent high-power cases from the chamber) and are chambered for .30in-30 rounds and the like as a result. Modern under-lever rifles which use similar actions are often chambered for popular pistol rounds such as the 9mm Parabellum, .38in Special, .357in Magnum, .44in Special or .44in Magnum.

It was the Marlin Company which developed the only current variation on the simple four-, five- or six-groove rifling system which became almost universal during the nineteenth century. In 1953 a patent was granted for a system known as Micro-Groove, which had many more grooves and lands (the exact number depended on the calibre) which were both of a different profile from, say, the Enfield rifling system, and were considerably shallower. Marlin claimed superior accuracy for its system, which grips the projectile more tightly while cutting shallower tracks in it. All Marlin rifles produced after the early 1950s were fitted with Micro-Groove barrels.

THE SAVAGE 99

The Savage 99, in contrast to its rivals, was a very much more 'modern-looking' design, despite having been conceived at

around the same time. Arthur Savage was a street-car superintendent in Utica, New York, when he devised his first rifle, in 1895; he modified the design in the light of experience over the following four years, and the Model 99, as the result was known, has changed only in a minor way since.

To start with, he dispensed with the under-barrel, tubular magazine and replaced it with a positively indexed rotary spool magazine very similar in character to that produced by Mannlicher and Schönauer, which was very much kinder to the ammunition and avoided the danger of the point of a bullet's nose impacting with the primer of the round in front of it and setting it off. He did away with the exposed hammer, too, and instead used a spring-loaded firing pin; the form of the lever he used meant that the action had a considerably longer throw and performed primary extraction, and could accommodate more modern cartridge forms as a consequence.

The only major improvement made later to the Savage 99 took the form of a re-designed safety catch, which was both more secure and very much easier in operation, sited like that of many shotguns, on the curved rear upper surface of the receiver where it fell easily under the thumb. The rotary spool magazine was also dropped in favour of a detachable, internal four-round box magazine, in the interests of economy.

It is interesting to note that Winchester's last under-lever-action rifle was a hammerless design with a four-round detachable box magazine which looked almost identical to the Savage 99 except for the fact that it had a rather longer fore-stock.

Savage Arms went on to become a major force in the market, and produced excellent shotguns and a range of bolt-

action hunting rifles at very competitive prices in addition to the Model 99.

THE BROWNING LEVER-ACTION

The Browning lever-action rifle is a very different design, with a rotating bolt head locked by conventional lugs, the cylinder being thrown back by means of a rack and pinion gear which allows a long bolt travel for a short throw of the actuating lever (this was not a new departure; the same method was first employed by a gunmaker in Connecticut, named Bullard, in the 1870s). It harks back to the original Winchesters and Marlins in that its hammer is exposed– a feature which some shooters prefer, since it both gives a clear visual check of the gun's status (though the Savage, for example, has an indicator pin which is pushed up out of the surface of the receiver to show when it is cocked) and allows it to be held at half-cock.

Curiously, given that it is very appropriate for short, low-powered cartridges, the under-lever action was rarely used for .22in calibre rim-fire rifles, save by Marlin, who produced one in 1891, revised it in 1897 and again in 1939, when it became the Model 39. During the 1950s, Marlin's competitors caught on, and Browning began producing the BL-22 and Winchester the Model 9422 (which was still available half a century later in the very different .22in Magnum chambering). Winchester also produced a variety of self-loading .22in rim-fire rifles, the first of them in 1903, and not a few slide- or pump-action rifles in the same calibre. Remington produced .22in calibre pump-action rifles too, as well as the Model 7600, chambered for centre-fire cartridges in up to .30in-06 calibre – the only manufacturer to offer a heavy-calibre rifle with this type of action despite its

popularity in shotguns (though others were produced chambered for heavy pistol rounds).

Equally curiously, Remington– which is the longest-established private gunmaker in the United States, having been in business since 1816– only ever made one under-lever-action rifle, a .22in rim-fire rifle launched in the 1960s and very soon withdrawn from sale.

BOLT-ACTION SPORTERS

Despite the huge sales of under-lever-action rifles, development in the twentieth century was concentrated on bolt-action utility and sporting rifles. It is suggested that the first sporting bolt-action rifle ever produced was an M1903 Springfield, modified in the year of its introduction to the order of President Theodore Roosevelt, by cutting down the fore-stock and removing the handguard and fitting a blade foresight and Lyman backsight. It is conceivable that some – if not many – of the M1903s which became available via the NRA after 1910 were modified in a similar way. In 1920, the Springfield Armory itself began offering modified M1903s via the NRA as the NRA Springfield Sporter, and the following year Remington launched the first custom-built sporter rifle with a bolt-action as the Model 30 and the rather better-finished 30S. It was actually a modified M1917 Enfield, which, we may recall, the company had manufactured in great numbers during the war just ended. It had its weaknesses – its rather heavy cock-on-closing action chief among them – and its strengths, such as a low-set bolt handle which did not need modification to accommodate a telescopic sight, in the way the Springfield (and the Mauser, from which it was derived) did, and an excellent safety system, but was soon to be

popularly perceived as out of date, thanks chiefly to rather poor stocking on the utility model.

Winchester followed its chief rival in 1925 with the mediocre Model 54 and then, 12 years later, brought out a masterpiece, the Model 70, which was still going strong 60 years on, by which time it was selling for between US$500 and US$1000, depending on the actual construction, the standard of finish, the calibre, and the length of its barrel. (And the Winchester Model 70 wasn't 'just' a hunting rifle: a year after its introduction, a suitably-sighted Model 70 won the Wimbledon match at Camp Perry, which was shot over 1000 yards/910m.)

There were relatively few sporting rifles produced in Europe during the inter-war period; many of those that were used Mauser actions supplied by the Oberndorf factory or by FN in Liège, though there were also inferior copies, often with misleading names, many of them actually salvaged from rifles and carbines which had been issued during the war. Some American custom gunmakers also bought the actions they used from Europe, among them one who was to become famous as an innovator and a producer of very fine rifles indeed, Roy Weatherby. Weatherby went on to develop and produce a bolt-action system of his own, known as the Mark V, which had nine locking lugs arranged as three triples, almost in the form of an interrupted thread, at the head of an over-sized cylinder (so that the body of the bolt was of greater diameter than the lugs, which allowed him to dispense with the lug slots found in other boltways); this made for a much smoother action, while the positioning of the lugs, at an angle of 120 degrees, meant that the bolt handle had to be lifted through 60, rather

than 90, degrees to free them. The lug system, though not the over-sized cylinder, seems actually to have been the invention of Charles Newton, in around 1910; Newton also developed a number of alternative rifling systems which, while they were effective, were not so much better than the existing types as to justify considerable extra cost. Weatherby also developed a series of long, powerful 'magnum' cartridges in a variety of calibres from .224in to .378in; Mark V rifles are still on sale today, and have been joined by complementary models to make a comprehensive – and enviable – product line at prices from below US$500 to more than US$5000.

A BROADER MARKET

As the market in the USA broadened, so more and more manufacturers began producing bolt-action hunting rifles to satisfy it. Some, like Weatherby, were excellent, and made a real, positive (if actually minor) contribution to the gunmaker's art; some were content to stick to existing, tried-and-tested designs and simply produce well-engineered, workmanlike rifles made to last a lifetime or two. Few, if any, gunmakers offered full-power rifles at bargain-basement prices since it was impossible to compete with military-surplus stock being sold off at much less than cost price. This was – and is – in direct and welcome contrast to the market for handguns, which has been flooded with cheap 'Saturday night specials' since the advent of the brass cartridge. There were considerable numbers of small-bore rifles, as the .22in calibre was often known in the United Kingdom, which certainly didn't qualify as great rifles by any stretch of the imagination, however, and it was to be some considerable time until quality of design, manufacture, and finish became as important in that market as it had long been in the wider field. As late as the mid-1970s, a well-respected (American) gunsmith and author could suggest, without much exaggeration, that it was 'a damned shame' that no-one made a 'decent .22in-calibre bolt-action rifle anymore', and go on to suggest that, if his readers could recognise one, they should buy it; that state of affairs had certainly changed by the time two decades had passed, with a very good selection of fine rim-fire bolt-action rifles available from most good manufacturers.

And during the same period, there were worthwhile advances being made in the bigger-bore bolt-action rifles, too, many of them from Germany and Austria, which had at long last regained their position in the forefront of firearms development. Mauser and Voere in Austria both developed three-lug front-locking systems, the latter's locking into a stellite insert in the barrel extension, which allowed the bolt rotation to be reduced to 60, rather than 90, degrees,

■BELOW: The Mauser Model 91 (bottom) and Heym Magnum Express represent the two wings of the market for high-quality hunting rifles: the former the small calibres, the latter the heavy.

while Sauer, which has more recently become very closely associated with SIG, produced a system for its Model 80 and 90 rifles which used conventional, rear-set tenon-like lugs but had them retract entirely into the cylindrical body of the bolt on unlocking. The same system was later used in the SIG-Sauer SSG 2000 sniper rifle. Heym of Suhl came up with a similar system but used retractable balls instead of square lugs for its beautifully finished SR30 rifle, which in 1997 sold complete, stocked in walnut and rosewood, for £1300 Sterling/US$2200, or for £350 Sterling/US$575 as a bare action and barrel, and which was a fitting successor to a long line of extremely well-made Mauser-style weapons.

SELF-LOADING HUNTING RIFLES

Most centre-fire sporting rifles have been either under-lever- or bolt-action weapons, but self-loaders have been available in limited numbers since around 1906, when Remington introduced the John Browning-designed Model 8, which was unusual in that it employed the long-recoil method of operation, its barrel enclosed in a protective tube. Gas-actuated systems as used in the majority of military rifles developed since World War I have always been more common; since the 1970s almost all the commercial suppliers of military weapons of this type have also produced versions for the open market, while Browning, Remington, and Winchester have all produced purpose-

built gas-actuated hunting rifles, with Remington very much the front runner with its 740/7400 series, which appeared originally in 1955 – a truly excellent, accurate, self-loading rifle at a price tag of not much more than US$500 thanks to the application of modular manufacturing techniques; many of the parts of the Model 740 and 7400 were interchangeable with those of the pump-action Model 760 and 7600, which allowed considerable economy of scale. Not surprisingly – and for identical reasons – the modified military weapons are usually only available in .223in Remington and .308in Winchester

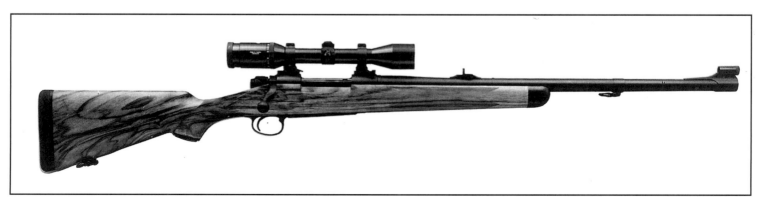

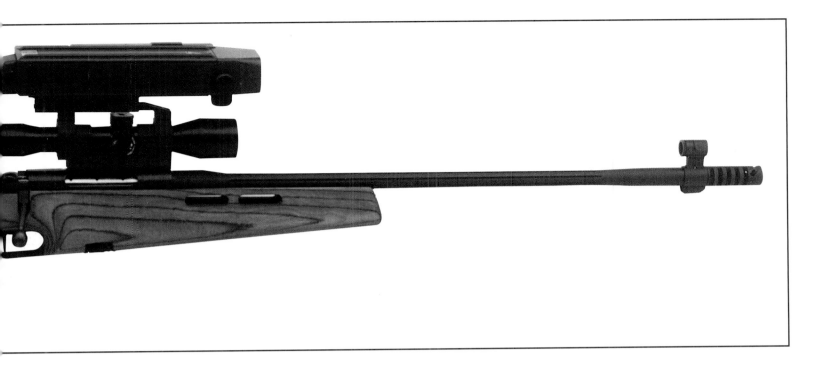

■ABOVE: The Mauser Model 86 SR is intended as a sniper's weapon. The box-like structure atop the telescopic sight is a laser range-finder for the process of sighting-in on a target.

chamberings, these being dimensionally identical to the 5.56mm and 7.62mm NATO rounds for which the rifles were originally designed, while the purpose-built auto-loaders were produced in a wider range of calibres. Many later semi-automatic rifles (though they are probably better described as carbines) were chambered for the 9mm Parabellum or other heavy pistol cartridges, designed, quite clearly, for the 'law enforcement' market, since they have ballistic properties quite unacceptable on the hunting field.

There were military-replica SLRs, too – the most popular were copies of the M1 carbine and the M14 rifle, and the best of the latter was actually manufactured by the Springfield Armory. One of the most popular of the commercially available gas-operated self-loading rifles was based on the action Garand designed for the M1 and which found its way into the M14 by default – the Ruger Mini-14, from a company which was originally better known for its revolver pistols but which has since gone on to produce an extensive range of high-quality bolt-action rifles, too. The Mini-14 was chambered for the .223in Remington round, and was probably aimed originally at the law-enforcement, rather than the hunting, market; its career was unusual in that it actually made the cross-over into the

military market when the Mini-14/20GB appeared, with such accoutrements as a bayonet lug and flash suppressor. During the late 1980s, Sturm, Ruger & Co. went all the way with this rifle, and developed the AC-556, which was externally identical but which had a selective- and burst-fire capability. It also produced a version chambered for the intermediate 7.62mm x 39 Soviet round as the Mini-Thirty.

SNIPERS AND THEIR RIFLES

The two very different arms of sport shooting – match shooting at targets and hunting in the field – come together and find a military application in the work of the sniper, a man whose task is to dispose of the enemy's most precious assets by means of an accurately placed rifle shot at long range.

The first time there was widespread use of snipers was probably during the American Civil War, when both sides employed them to questionable effect, usually against troops drawn up in static defensive positions; they were most

■ABOVE: The McMillan M87 sniper's rifle is a reversal of the normal process – a militarised version of a rifle built for the hunting market, the Talon Safari. It has a glassfibre stock.

commonly armed with rifles made by Christian Sharps (or good copies thereof), fitted with long telescopic sights, and could be effective at surprisingly long ranges – up to 910m (1000 yards) under ideal conditions – even though the ballistic properties of black powder rifles were far from ideal. The British were sorely troubled by snipers during the wars against the Boers in South Africa – men who had a tradition of marksmanship ('What range do you make it?' poet Rudyard Kipling asked Bennett Burleigh, the *Daily Telegraph*'s correspondent, when they observed British troops coming under accurate long-range fire at Karee Sidings, Bloemfontein, in March 1900. 'Eight hundred [yards] at the nearest', replied Burleigh. 'That's close-quarters nowadays. You'll never see anything

■ABOVE: The Parker-Hale Model 81
mates the tried-and-tested Mauser
action to a 610mm (24in) barrel. It is
available in a variety of calibres, from
.22in Hornet to .308in Winchester.

closer than this. Modern rifles make it impossible.') – but it was not until World War I, the static war to end them all, that sniping became an everyday pastime, initiated first by the Germans but taken up wholeheartedly by their adversaries, too, as much as anything to relieve the boredom of life in the trenches.

GERMAN SNIPER RIFLES

The first German attempts to supply sniper rifles took place in Bavaria, in the autumn of 1914, and actually consisted of what we now call a mail-shot to all the known (civilian) owners of 7.92mm Mauser hunting rifles fitted with telescopic sights, their identities and addresses laboriously gathered from gunsmiths all over the country; there were few positive responses, and just some dozens of rifles were collected as a result. They were supplemented with rifles ordered from gunsmiths, the majority of which were fitted with 4x magnification sights by Gérard or Goerz of Berlin, at a cost of around 330 Marks each. The first consignment, of 60 rifles, reached the front just before Christmas, but were only of limited use, and thereafter sniper rifles were produced by the primary supplier, the Royal Rifle Factory at Amberg. Meanwhile, in Prussia, the War Ministry had adopted a more controlled approach, and ordered 15,000 Gew98 rifles fitted with telescopic sights by Goerz, Zeiss and Luxor from the Spandau factory, deliveries of which commenced before the end of the year. By August 1916, each infantry or Jäger company of the German Army had at least three sniper rifles – 20,000 in all.

The Prussian and Bavarian conversions (each army had a degree of autonomy) differed in one main sense only. The Prussian rifles had their sights mounted on the axis of the barrel, directly above the receiver, which prevented the use of charger clips and meant that the rifles had to be loaded with individual rounds, one at a time. The decision to adopt this arrangement was taken because parallax was reduced to a minimum, the eyepiece being in the plane of the conventional sights. In the Bavarian rifles, the sights were offset slightly to the left of the axis of the barrel, which permitted clip loading. The rifle-and-telescope combination was very good indeed – it was re-adopted unchanged at the start of World War II and was only superseded (and then not entirely) by the self-loading Gew43 fitted with the *Zundblickfernrohr* 4 sight.

BRITISH SNIPER RIFLES

The first official British sniper rifles (a few officers brought their own Mauser and Mannlicher hunting rifles to the front, and others were raised from the public or were captured during raids on enemy trenches; ammunition for them was hard to come by) were not issued until 1915 and did not come into general use until the following year. They did not have telescopes in the normal sense at all, but instead were fitted with a pair of lenses, one which incorporated an aiming notch at the position of the backsight, the other in front of the foresight, its blade still being used as the aiming mark. Most of the optics were produced by Lattey or Neill at very low cost, and a total of about 13,000 were procured officially, though many sets were also bought privately. They gave two- to three-power magnification, but only over a very narrow field of view – just one to one and

a quarter degrees; about two metres per 100m of distance (a little over six feet at 300ft) – which meant that shifting onto a target was not at all easy, and they were much affected by dust and extraneous light.

The rifles to which they were fitted were standard SMLEs, usually with

Mark III or Mark III actions (introduced in 1907 and improved in 1916, the Mark III rifles were the most common in British and Empire service during World War I; Enfield made about 2,300,000 and BSA another two million, while the Ishapore factory in India and the Lithgow factory in Australia contributed a further two million between them, and went on producing them until the 1950s) which were really no more than adequate at very long ranges, though it was very late in the war before they started to be replaced by rather better P'14 rifles,

■BELOW: The Remington 700 series is another hunting rifle good enough for use as a sniper's weapon. It saw regular service in Vietnam and was still in service three decades later.

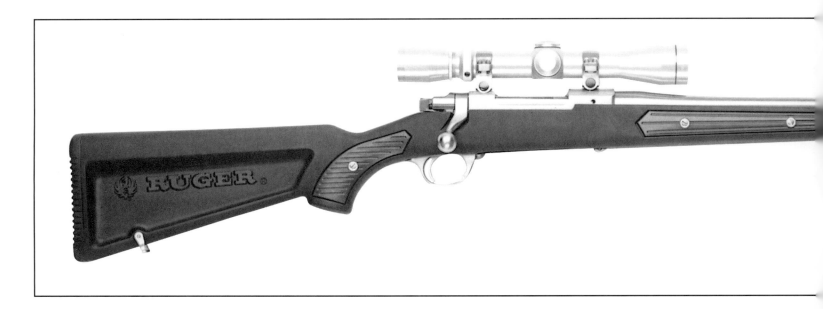

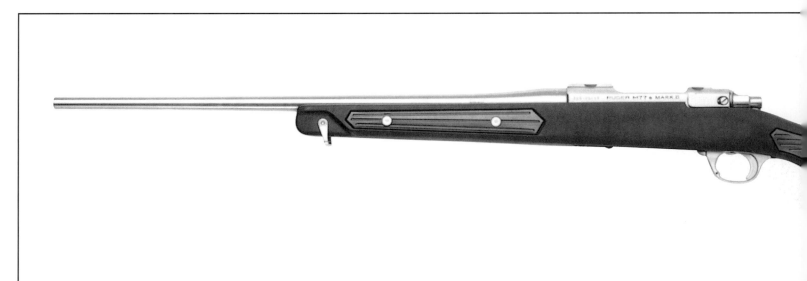

which became the standard sniping rifle and remained so until the late 1930s. The paired Galilean lenses were eventually replaced by conventional telescopes, most of which were supplied by the Periscope Prism Company or Aldis; they amounted to somewhat less than 10,000 in total. Most British sniper rifles had their telescope mounted to the left hand side of the receiver, which both allowed the standard iron sights to be used for snap-shooting and for the rifles to be recharged from clips. Around 1000 Winchester telescopic sights, instantly recognisable by their length, were procured from the USA for use by the British Army, and these 4x and 5x units, which had a field of view of almost six metres per 100m of range (20ft per 328ft), were also specified for the US Marine Corps for fitting to the M1903 rifle.

During World War II the British Army and Royal Marines, who first became involved in 'special operations' during

that conflict (carrying out what Prime Minister Winston Churchill, with his usual eye to a good headline, called 'butcher and bolt' raids), conceived a need for a silenced carbine to be effective at up to 250m (820ft). The result was the De Lisle carbine, which chambered the .45in ACP (Automatic Colt Pistol) round devised for the self-loading handgun John Browning designed and Colt's manufactured and which the US Army adopted as the M1911 in the Lee-Enfield action. With a 185mm (seven inch) barrel enclosed in a full-length suppressor, and employing a round which (at a muzzle velocity of 260 metres/853ft per second) is sub-sonic anyway, the De Lisle is widely held to have been one of the quietest and most effective silenced weapons ever produced, the only sound it made being the mechanical component – that of the firing pin falling on the primer cap (though, unfortunately, nothing could be done to quieten the cycling of the bolt

■ **ABOVE: Like most modern hunting rifles, the Ruger M77 is delivered without sights of any kind, but with its receiver drilled and tapped to take standard mounting rings.**

action). Two models were produced, one with conventional wooden furniture from the Lee-Enfield No. 4 rifle, the other with a pistol grip and a folding butt-stock similar to that found on the later Sterling sub-machine gun. The De Lisle is a very rare item today, most of those produced having been destroyed at the end of World War II, but it is to be supposed that a few are still to be found in the armouries of special forces units.

US ARMY AND US MARINE CORPS

The US Army had begun experimenting with telescopic sights in 1900, fitting 8x, 12x and 20x tubes to Krag rifles; in 1906 it was recommended that expert riflemen (who usually amounted to about two per

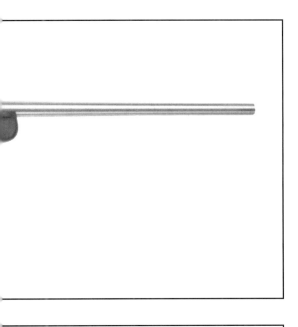

LEFT: The Ruger M77 Mark II All-Weather rifle is somewhat unusual in that it is constructed from stainless steel and Du Pont's Zytel glassfibre-reinforced plastic.

BELOW: Savage has been producing workmanlike rifles ever since the last decade of the nineteenth century, and the recent Model 111 FCXP3 is no exception; an excellent 'starter' rifle.

company) were to be issued with rifles so equipped, and by early the following year the Frankford Arsenal had produced working prototypes, on the prismatic principle. There was just one problem: at US$80 each, they cost three times the price of the rifle on which they were to be mounted. It was 1908 before a simplified version was devised, with six-power magnification and a 20mm (three-quarters of an inch) objective lens with a theoretical 'brightness' rating of 11 (ideally, a telescope of this power should have a 30mm objective – a little over an inch – and a rating of 25) which was further diminished by light loss in the prisms. An improvement in 1913 saw the magnification reduced to 5.2x, which upped the brightness to 14.8. Like most of the other sights we have considered so far, the M1908/M1913 was mounted out to the left of the receiver; it weighed 900g (two pounds), and unbalanced the rifle as a result.

In 1914 the German Goerz Certar sight was selected as a replacement, and since Goerz couldn't supply them, a copy was produced at the Frankford Arsenal which was the equal of it in every sense. The design specification was passed to the Winchester Repeating Arms Co., which produced prototypes. After cursory testing, a contract for 32,000 sights was placed on 12 June 1918, using lenses to be supplied by Eastman Kodak. Happily, as it turned out – for the sights were actually next to useless – the machinery

to grind the lenses was unavailable, and the war was over – and the contract cancelled – before a single sight had been delivered. Prolonged testing in 1920 showed that the sights broke up in use, and the rifles which had already been fitted with mounts for them were restored to their original state and returned to storage, as were the 1000 or so which had been fitted with M1908/M1913 sights. The US Army had no rifle with telescopic sights from then until the start of World War II.

The US Marine Corps went by a different route, having adopted Winchester A5 sights for its shooting teams in 1914, mounted axially, in rings which permitted them to slide forwards, out of the way of the bolt handle (the US Army's Frankford/Winchester sights, which were also mounted axially, did not slide, and the bolt handle of the rifles fitted to receive them had to be modified as a result). Some 500 A5 sights were procured in all; they were used in training but not, as far as can be ascertained, in action. This sight became the Lyman 5A between the wars, and was the first to be adopted by the US Marine Corps during World War II, though it was soon replaced by the Unertl 8x, which was 610mm (24in) in length and had a field of view of little more than three metres (10ft).

It was to be hard to find a single marine (or seaman – M1903 rifles so equipped were also issued to the US Navy, specifically to detonate surfaced mines) who had anything like a good word for them; they were 'obsoleted' in 1944 and replaced by Weaver 330 sights with the military designation M73B1, which were also fitted to some M1C

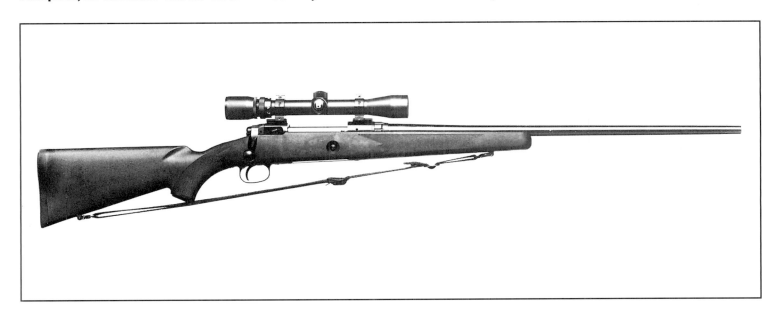

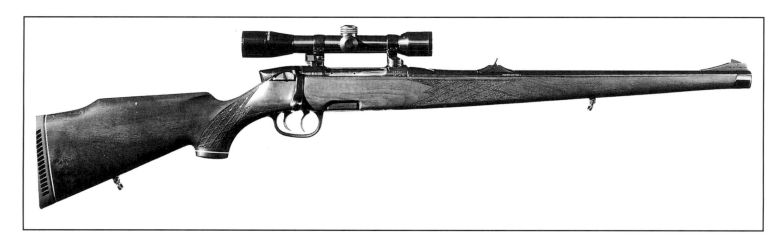

■ABOVE: The modern Mannlicher rifles retain the famous Mannlicher rotary magazine and are available with a full stock and a left-hand action; the Sporter, shown here, has a set trigger.

Garand sniper rifles. Most of the latter got M79/M81/M82 sights (the difference between the three was minor, and related to the form of the graticule or aiming marks), which were the military version of Lyman's Alaskan, with two and a half-power magnification, a field of view of 15m per 100m (49ft per 328ft) and 'eye relief' (the distance between the shooter's eye and the eyepiece) of 100-125mm/four-five inches (where earlier sights had half that or less, as many a sniper found out to his cost when the eyepiece rim smashed into his eyebrow. . .). The Canadian Army also acquired some Lyman Alaskan sights for its Lee-Enfield No. 4 Mk. 1 rifles during World War II, the P'14 rifles which had been adopted as snipers' weapons throughout the British Empire at the end of World War I having been superseded and largely declared obsolete in the intervening period, but most of the British Army's sniper rifles of the period – specially-selected Number 4s – were fitted with No. 32 sights, a new telescope which had originally been designed for use with the Bren LMG. The sights were fitted to this rifle at the time of its selection and setting up, and were never to be separated from it; if either needed adjustment, both were returned to the armourers (the number of the sight was stamped into the butt of the rifle, but that wasn't the end of the procedure – even the paired clamping rings had identifying numbers on each part). The telescope itself gave three-power magnification and a nine degree field of view – around 18m per 100m (59ft per 328ft). Much of the conversion work to fit the sight mounts and the sights themselves was carried out by Holland & Holland, using rifles manufactured by BSA, at the rate of about 800 per month, though some 1400 were converted at Enfield. Holland & Holland converted a total of 23,177.

The No. 32 sight was very much state-of-the-art at the time, and the Mark III version, approved in October 1944, was fitted to the later L42A1 sniper rifle which came into service when the British Army switched over to self-loading rifles. Its elevation and windage adjustment drums were set up on the forward mounting ring, each 'click' of adjustment in early models being equal to two

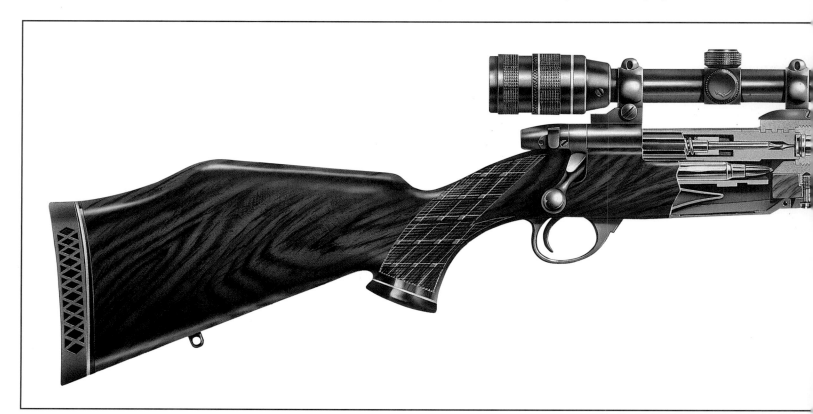

minutes of angle or 50mm per 91m (two inches per 300ft), though experience showed this to be inadequate over longer ranges, and it was halved in subsequent marks.

World War II-vintage snipers' rifles were sometimes fitted with bipods (and a monopod was developed, and then rejected, for the Lee-Enfield) but most snipers found a sling, which either wrapped or was looped around the left arm, to be a more satisfactory means of steadying the rifle in the prone position as well as when kneeling or standing.

THE MODERN SNIPER'S RIFLE

The majority of snipers' rifles of the two world wars were designs which dated from half a century earlier, when riflemen were expected to be able to hit a man-sized target at anything up to 600m (1970ft), and as a result they didn't need much setting up or modification to do the job they were devised for. Later rifles, such as the auto-loaders which came to dominate in the 1950s, were different, having been designed with a different set of criteria in mind, for assault firepower rather than ultimate accuracy, and as a result few of them were any good in the sniper role (though there were exceptions, like the otherwise unremarkable M14).

The solution for most nations' armed forces was to retain the rifles they were already using, and we have noted how the British Army, for example, relied on reworked Number 4 Lee-Enfields, re-chambered for the new NATO-standard 7.62mm rim-less round. But as time wore on, it became clear that modern manufacturing methods allowed considerably more accurate rifles to be produced economically, and this led to a rash of new designs. There was a further development, too, driven by the search for a better ballistic profile: a move towards 12.7mm/.50in as a more suitable calibre, a direct contrast to the shift the other way, to smaller rounds, for the 'everyday' infantry rifle.

A NEW MANNLICHER

One of the first to adopt a new purpose-designed sniper rifle was Austria, which took on Steyr-Mannlicher's fairly conventional-looking SSG (*Scharfschützengewehr* – Sharpshooter's Rifle) in 1969. Not entirely unsurprisingly, this rifle used the rear-locking Mannlicher bolt system, not the more widespread front-locking Mauser, which consisted in this case of three pairs of lugs, permitting a 60 degree rotation, and it also employed the Mannlicher rotary magazine, holding five rounds of 7.62mm NATO ammunition. Its heavy barrel was cold-forged – a method pioneered in Germany by Dr-Ing Gerhardt Appel for the production of hypodermic needles during the inter-war period and then applied to gun barrels, specifically, those of the MG42 machine gun, during World War II.

Appel's method, which is now the industry standard, starts off with a drilled and reamed steel bar, shorter and considerably greater in external dimensions than the finished barrel. A mandrel, which is exactly the internal form and dimension of the finished barrel in reverse, is placed inside, and then the blank is beaten by a bank of hammers, so rapidly and with such force that the steel actually becomes plastic, over the mandrel, reducing the blank in diameter and elongating it by 50 per cent; the interior takes the form (and the dimensions) of the mandrel exactly and the exterior takes the form of the hammer heads. The chamber can be formed simultaneously, and there is no restriction on the use of super-tough stainless steels and alloys, which are notoriously difficult to machine. In the case of the SSG 69, the bore was minutely tapered.

The SSG 69, which was factory-fitted with a matched Kahles Helia 6S2 or ZF69 6x telescopic sight (infra-red and light-intensifying sights were also available), was perfectly capable of producing consistent 400mm (16in) groups at 600m (1970ft). It was fitted with a plastic stock (and was one of the first examples of the application, though a competition version, fitted with aperture sights, was stocked in walnut)

Weatherby Mark V

Calibres: .22-250, .224in, .240in, .257in, 270in, 7mm, .300in, .30-06, .340in, .378in, .416 Win. Magnum, .460 Win. Magnum
Weight: 2.95kg (6lb 8oz) to 4.75kg (10lb 8oz)
Length: 1105mm (43.5in) to 1180mm (46.5in)
Barrel length: 610mm (24in) or 660mm (26in)
Effective range: Over 1000m (3250ft), according to chambering
Configuration: Five-round integral box magazine, bolt-action
Muzzle velocity: According to chambering
Country of origin: United States

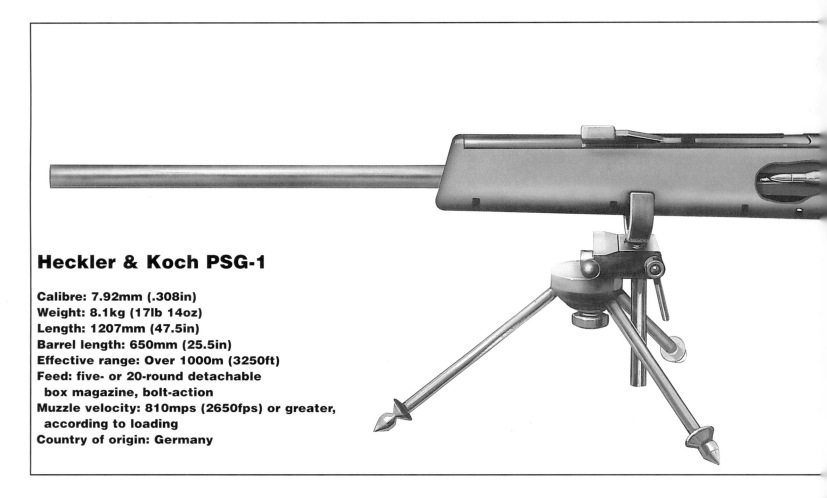

Heckler & Koch PSG-1

Calibre: 7.92mm (.308in)
Weight: 8.1kg (17lb 14oz)
Length: 1207mm (47.5in)
Barrel length: 650mm (25.5in)
Effective range: Over 1000m (3250ft)
Feed: five- or 20-round detachable
  box magazine, bolt-action
Muzzle velocity: 810mps (2650fps) or greater,
  according to loading
Country of origin: Germany

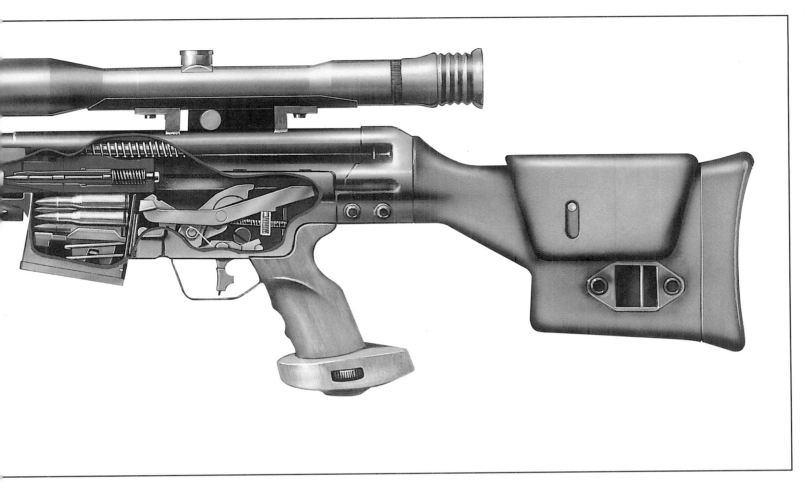

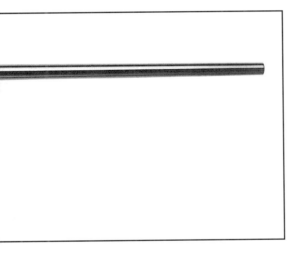

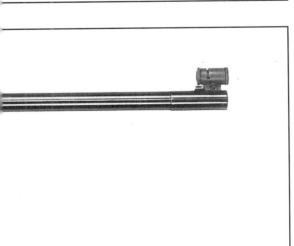

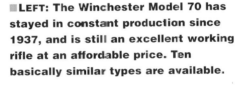

■LEFT: The Winchester Model 70 has stayed in constant production since 1937, and is still an excellent working rifle at an affordable price. Ten basically similar types are available.

which could be adjusted at the butt for length by the insertion of spacer pieces. There was a choice of a single trigger or a double set trigger, both of them externally adjustable. The rifle was also available in short-barrelled form, and a silencer system could be factory-fitted. A very similar rifle was available commercially in a variety of calibres, from .222in Remington to .458in Winchester Magnum, at prices just short of £1200 Sterling/US$2000.

A NEW REMINGTON

The US Army and US Marine Corps also adopted a quite ordinary looking hunting rifle as a sniper rifle, in their case a 'militarised' version of the Remington 700 which was the first bolt-action rifle to introduce recessed engagement of the bolt

■LEFT: The Anschutz range of small-bore competition rifles – this is the top-of-the-range Model 1913 Super Match – are some of the finest available in the world today.

head, a safety measure primarily, which reduced the chance of a penetrated primer cap (or worse still, a split cartridge case head) from leading to an uncontrolled escape of gas at high temperature and under enormous pressure, either into the receiver or into the shooter's face. First taken up in the 1960s as the M40, it was updated a decade later, given a stainless steel barrel and camouflage-pattern GRP stock and a more powerful telescope, and known as the M40A1. In the 1980s, a more thorough revamp saw the original action re-stocked in Kevlar to a more futuristic pattern with a built-in bipod and a butt adjustable for length, when it was re-designated the M24. By way of an indicator, M24 rifles sell for around £1500 Sterling/US$2500 on the commercial market.

BRITAIN'S PM

As a replacement for the L42A1, the British Army's snipers adopted another bolt-action rifle, designated as the L96A1, developed by a specialist company, Accuracy International, as the PM. This was also chambered originally for the 7.62mm NATO round (though versions firing more powerful ammunition, such as the .338in Lapua Magnum, with a much greater effective range, were also produced). It made extensive use of aluminium and high-performance reinforced-plastic composites and had a stainless steel barrel which came as close to being self-cleaning as any – a feature it shared with similar rifles from McMillan and others. It had an integral bipod fitted at the extremity of the fore-

stock, and a monopod in the butt-stock. Fitted with a Schmidt & Bender 6x or 10x sight, it was easily capable of a first-round kill at up to 600m (1968ft) in trained hands. A version with an integral silencer, which utilised low-power, sub-sonic ammunition with an effective range of 300m (985ft), was also offered. An improved version known as the Model

■ABOVE: **ABOVE: Krieghoff combination guns are available as rifles or shotguns, configured over-and-under or side-by-side, with the option – as here – of different chambering for the barrels.**

AW was later produced, chambered for saboted ammunition such as Winchester's 7.62mm SLAP (Saboted Light Armor Piercing) round.

FRANCE'S FR-F1/F2

In 1966, the French Army adopted a rifle known as the FR-F1 (*Fusil à Repetition, Modèle* 1), based on the action of the MAS 36 infantry rifle and chambered for the same 7.5mm round, with the addition of a pistol grip, spacer pieces for the butt, a longer, heavier barrel with a flash hider/muzzle brake, a bipod (mounted well back in the fore-stock, where it could be adjusted easily) and an APX Model 804 telescopic sight. It was superseded in 1984 by the FR-F2, which was basically similar but with its barrel protected by a plastic thermal sleeve which was said to prevent it bending in strong sunlight,

Parker-Hale M-85

Calibre: .308in (7.92mm) Winchester
Weight: 5.7kg (12lb 8oz) with sights
Length: 1145mm (45in)
Barrel length: 615mm (24.25in)
Effective range: Over 1000m (3250ft)
Configuration: 10-round detachable box magazine, bolt-action
Muzzle velocity: 810mps (2650fps) to 1160mps (3770fps) according to projectile weight
Country of origin: United Kingdom

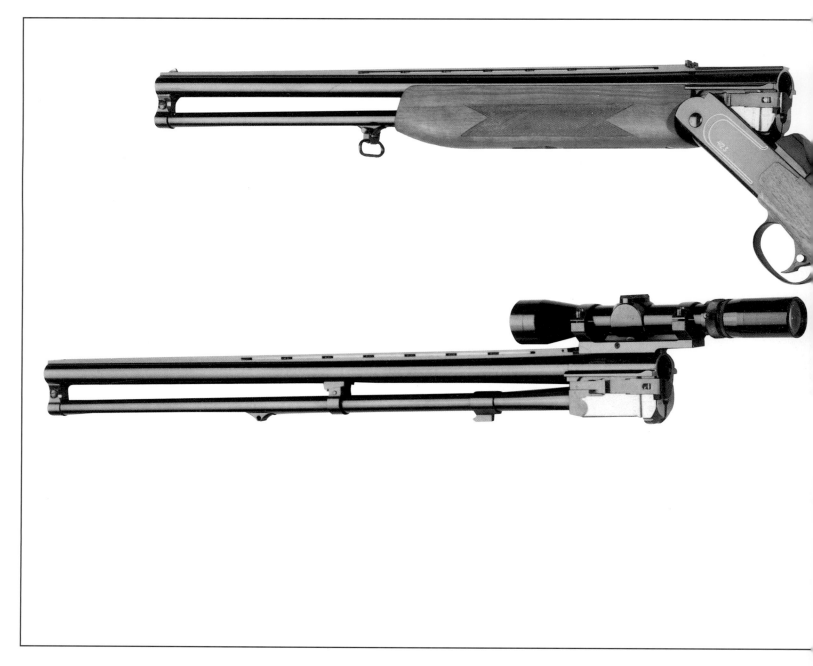

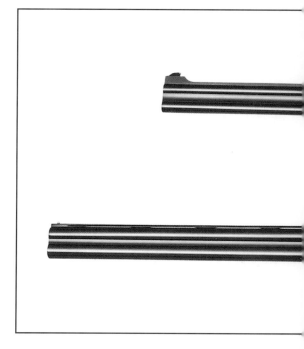

■ABOVE: Combination guns like the Finnish Valmet and the Beretta, opposite, are often supplied with 'extra' pairs of barrels in different chamberings.

improve the sight picture by cutting down heat shimmer immediately in front of the objective, and reduce the infra-red signature. The revised model was chambered for the 7.62mm NATO round.

FINNISH TRG-21 AND SWISS SSG

One of the best of the new breed of bolt-action sniper rifles came from Sako in Finland – a company which has also cornered a significant slice of the market for high-quality mass-production hunting rifles priced at between US$1000 and US$1500. The TRG-21 was introduced in 1989 and is unusual in that not just its

(stainless steel) barrel, but also its receiver are produced by the cold-forging process. The barrel and receiver are attached to an aluminium sub-frame to which the plastic stock (injection-moulded polyurethane, in this case) is also attached, making the two virtually independent of each other, and the three-lugged front-locking bolt-action incorporates a silent safety and a cocking status indicator. The TRG-21 is produced in 7.62mm NATO chambering, but a heavier version, the TRG-41, is chambered for the considerably more powerful .338in Lapua Magnum cartridge for improved accuracy over longer ranges.

In Switzerland, SIG produced two quite different bolt-action sniper rifles, the SSG 2000 and 3000. The former used the retractable-lug system Sauer, SIG's close partner in Germany, developed for

its Model 80 and 90 hunting rifles, mated to a SIG-developed trigger and three-way safety system and a cold-forged barrel, with either a Zeiss Diatal 8 x 56 or a Schmidt & Bender variable 1.5-6 x 42 telescopic sight. This was fitted with a two-piece walnut stock, adjustable for length and depth in the butt and with its forward sling-swivel mounted in a channel which stretched from just ahead of the four-round box magazine right to the forward extremity of the fore-stock.

The Model 2000 was available in 5.56mm NATO, 7.62mm NATO, .300in Weatherby Magnum or 7.5mm Swiss chamberings, while the Model 3000 was chambered for the 7.62mm NATO round only. The Model 3000 also differed in being stocked in black plastic (though with no less a degree of butt adjustment available, and with a lighter, ventilated fore-stock), with a bipod fitted as standard. Internally it was substantially different, with a front-locking bolt with three pairs of lugs, a 60 degree throw and an over-sized cylinder, which was, it was claimed, almost silent in operation. Its fully-floating barrel was fitted with a flash hider/muzzle brake; the Hensoldt 1.5-6 x 42 telescopic sight (which could be exchanged for all the standard NATO variants, a common requirement) was factory-matched to the rifle.

SELF-LOADING SNIPER'S RIFLES
As well as its two bolt-action sniper's rifles, SIG also produced a version of the self-loading SG550 rifle with a heavy cold-forged barrel and extensively modified furniture, fitted with standard

dovetails to accept a variety of telescopic and vision-enhancing sights, fitted with a bipod and a thermal screen above the handguard, to prevent distortion of the sight picture by the hot propellant gases. Somewhat unusually, it was available only in 5.56mm calibre, which went decidedly against the trend. Indeed, when Israeli Military Industries, which manufactured the Galil assault rifle, came to produce a version for snipers, it chose to base it on the export version, chambered for the 7.62mm NATO round.

The rifle in question was, like the assault rifle, developed in very close consultation with the Israel Defense Forces, which ensured that 'grass-roots' opinion played a part in deciding on its form. The first move was to delete the selective-fire option, and replace the trigger mechanism with one which was both progressive in action and individually adjustable for pull. The barrel was replaced, too, by a heavy, fully-floating tube fitted with a flash hider/muzzle brake, which could be swapped for a silencer. Somewhat unconventionally, the 6 x 40 telescopic sight is mounted to the left of the receiver, not axially, in a fitting which permits rapid removal and replacement without effecting the zeroing. Unconventionally, too, for a rifle designed for ultimate accuracy, the butt-stock is

■BELOW: Like all the best custom-made guns, Beretta's combination over-and-unders are fitted carefully to the owner. Many shooters specify more than one pair of barrels.

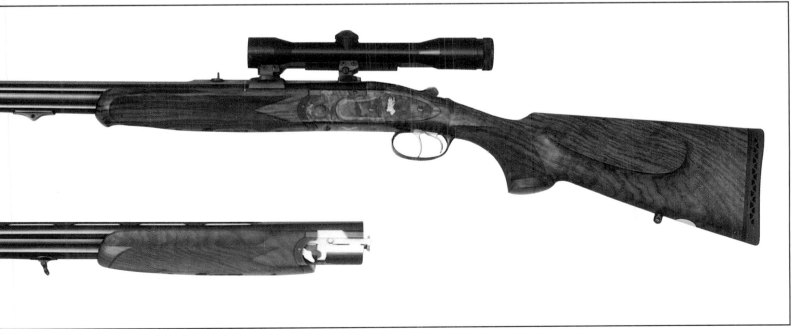

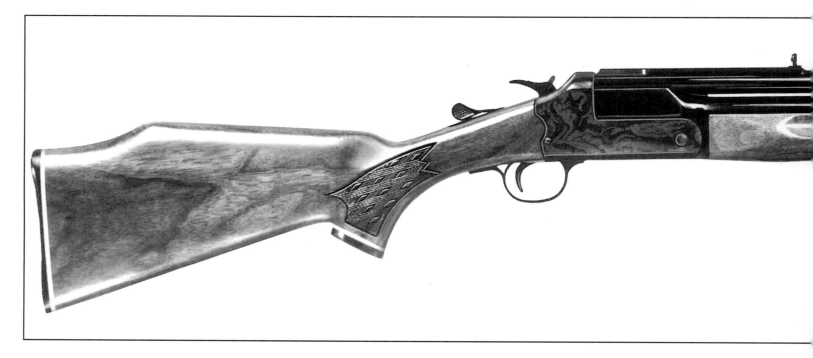

■**ABOVE: Towards the other end of the scale from the US$20,000-plus Berettas is the Savage Model 24, an over-and-under combination gun with a rifled barrel over a smooth-bore.**

hinged, and is normally folded down the right hand side of the rifle for transportation. Like the French FR series, the Galil bipod is located immediately in front of the magazine.

SOVIET DRAGUNOV

The USSR was often very adventurous in the weapons it adopted, and frequently was the first to take up a new type; the Dragunov sniper's rifle – properly known as the *Snayperskaya Vintovka Dragunova*, or SVD – was no exception, being the first precision self-loading weapon to appear, post-World War II. It may well be that the Red Army's hand was forced by the fairly abysmal performance of the AK assault rifles over a range of more than about 400m (1310ft). Not surprisingly, the SVD is based on the same rotating-bolt action which Kalashnikov designed, simplified by deleting the sustained-fire option and modified to take the old long 7.62mm x 54R Model 1891 cartridge, which always was a powerful round with a satisfactorily flat trajectory thanks to a muzzle velocity of 830 metres (2725ft) per

■**RIGHT: The Springfield M6 Scout is very rudimentary and was designed originally as a survival rifle for US Air Force crewmen to enable them to live off the land until rescued.**

second and also to reduce the cyclical rate, and thus the degree of movement during reloading. Most unusually, the extra-long barrel (610mm/24in in place of the 415mm/16in of the standard AK) was fitted with a mount for a bayonet. A PSO1 telescopic sight was factory-fitted and matched to each rifle, but could be swapped for other types without loss of zeroing. For clandestine operations over short ranges, the Soviet Union also developed a special-purpose sniper rifle, the VSS, in 9mm Makarov chambering (the standard Soviet military pistol round; it is somewhat less powerful than the 9mm Parabellum round standardized by NATO) with a reduced charge, to give a sub-sonic muzzle velocity. The VSS had a Kalashnikov-type action, and was fitted with a barrel with an integral silencer; it was designed to be used at ranges of up to 400m (1310ft), and could be fitted with

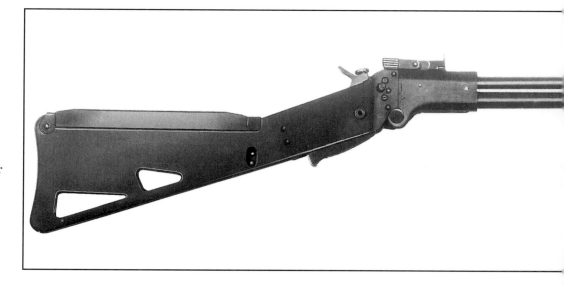

the same variety of vision-enhancing sight units available to the Dragunov.

THE WALTHER WA 2000

By far the most unusual of the modern sniping rifles – and not just in its appearance – was the bullpup design developed in Germany by Walther as the WA 2000 and introduced in 1981. The WA 2000, just 905mm (35.6in) long as opposed to the 1125mm (44in) of the British L96A1 or the 1140mm (45in) of the more conventional SSG 69, still managed a 605mm (24in) barrel, only 40mm (one and a half inches) shorter than either of those two comparators, and to improve its stability was clamped between massive upper and lower supporting elements, both of which continued through the receiver, right to the extremity of the butt-stock. The objective was both to prevent the torque

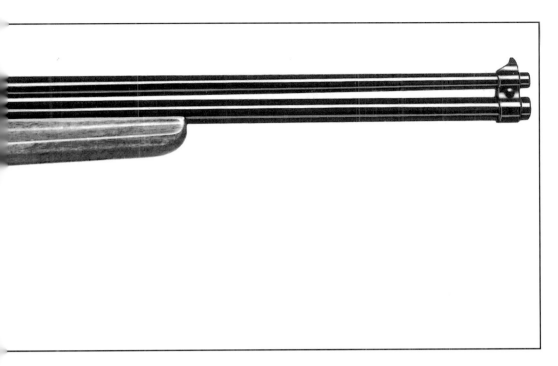

converted from right- to left-hand operation by swapping over the cheek-piece and one bolt head for another.

HEAVY-CALIBRE SNIPER RIFLES

The sniper's real effectiveness on the battlefield is measured in terms of his ability to destroy his target without warning. Traditionally, much of that was achieved by means of fieldcraft – getting into position unobserved and remaining there undetected, before, during, and after the fire mission. It stands to reason that the greater the range at which a target can be engaged effectively, the

■ BELOW: The M6 scout has a .22in Long Rifle (LR) rifled barrel over a .410in smooth tube, and literally folds in half; with a 457mm (18in) barrel it is accurate out to over 100m [328ft].

induced by the rifling from lifting the muzzle away from the point of aim and to direct the recoil in a straight line through the axis of the weapon. The barrel was formed with external longitudinal flutes, which both helped to reduce vibration and improved heat dissipation by increasing the surface area. The geometry of the rifling was different for each of the three standard calibres (.300in Winchester Magnum; 7.62mm NATO and 7.5mm Swiss) in which it was supplied. Gas-operated by the action of the piston on the bolt carrier, and with the familiar seven-lug rotating bolt pioneered by Stoner, the WA 2000 was of largely modular construction, not unlike the Austrian AUG, though the impetus in its case was to be able to perform routine maintenance without disturbing the relationship between barrel and stock. Like the FA MAS, it could be quickly

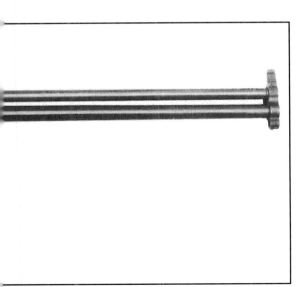

better the sniper's chances of success will be, and to that end there was a move during the 1980s to adopt a heavier calibre with a greater effective range – the 12.7mm/.50in round previously used only by heavy machine guns such as the American M2 Browning or the Russian NSV. The 12.7mm/.50in round – which is available in a variety of forms – has a projectile more than 10 times the mass of a 5.56mm round, six to seven times that of a 7.62mm round, which it fires at a muzzle velocity somewhat higher than the latter – around 855 metres (2805ft) per second. Accordingly, it is effective over a considerably greater distance

have the field to itself, however, and at around the same time, Barrett Firearms produced its self-loading Light Fifty, Model 82 A-1, which despite its name was somewhat bigger still, at 13kg (29lb) and 1450mm (57in) overall length. Eventually, as a result both of firing trials and combat experience in Iraq, the Barrett rifle, recoil-operated and with a recoiling barrel, which combined with a sophisticated muzzle brake to reduce the impact on the shooter's shoulder to manageable proportions, was judged to be marginally the better, and late in 1991 the Murfreesboro, Tennessee, company won a contract to supply 300 to a variety

devised as they were to carry out exactly the same task: the nature of the barrel and its rifling haven't changed, and neither has the mechanism of the trigger – or at least, not out of all recognition: the frontiersman of 200 years ago would certainly know exactly what the Barret M82 was for. But how he would wonder at its range and its accuracy, at the quality of its engineering, and at the very materials of which it was made, let alone at the ease of loading it.

FUTURE DEVELOPMENT

The rifle's development has kept pace remarkably well with that of technology

■ABOVE: The Steyr-Mannlicher Match rifle was specifically designed for UIT competitions, hence the eccentric-looking stock which ensures that no external forces deform the barrel.

(a .50in sniper rifle in American hands recorded a confirmed kill at 1800m/5900ft range during the Gulf War of 1991, far in excess of anything possible with a 7.62mm rifle) and is effective against so-called 'material' targets – vehicles, helicopters and fixed-wing aircraft, and even buildings – as well as personnel.

In the mid-1980s, the US Navy asked McMillan Gunworks, which produced GRP stocks for M40 sniper rifles as well as a range of well-respected hunting and match rifles of its own, to develop a weapon in .50in (12.7mm) calibre for its SEAL special forces units, and the result was the single-shot, bolt-action M-87 with stainless steel receiver and chrome-molybdenum barrel, which later metamorphosed into the M-87R, with a five-round box magazine. Tests showed that the new weapon was a significant step forward in the right circumstances, despite its considerable size (1345mm/53in overall) and weight (almost 10kg/22lb). McMillan did not

of US military units. A somewhat futuristic design with a composite plastic tube and an absorbent rubber pad in place of a normal butt-stock, the Barrett M82A1 is fitted with a 10-power telescopic sight and a thermal sleeve over its 737mm- (29in) long barrel. In addition to standard M33 ball ammunition, it could fire M8 armour-piercing incendiary (API) ammunition, and potentially the Winchester-developed .50in SLAP round with its tungsten penetrator, capable of perforating 19mm (three-quarters of an inch) of armour at 1500m (4920ft) range, though that would probably require a stellite-lined barrel.

COMING FULL CIRCLE

There is a certain symmetry here. We began our study of the evolution of the modern rifle looking at weapons which originated from the new American colonies like Tennessee, a metre and a half (five feet) in length and firing half-inch-diameter bullets. And after two centuries of development, we find ourselves considering rifles from the same part of the world which are very similar in those two basic respects! There are other similarities between the two very different rifles, too, of course,

and materials science in general. There were times when, as we have seen, its progress seemed to stagnate, and there were a number of occasions when influential developers took a wrong turning, but that has been true of virtually every other product of modern man, too, for there's very seldom trial without error, and few successes are not built on failure. As for the future, as long as there is a need for projectile weapons, the basic nature of the rifle will remain unchanged. We may see far-reaching changes in the nature of ammunition, both in terms of the chemical composition of propellants and the way in which they are packaged and delivered, as well as in new types of projectile, and we are very likely to see some form of laser target designation taking over from conventional sights, just as it is becoming more and more common in the associated field of handguns, though the problems provoked by the much longer ranges involved still remain to be addressed. In general, however, the similarities between the weapons of today and those of tomorrow will far outweigh the differences between them, just as they do between those of our time and those from the past.

INDEX